T0326622

EXOTIC ALTERNATIVE INVESTMENTS

EXOTIC ALTERNATIVE INVESTMENTS

STANDALONE CHARACTERISTICS, UNIQUE RISKS AND PORTFOLIO EFFECTS

KEVIN R. MIRABILE

ANTHEM PRESS

Anthem Press
An imprint of Wimbledon Publishing Company
www.anthempress.com

This edition first published in UK and USA 2021
by ANTHEM PRESS
75–76 Blackfriars Road, London SE1 8HA, UK
or PO Box 9779, London SW19 7ZG, UK
and
244 Madison Ave #116, New York, NY 10016, USA

British Library Cataloguing-in-Publication Data
A catalogue record for this book is available from the British Library.

Library of Congress Control Number: 2020951326

ISBN-13: 978-1-78527-610-1 (Hbk)
ISBN-10: 1-78527-610-7 (Hbk)

Cover Image: Tendo/Shutterstock.com

This title is also available as an e-book.

DISCLAIMER

Please note that this book is not intended to provide investment advice. It is not a
solicitation to buy or sell any security, nor is it intended to advocate for a specific
investment in any asset class or product. It is intended to provide observations and information
only. Individuals who wish to invest in any product discussed in this book should speak to an
appropriate financial advisor, accountant or attorney before investing and should not rely on any
information presented as a basis for any investment decision. Alternative investments, particularly those covered in this book, have substantial risks, including many which may not have been
discussed in this book or known by the author at the time of this book's publication.

CONTENTS

ILLUSTRATIONS

Figures

Tables

PREFACE

This book is intended for individual investors, financial advisors, institutional investors, academics and students who have a desire for information and knowledge about investment products that go beyond just stocks and bonds or vanilla hedge funds, private equity and real-estate investments. It is for those individuals who are actively seeking to learn about new sources of return, how to reduce risk or diversify their portfolio. Investors already have access to a wide range of books and materials on hedge funds, private equity, real estate and alternatives. This book is designed to provide information about a unique subset of those asset classes and to explain the value and opportunities available from these bespoke investments about which there is much less published information. Investments in so-called exotic alternatives—such as artwork, insurance-linked products, farmland, cryptoassets, collectibles, alternative medicines, storage units, litigation finance, intellectual property, vintage watches and wines—will be explained in plain language. This book is for those investors interested in better understanding the economic drivers and investment vehicles related to these new exotic investment opportunities, as well as the impact of adding these exotic alternatives to traditional portfolios.

This book is the product of many hours of independent interviews and subject matter research. I am very grateful to all those firms and individuals who provided background research and interviews for this book and who helped make this book possible. I would like to specifically thank Cynthia Sachs, Rajiv Rebello, Beat Hess, Eva Shang, Dr. Evan Bedil, Philip Belardi, Carter Malloy, Barbara Keady, Richard Travia, Michael Bucella, Peter Brady, Tom Ehrlein, Ken Shoji, Ron Suber, Seth Weinstein and Greg Kiernan for their respective insights and contributions.

This book also reflects background research by many of my students in the alternative investment program at Fordham University's Gabelli School of Business, the alternative investment club research team, most notably Jonathan Josef, who prepared the data analysis for this book, and my research assistant Tyler Eufer, who provided analysis of academic research on exotic alternative investments. Also, a special thanks to my daughter, Sarah Mirabile Blacker, for her extraordinary editorial work and constant motivation and encouragement during the writing of this book.

Chapter One

INTRODUCTION

Understanding exotic alternative investments requires in-depth knowledge of both traditional investment products such as stock and bond investing as well as alternative investments like hedge funds, private equity, venture capital, real assets and real estate. Let's start with some basics of asset allocation and the characteristics of traditional stock and bond investing before exploring the role of alternative investments and the unique subset of alternative investments we now refer to as exotic alternative investments.

All investors or their advisors must make choices about how to invest their funds. Historically this was done by merely picking the right mix of large-capitalization stocks and investment-grade bonds. Many asset allocators have used a simple 60–40 allocation to stocks and bonds as a baseline or benchmark for their portfolio recommendations to clients. More sophisticated advisors include a wider range of stocks and bonds including small-capitalization stocks, high-yield bonds and international securities. Others still might also include an allocation to commodities or inflation-linked securities to further diversify away risk or improve returns. The appropriate weights for each asset class in a portfolio are based on the risk tolerance and time horizon of any individual or institution and the liquidity of the underlying investments, among other factors. Portfolio asset allocation models for both individual investors and institutional investors are normally updated at least annually to take on more or less risk as investment objectives or risk tolerances change or to reflect shifts in correlations or return outlooks for various asset classes or simply to rebalance the portfolio.

Over time, the asset allocation process has become much more sophisticated. Portfolios today include dozens of categories and subcategories or derivatives that investors and allocators believe can help them improve their risk-adjusted returns or meet other portfolio management objectives. In addition, many investors now use passive investments and index funds to obtain exposure to various asset classes like stocks, bonds and commodities, at the expense of active fund management and individual security selection. These index products offer a wide range of asset class exposures and returns, with much lower fees than active funds.

Today we are also at a bit of a crossroads when it comes to the outlook for traditional stock and bond returns, whether passively or actively generated. Equity valuations are relatively high, interest rates are relatively low and inflation is muted. This will make it difficult for investors to generate double-digit stock and bond returns. It may be a challenge to earn returns above the low single digits from investing in just stocks and bonds. This somewhat sanguine outlook comes at a time when many investors need to achieve a target rate of return of 7% or more to fund their liabilities or achieve their retirement goals.

Alternative investments are sometimes hard to define and vary from institution to institution or advisor to advisor. Sometimes alternatives are described as anything that is not a stock or a bond or anything that cannot be immediately converted into cash. This definition by exclusion is not very specific and seems way too broad. Most investment management firms have their own definition of what is or is not included in the definition of alternative investment. The definition almost always includes hedge funds and private equity, sometimes real estate and real assets, and other times not. The approach recommended here is to define alternatives by including those asset classes that I believe are most often captured in practice by institutional and individual investment advisors when defining alternatives. In this book, we intend any references to alternative investments to mean investments in hedge funds, private equity, venture capital and real estate.

For several years now, investors and their advisors have been preparing their portfolios for the inevitable return of market headwinds and an increasingly challenging outlook for investing in traditional stock and bond portfolios. This is, of course, after a remarkable period of extended growth and mostly positive returns for both stocks and bonds. Investors have been increasingly turning to alternative investments such as hedge funds, private equity, venture capital and real estate to protect principle, diversify risk and improve returns.

Over the longer term, adding alternatives to a traditional portfolio had very positive risk-reduction and return-enhancement effects. Taken as a whole, these alternative investments were able to add "equity-like returns with bond-like volatility". Allocating to alternatives had the effect on traditional portfolios of lowering portfolio standard deviation with sacrificing returns, thereby improving Sharpe ratios, lowering worst-case drawdowns and improving other risk measures. That is no longer the case.

Unfortunately, since the financial crisis of 2008, alternative investments have had many issues. In many cases, they have not delivered the diversification and added return that many investors were hoping to obtain. Hedge funds have dramatically underperformed since 2008 and face a number of issues related to rising correlation to stocks, fees and lack of transparency. Private equity valuations and returns have also been a challenge, and real estate investing returns appear to be approaching the end of a long upward cycle with issues related to rising property taxes and limits on deductibility. Liquid alternatives such as hedged mutual funds have struggled to deliver alpha and to fulfill their promise of delivering alternative investment returns to retail investors. While many alternative investments have continued to benefit from both institutional and retail investor allocations and flows recently, assets have been growing at a slower rate and with longer lead times for the decision making of investors.

Many hedge funds and funds of hedge funds have been unable to deliver on their promise to investors. Many have been forced to close their funds. Investors have demanded lower fees, putting pressure on many firms to remain solvent. In almost all cases, returns have been much lower than during the pre-crisis period. Since 2010, there have been less new large-scale hedge fund launches. More hedge funds than ever have gone out of business or have closed since 2008. The COVID-19 crisis is also likely to cause less new hedge fund formation and more hedge fund failures. Of course, great performance is always available from the best alternative hedge fund managers, but the persistence of any outperformance is not consistent. The amount of time and resources needed to identify true alpha-producing strategies and managers takes much longer than before and is becoming increasingly more expensive.

Many alternative investment managers have suffered from some of the same issues and problems that other active stock and bond managers have experienced since 2008. They too have been unable to consistently beat their benchmark or generate absolute returns or low correlation due to some of the same headwinds facing traditional active managers. Hedge funds have also faced some unique challenges that adversely impact their strategies, such as the effect of central bank intervention, increased regulation, low dispersion of equity returns, bank balance sheet contraction, improved market efficiency and too much money chasing too few opportunities. These additional headwinds have weighed heavily on hedge fund strategies using arbitrage or leverage or short-selling to generate performance. Hopefully, this situation will change. However, for now, it has led more than a few large institutional investors to reexamine or reduce their allocation to these heretofore growing segments of their portfolios.

Private equity firms have been more successful when it comes to raising assets, but now suffer from a significant overhang of dry powder and uninvested funds. This is causing competition for deals and compression of returns. Difficulty realizing value via initial public offerings (IPOs) due to lower public price to earnings multiples are increasingly significant issues for investors in private equity funds. Large IPOs like Uber and Lyft have failed to live up to the expectations of public market investors and have performed poorly.

Real estate funds are also challenged. A slowdown in new housing starts, rising interest rates and peak valuations are slowing demand for housing and putting pressure on returns. Since the 2008 financial crisis real estate has performed better than hedge funds and has faced fewer issues than private equity. At least until the recent COVID-19 crisis. Real estate values and returns are very exposed to a downturn in the economy and will suffer during any recession or economic downturn, including an extended COVID-19-related recession.

So, what is an exotic alternative investment and why is it relevant? While there is no standard definition of an exotic alternative investment, we generally can take the approach that we will know an exotic alternative investment when we see one. Exotic alternatives are hybrids that share some of the return and risk characteristics and structures commonly associated with stocks, bonds, exchange-traded funds (ETFs), mutual funds, hedge funds, private equity, venture, real asset investments and real estate. Many of the investments we are now referring to as exotic alternative investments are getting attention from investors and their advisors. Why? The answer is simple: these investments offer the potential to do what hedge funds and other alternatives were supposed to do, that is, to provide investors with positive risk-adjusted returns and diversification, the characteristics that they had previously obtained from hedge funds, private equity and real estate. Today, many exotics are now able to deliver higher returns and lower correlation than hedge funds, private equity or real estate. Many exotic opportunities come from new or emerging investment categories; however, many also have been around for decades. Some have very short track records and no benchmarks or indices, while others have multi-year track records and more than one index to follow.

Exotic alternatives can be found in many corners of the investment world. Exposure can be obtained either by directly owning the asset or by owning the stocks or bonds issued by firms who own or service the underlying asset class. Exposure to farmland can be obtained by owning a farm, owning a corporation that manages farmland or owning firms that sell seed and fertilizer. Exposure to all sorts of collectibles can be obtained by owning the baseball, comic book or artwork directly or by owning shares of companies that sell or auction them for a fee. Exposure can also be obtained by owning commingled vehicles such as ETFs that invest passively in the underlying asset or commodity. Today you can invest in ETFs or real estate investment trusts (REITs) that own a portfolio of storage facilities, gaming stocks or that hold Bitcoin or medical marijuana licenses or sports franchises. In addition, there are limited partnerships (LPs) or limited liability companies (LLCs) that create exposure to life settlements, water rights, air rights, tax credits or third-party litigation claims.

The definition of exotic alternatives is obviously fluid, subject to debate and is evolving. Hopefully, some of the principles discussed above can be used to identify and differentiate exotic alternative opportunities from more traditional ones. The approach taken in this book is to review and discuss the characteristics of these new, emerging and often more complex investments both individually and from a portfolio perspective. Exotic alternatives, despite higher volatility and less liquidity, often have lower correlation to traditional stock and bond indices than other alternative investments and positive portfolio effects.

As traditional hedge fund and private equity markets and strategies mature and attract increasingly larger investment, it is natural for their returns to slow and for correlations to increase. The smaller, more niche-oriented strategies and products included in the category of exotic alternative investments naturally pick up where hedge funds and other alternatives started some 30 years ago. At that time, they were considered niche strategies and provided a low correlation and higher returns relative to traditional investing in stocks and bonds.

Investing in alternatives involves understanding and evaluating a broad spectrum of opportunities, structures and risks. It is important to recognize that all alternative investments represent a continuum of risks and rewards. Perhaps it is useful to think of today's exotic alternative investments and the opportunities they present in a way that is similar to how investors viewed hedge funds, real estate and private equity, credit or venture capital in the 1990s. We can also think of hedge fund investing in long and short equity hedge fund strategies or using REITs to gain exposure to real estate as the more mature version of alternative investments, and of farmland, life settlements, cryptoassets or catastrophic risk securities (or any of those we call exotic) as the less mature, not quite ready for the institutional investor, version of alternatives. Today, many of what we once called alternative may in fact be considered traditional, and what we call exotic may one day be considered more mainstream as well.

Financially oriented investors can profit by buying into assets such as artwork or vintage clothing or jewelry during periods when demand for the asset is increasing while the supply of the asset remains fixed or is growing more slowly. The financial investor is one who is dispassionate about the artist or period of the asset and is only interested in the artwork as a store of value and source of appreciation and financial gain. Exotics such as rare earth minerals, batteries, uranium or Bitcoin derive their value not from any pleasure taken in viewing the asset or commodity but from the fact that the demand for use of the particular commodity exceeds supply over an extended period, often well into the future. If the demand to use Bitcoin as a transaction currency goes up faster than the supply of Bitcoin, then prices rise. They fall when the opposite is true, often dramatically. Financial investors who can forecast trends related to pure supply and demand imbalances can profit handsomely. In other types of exotic investments, value can also come from the right to future income streams, future cash flows or rent. Intellectual property rights, storage containers, life insurance and litigation settlements all offer an investor future cash flow. Sometimes the cash flow is known and sometimes it is uncertain or has credit risk. Those who can purchase these cash flows at attractive discount rates or those who can better estimate cash flows can profit handsomely. Some investments are hybrids. Farmland derives its value from the fixed supply of land, from collecting rent and from the value of the commodities the land can produce. Other times, value comes from disrupting an industry and capturing a market share, such as when fintech or cannabis products displace traditional food and beverage or banking products. Financial investors can often return double-digit yields with minimal credit risk due purely to the fact that there is more demand for cash to finance business than there is supply at a particular point in time. In many cases, value can come from a combination of intrinsic value, supply-and-demand imbalances and the opportunity to buy cash flows at an attractive discount rate.

Exotic alternative investments are quirky, less understood and can often involve more complex risk. At times this risk can be quite significant. Sources of risk can come from valuation challenges, illiquidity, fraud, a lack of insurability and difficulty forecasting supply and demand or cash flows or a lack of regulation or higher taxes. Discount rates on cash flows or rents have to cover expected loss or credit risk and a premium for illiquidity. Anyone who has followed the prices associated with Bitcoin and other cryptocurrencies certainly knows this to be true.

Due diligence is also an important element of any exotic alternative investment. Due diligence is twofold. There is due diligence on the investment itself. There is also, perhaps more importantly, a need for due diligence on the manager, platform, broker, exchange or advisor used to create a portfolio. Due diligence on the asset class itself involves studying the metrics associated with supply and demand, using indices as proxies for returns, forecasting imbalances into the future, evaluating the legitimacy of future cash flows as well as any credit risk or uncertainty associated with them and understanding the liquidity of any direct or commingled investment that is trying to profit from increases in value over time. Due diligence also involves evaluating the track record and skill set of the manager, broker or platform hired to acquire or invest in exotic alternatives, as well as their terms and fees.

One goal of this book is to evaluate these more complex and less liquid investments from a purely financial perspective, divorced from any affinity toward the asset class itself or the intrinsic value associated with ownership. The approach is to separate personal perspectives on the underlying art or collectibles or the opinion about the nature of a litigation claim from the investment opportunity and risks themselves.

The motivation to explain how exotic alternatives work comes from a desire to promote and discuss investments that can further diversify portfolios and generate outsized returns. It is an extension of my previous books, research and lectures on the benefits of adding more traditional alternatives such as hedge funds, private equity and venture and real estate to traditional stock and bond portfolios.

The focus of this book is on those categories of exotic alternatives that make for sound financial investments and qualify for inclusion in a diversified portfolio owned by high-net-worth or institutional investors. Intrinsic value comes from viewing or showing an asset like a painting or can be derived from driving a vintage sports car. That is where demand from the enthusiast or collector originates. It is not financially motivated per se. It makes the investor feel good. Sometimes, these are referred to as passion investments. Here, profit is a secondary consideration, if even a consideration at all. The focus of this book is not on investments made by individuals purely for their intrinsic value, such as the pleasure derived from consumption or personal enjoyment, divorced from any financial motivation. The focus of this book is on those exotic alternatives that are attractive from a financial perspective, that can be traded and valued and can be included as part of an investment portfolio. The approach is to think about an asset in terms of its underlying value drivers and their probable financial implications.

This book is intended to provide a quick reference guide for advisors, investors, academics and individuals who are curious about some of these new and exciting investments. The chapters alternatively discuss a wide range of investments with varying value propositions such as supply and demand, usage cases, cash flow or some combination.

The value of this book is in its consistent approach to discussing value creation, operating metrics, data sources, investable vehicles, direct investment platforms and risks related to a wide range of exotic alternative investments. It is not meant to be a specialized guide to any one asset class or exotic investment category. It is intended to provide a framework for evaluating any new, complex or exotic investment that is available today or comes along in the future. I hope you enjoy it!

Chapter Two

ARTWORK AND ART FINANCE

Introduction

Artwork and other collectibles like vintage automobiles, baseball cards, wines and whiskey represent an asset that produces no cash flow, is lightly regulated and whose valuation is purely a function of the tastes and preferences of collectors and consumers. They are also very illiquid and difficult to value. The collectibles market is not one single market. It is segmented by the type of collectable and the styles or offerings within a particular collectable. Artwork is broken down into historical periods and the type of art, such as sculptures and paintings, various artistic styles or schools and specific artists. Automobiles can include Italian, American, classics or muscle cars. Wines can be French or Italian and of various vintages.

Despite the unique and bespoke nature of any specific collectable, there has been a great deal of progress in the creation of investment vehicles and platforms or the securitizations of various collectibles. This progress has the effect of moving many collectibles from being considered an investment limited to enthusiasts and collectors to an asset class suitable for investors who are purely motivated by financial considerations. In this chapter, we will examine artwork as a specific type of collectible that can be used as a source of investment and to generate returns not highly correlated with traditional stocks and bonds.

Artwork

Today there are opportunities to profit off artwork by investing in art funds, auction houses, art-lending services and risk management services or financing and insurance products related to fine art and other market segments. Many private banks and wealth management firms already offer their clients art advisory services related to acquisition, financing and insuring artwork that is held for personal aesthetic preferences and/or its own intrinsic value. Therefore, treating art as part of a diversified portfolio holding for non-enthusiasts and including art and collectibles as a component of asset allocation for all investors seems like a logical next step.

A Few Definitions and Key Terms

Art collectors buy artwork to adorn offices or buildings or to display in their home. Collectors may loan their works out to museums and sometimes donate them outright to museums upon their death.

Art investors are interested in portfolio diversification by using art as an investment. Investments are considered long-term buy-and-hold components of a portfolio and often span very long periods. Art investors are looking for long-term appreciation and preservation of capital from owning art.

Art speculators try to invest in artwork where they see opportunities for either short-term gains or medium-term opportunities to capture artwork whose value will appreciate. Speculators often will try to invest in new artists at an early stage of their career, when pieces can be purchased more inexpensively and with significant upside.

The provenance of a piece of art is a reference to the chain of custody or trail of ownership associated with a potential investment.

Abstract art is a type of art that does not purposefully intend to represent anything that is easily recognizable and which has no clear subject and may simply be a collection of colors, shapes and textures subject to individual interpretation.

Fine art includes paintings, sculptures, printmaking and other works created for their beauty and which originate from an artist's unique skill or innate qualities.

An art auction house or fine art auction refers to a place where artwork is bought and sold in a competitive setting, as opposed to art galleries where artists showcase their work and purchases are negotiated bilaterally.

An appraisal is an auction house's evaluation of an artwork's market or insurance value. There are many useful websites where the language and terms used in the art community can be studied, including sites managed by the Metropolitan Museum of Art in New York and the Tate Gallery in London.

Market Participants and Industry Players

There is both a primary and secondary market for artwork. Galleries are where many original pieces of art get sold. Artwork can also be bought and sold on the secondary market, using auction houses and other listings to match buyers and sellers or previously purchased works. The art world is also changing as new technology begins to impact more traditional structures and ways of doing business.

The primary market for art includes the purchase of original work by collectors, designers and consumers. Buying original artwork directly from the artist is supported by a network of individual buyers from many demographics and galleries that bring multiple buyers together with artists looking to sell their work. The largest demand for art comes from buyers in the United States, the United Kingdom and China.

Art galleries are private businesses that work with one or more artists to promote their work. Artists get paid when a piece of their work is sold, and they must pay a fee or commission to the gallery for its services. The gallery will devote significant time to promoting an artist to its clients or followers. There are more than 1,500 art galleries in New York City, spread across all five boroughs, making it the largest concentration of galleries in the world.

The secondary art market is supported by a network of auction houses, museums, consumers, appraisers, advisors, dealers and retailers, collectors and speculators interested in facilitating the purchase and sale of artwork between buyers and sellers. The largest auction houses in the United States include well-known names like Sotheby's and Christie's. Other popular auction houses include Skinners in Massachusetts, Heritage in Dallas, and Bonham and Butterfield's in Los Angeles. Auction houses help sellers set reserve prices and facilitate in-person, online and over-the-phone auction processes, including previews and early bidding. Auction houses can charge a percentage of any sale, called a buyer's premium, which can range from 15% to 30% of the sale price and which is subject to a minimum commission value as well. Auction houses also get paid a fee from the seller for offering the artwork and running the auction. This fee is normally another 5%–10% of the value of the sale.

Museums are another important component of the art market. Yet, unlike a gallery, a museum is not in the business of selling art. They rely on their benefactors and on donations, grants or artwork loans to present art to the public for viewing. They usually charge admission to visitors entering the museum to cover operational costs.

We must also consider that technology is also beginning to have an impact on the art market. Artists can leverage new technology to create a brand and showcase original works. Social media is opening the art world to younger, more technology-savvy consumers, impacting how galleries drive traffic to events and how auction houses broadcast their collections for sale. Today, social media sites such as Facebook and Instagram, technology platforms such as Saatchi Art and alternative investment platforms such as Yield Street are gradually becoming increasingly relevant to investors in all sorts of collectibles.

Industry Associations and Best Practices

The Art Dealers Association of America (ADAA) is a nonprofit membership organization comprised of the nation's leading galleries in the fine arts. Founded in 1962, the ADAA seeks to promote the highest standards of connoisseurship, scholarship and ethical practice within the profession. For further information, please visit https://www.artdealers.org.

The Art Fund Association is one trade group of investors, advisors, service providers and other professionals. The association was founded in 2009. The mission of the association is to establish best practices and promote the growth of art as an investment by establishing a forum of like-minded individuals so that the art fund industry can come together for the advancement and promotion of the art investment industry. Please see the association website for information at http://www.artfundassociation.com/_who_we_are/mission.html.

There are numerous regional art dealer associations in almost every major city where art is displayed or offered for sale to the public. The following link has a comprehensive list of regional art dealer associations and other websites with information about dealers and various services supporting the art industry in the United States: http://art-collecting.com/artassociations.htm.

Market Size

In 2018, over $12 billion of art was sold by the top global auction houses, according to Sotheby's Mei Moses index data. This index data contains information about the broader art market from 1950 to 2018. According to the Artprice "blue-chip" art-work index, the paintings created by the top 100 artists have outperformed the S&P 500 by more than 250% between January 1, 2000, and December 31, 2018.[1] The 2017 *Deloitte Art and Finance Report* estimates that approximately $1.62 trillion worth of art is held privately and that 88% of wealth managers now suggest art acquisition as a component of wealth management strategies. In addition to owning art as an investment, investors can also profit from financing artwork. According to Deloitte, the value of art finance is relatively small, but growing rapidly and is currently estimated to be between $17 billion and $20 billion.[2]

According to Citigroup's 2019 sales report on the state-of-the-art market, its 2018 volume of artwork sold set a new record high, with postwar and contemporary art topping the list. The report noted that Christie's reported its best year ever in 2019, with gross sales of $7 billion. Online sales were highlighted as a component of increasing importance to Christie's sales for 2018 as well. Sotheby's sales for 2018 were over $6 billion, up 15% from the previous year.[3]

The *Wall Street Journal* called art one of the best investments of 2018.[4] In 2018, the S&P 500 declined by 5.1%, while the art market increased by 10.6%. However, it should be noted that art-related data and indices tend to have a great deal of volatility. Index averages can be misleading since there are often a small number of extraordinarily good years within any period of analysis, with most years having only average to below-average performance.

Global sales of art and antiques reached an estimated $64.1 billion in 2019, which is down 5% year over year. The United States, the United Kingdom and China account for the majority of the value of global sales in 2019, with a combined share of 82%. In the gallery and dealer sector, 2019 sales grew 2% year over year to $36.8 billion. In auctions, 2019 sales fell 17% year over year to $24.2 billion. Works selling for more than $1 million accounted for 55% of the value of fine art auction sales, with less than 1% of the lots sold. Gallery works sold over $10 million were the worst-performing in 2019, declining 39% in value with 35% fewer lots sold. In the art fair sales sector, 2019 sales reached $16.6 billion. Dealers reported that 15% of these sales were made before the fair, 64% during the fair and 21% after the fair as a direct result of exhibiting at the fair.

1. "Artprice Launches Its 'Blue-Chip' Art Market Index," Artprice, Feb. 2, 2018, https://www.artprice.com/artmarketinsight/artprice-launches-its-blue-chip-art-market-index-artprice100-designed-for-financiers-and-investors-2.
2. *Deloitte Art and Finance Report 2017*, Deloitte, 2017, https://www2.deloitte.com/content/dam/Deloitte/lu/Documents/financial-services/artandfinance/lu-art-finance-report.pdf.
3. Suzanne Gyorgy et al., *State of the Art Market*, Citigroup, Spring 2019, https://www.privatebank.citibank.com/pdf/State-of-the-Art-Market-Spring-2019.pdf.
4. Avantika Chilkoti, "The Best Investments of 2018? Art, Wine and Cars," *Wall Street Journal*, Dec. 2018, https://www.wsj.com/articles/the-best-investments-of-2018-art-wine-and-cars-11546232460.

Total Revenue in 2019	Annual Growth 2014–2019	Annual Growth 2019–2024	Profit Margin In 2019	Wages as a share of Revenue in 2019
$11.8 bn	3.8%	0.1%	12.3%	11.2%

Figure 2.1. IBISWorld revenue, growth and profit of US art dealers in 2019.

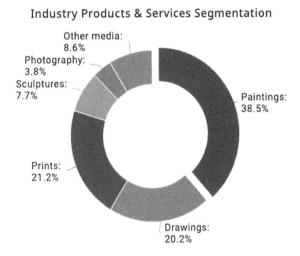

Figure 2.2. IBISWorld art dealer revenues by type of art sale for 2019.

According to IBISWorld data, as shown in Figure 2.1, US art dealers generated $11.8 billion in revenues in 2019. The industry profit margin in 2019 was 12.3%. Growth is expected to slow between now and 2025.

The sale of paintings, drawing and prints in Figure 2.2 made up approximately 80% of all art dealer sales in the United States in 2019. The remaining revenue came from sculptures, photography and other art forms.[5]

According to the Art Basel and UBS Art Market 2020 report, the 2019 online sales of art globally reached $5.9 billion. For those dealers who made online sales in 2019, 57% were to new buyers, and for second-tier auction houses new buyers accounted for 34% of their online sales.[6]

---

5. Anna Miller, "Art Dealers in the U.S.," IBISWorld, Dec. 2019, https://my.ibisworld.com/us/en/iexpert-risk/45392/iexpert-risk.
6. Clare McAndrew, *The Art Market 2020*, Art Basel and UBS, Mar. 2020, https://www.artbasel.com/about/initiatives/the-art-market?gclid=CjwKCAjw4KD0BRBUEiwA7MFNTVW2hw pDMVr4dQ599XgIoRRFagtwEJ3Jxs3dnxnGekTB3yORgC9PehoCkyoQAvD_BwE.

Opportunities and Strategies

Just as other asset classes with many segments and securities or individual offerings, investing in artwork can be done actively or passively. Passive investing involves buying known artworks and holding them for a relatively long term. This usually involves owning a diversified portfolio of an established artist's work. This would be akin to owning a portfolio of large-cap equities. A high-risk and active strategy might involve buying a particularly new artist's work and speculating on its increase in value over a relatively short period. This would be similar to small-cap investing, venture capital or investing in start-up hedge funds. There also may be arbitrage opportunities to buy artwork in one market and sell it in another at a higher price, resulting in quick and relatively risk-free profit.

Lending is another way to profit from art as an asset class. An art portfolio is an asset that can be leveraged. Individual art pieces or entire portfolios can be used as collateral to secure a loan. Many private banks provide services to individual, high-net-worth clients to facilitate art lending. Loans raised against the value of artwork can provide liquidity or allow proceeds to be reinvested in income-producing assets or to reduce other higher costs, unsecured debt or to generate growth from investing in equities. Investors or funds organized to provide loans collateralized by artwork can earn a substantial liquidity premium. A loan made by an investor can generate yields greater than 10% and will normally include over-collateralization and a low loan to value ratio to mitigate risk. Loans can be relatively short-term or longer-term in nature. Collateral is valued by third-party appraisers and is insured. Loans should have a first lien on the artwork. The lender should also know the location and provenance of each of the pieces of art against which a loan is taken. The primary borrowers are collectors, dealers and corporate clients looking for liquidity or to finance additional acquisitions. According to the 2017 *Deloitte Art and Finance Report*, the American art-secured lending market grew by 13.3% in 2017, to reach a peak of an estimated $17 billion to $20 billion.[7]

Insurance

Insurance is a major component of art investing. The risk related to fraud, damage and aging are significant and can impair the value of any asset owned for appreciation. A home-owner- or business-owner policy will generally provide adequate coverage for a truly valuable art collection. Coverage, if it exists, may vastly undervalue artwork or cover only enough to buy a reproduction. Art insurance can cover a wide range of investments, including paintings and drawings, photographs and sculptures or other collectibles such as jewelry, automobiles and rare wine or coin and stamp collections. Dedicated art coverage needs to fit potential damage scenarios, such as fire and water damage, earthquakes, riots or theft. Policies may have preconditions requiring the policyholder to warranty that they have taken certain preventative measures to protect their fine art investments, such as having specific security systems or sprinklers. There may also be restrictions on how an

---

7. *Deloitte Art and Finance Report 2017.*

investor can display and store a collection to protect it from deterioration or theft. Title insurance may also be needed to ensure that the artwork is free of claims from previous owners or creditors or to protect against fraudulent conveyance.

Who Invests?

Individual investors who are classified as high-net-worth or mega-high-net-worth individuals from the fintech, private equity and hedge fund space are active, direct investors in this sector, as is the growing community of billionaires from emerging markets such as Brazil and China.

There are also over 700 art programs that are described in the International Directory of Corporate Art Collections. Banks such as UBS have been major investors in corporate art collections for many years. JP Morgan Chase has a significant corporate art collection that includes many famous names, including Andy Warhol. According to the International Directory of Corporate Art Collections, the largest corporate art collection in the world at one time belonged to Deutsche Bank. The auto-insurance company Progressive now has one of the largest collections of contemporary art in the world. This collection includes art by renowned artists such as Petah Coyne Richard Prince, Cindy Sherman, Kehinde Wiley and Shirin Neshat. Many of these collections are considered part of the company's corporate mission and not a purely financial investment. These companies may invest to promote interest in their community, enhance the workplace and/or to support new artists, in addition to achieving any financial returns.[8]

Speculative investment in artwork by individuals and private funds is also on the rise due to increase in transparency, the use of information technology and the low correlation of art portfolios to traditional investments.

How to Invest?

Historically, art investors would simply buy a piece of art and hang it on their wall for their own viewing pleasure and perhaps to raise personal prestige amongst friends and family. Buying art as an investment, independent of any intrinsic value to the owner, is something completely different. The process of identifying investable artwork is complex and requires significant expertise developed over many years or employing experts to advise and counsel potential investors. Most art investors are better off using third-party platforms to create diversified portfolios of art.

Many private banks have dedicated teams to assist investors interested in adding art to their portfolios. These advisors can guide investors through every step of the process and help them meet their long-term investment objectives by adding artwork to traditional and alternative portfolios. Some noteworthy private banks offering art advisory services are US Trust, Bank of New York, Citi Private Bank and JP Morgan Private Bank.

---

8. Shirley Howarth, *International Directory of Corporate Art Collection* (New York: International Art Alliance and Humanities Exchange, 2017).

According to its website, the Bank of America offers a wide range of art-related services, such as consignment services to facilitate acquisition or sale, valuation, art lending, planning for high-net-worth individuals, family offices and foundations, as well as a range of services for endowments and other not-for-profits and institutions.[9]

Investors can also source artwork directly using platforms, advisors and funds. The number of ways to acquire art is getting more creative and the process of including art in a portfolio appears to be getting easier. Today, many companies offer art lending, direct investing, portfolio acquisition and construction either separately or, in some cases, under one comprehensive roof.

Benchmarks and Indices

Artprice is a research and econometrics company that maintains several indices related to artwork as investments. The Artprice 100 index, shown in Figure 2.3, was up over 400% since 2000 and significantly outperformed the S&P 500. The Artprice Global Index appreciated just 30% since 2000. The Artprice 100 index was designed to smooth out the effects of the world's more volatile artists. It is intended to provide a better pricing source and benchmark for the art market's "blue-chip" artists than the original Artprice Global index. Please see the company's website for more information about these at https://www.artprice.com/artmarketinsight/artprice-launches-its-blue-chip-art-market-index-artprice100-designed-for-financiers-and-investors-2.

The AMR index is designed to track price movements across the international art market. By selecting a large sample of 10,000 artists whose paintings and drawings have been sold around the world, the All Art index captures a significant share of the auction market by value. The index is updated monthly. For more information, visit the company's website at http://www.artmarketresearch.com.

Historically, there has been a very low positive correlation between art and other asset classes. This is a compelling reason to consider art as part of a diversified portfolio. According to a recent report on the future of the art market by Citigroup, the long-term correlation coefficient between art and the S&P 500 index was a very low 0.11. In addition, segments of the art market, such as artwork by older masters compared to modern art collections, tend to have a low correlation to one another and to increase the diversification effects of well-diversified art portfolios.[10]

Firms, Funds and Platforms

Takung Art is a publicly traded company based in Hong Kong. TKAT offers shared ownership primarily in Chinese calligraphy, paintings and jewelry. It launched in 2012

---

9. Bank of America Private Banking, https://www.privatebank.bankofamerica.com/insights/art.html.

10. Suzanne Gyorgy et al., "The Global Art Market: Perspectives and Drivers of Futures Trends," Citigroup, Nov. 2015, https://www.citivelocity.com/citigps/global-art-market/.

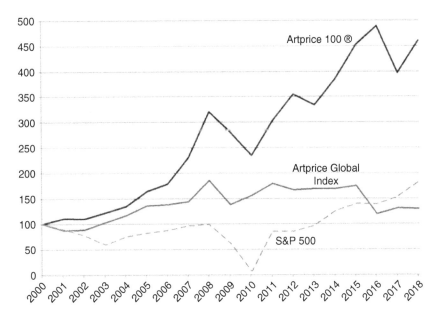

Figure 2.3. Growth of the Artprice100 index relative to the S&P 500 from 2000 to 2018. The base case of 100 is on January 1, 2000.
Source: Artprice.com

and has now grown to a market cap of $23.07 million. For more information, visit the company's website at http://www.takungart.com.

Scheryn Art Collectors' Fund is a private fund based in South Africa that was launched in 2015. It was founded by South African art collectors Herman Steyn and Dabing Chen, who provided an initial investment of about $1.6 million. It is the first contemporary African fund that exclusively invests in contemporary African art. The primary purpose of the fund is to promote African art, rather than generate returns. It accepts investments in the form of cash or artworks. For more information, visit the company's website at https://scheryn.com.

The Collectors Fund is a private fund based in Kansas City, Missouri, that was launched in 2007. It focuses on postwar and contemporary art. The fund manages two collections: the American masters collection and the twentieth-century masters collection. The minimum investment is $100,000, and by December 2010 it had raised approximately $30 million from about 100 investors. In 2011, it had sold 13% of its collection and reported a net annual return of 28.5%. For more information, visit the company's website at https://thecollectorsfund.com.

The Fine Art Invest Fund is a private fund based in Zurich, Switzerland, that was launched in 2010. It focuses primarily on contemporary photography. It mainly buys limited-edition prints, investing in established classics, rising stars and new talent. Unlike most art funds, the Fine Art Invest Fund often purchases works directly from artists. It is jointly managed by the KMS Fine Art Group and PMG Funds Management. In 2015, it had raised about $17 million from an unknown number of investors and reported a total return on investment of approximately 33%. It is an open-ended fund and allows investors to withdraw their investments on a quarterly basis. For more information, visit the company's website at http://www.thefineartfund.com.

The Tiroche DeLeon Collection is a private fund based in Israel that launched in 2012. It was created when art collectors Serge Tiroche and Russ DeLeon sold a collection of 230 works to Art Vantage PCC Limited Gibraltar. The fund focuses on artists from developing countries. The minimum investment is $500,000. The fund closed in 2017 and has a 10-year term. For more information, visit the company's website at http://www.tirochedeleon.com.

Anthea Contemporary Art Investment Fund is a private fund launched in 2013 and is based in Zug, Switzerland. It invests in postwar and contemporary artwork, which includes sculptures and photographs as well as paintings. In 2015, it reported a total return on investment of 28%. For more information, visit the company's website at http://www.anthea-art.com/fund.asp?idp=2&ids=3.

Athena Art Finance is a finance company specializing in art-based lending. Athena provides its clients with flexible options for debt financing secured by high-value artwork. Its clients are high-net-worth individuals, families, trusts and art market professionals, and Athena works closely with these individuals and their advisors, private bankers and wealth managers. Since 2015, Athena has provided over $225 million in financing for its clients around the globe. The company was acquired by Yield Street in April 2019 and is now part of the Yield Street alternative investment platform, offering secured lending products to qualified investors. For more information, visit the company's website at http://www.athena-art.com.

Artemundi Global Fund was a Cayman Islands fund launched in 2010. It focused on Old Masters, Modern and Modern Latin American art. The minimum investment was $250,000 for individuals and $1 million for institutions and it raised about $150 million. Artemundi closed on April 31, 2015, reporting a net annual return of 17%. For more information, visit the company's website at http://artemundiglobalfund.com.

Saatchi Art is a platform for those who wish to invest directly in art through the "invest in art" set-up run by Saatchi Art. The Saatchi Art website provides details regarding their previous recommendations for art investments as well as ideas for current investment opportunities. For more information, visit the company's website at http://www.saatchiart.com/invest-in-art.

Masterworks is a company that represents itself as an investment platform for fine art. It allows investors to purchase interests or shares in paintings similar to the way investors purchase shares in public companies or LPs. For more information, visit the company's website at https://www.masterworks.io/about/how-it-works.

Arthena is a venture-backed financial technology company that has pioneered quantitative strategies for artwork acquisition. Arthena is committed to bringing transparency to art investing, enabling investors to view and learn about acquired assets and artists. The Arthena team draws from a broad background of entrepreneurship, technology, mathematics, art, law and finance. The firm manages several funds, ranging from low-risk funds that invest in modern art and established artists to higher-risk funds that buy artwork from emerging artists. For more information, visit the company's website at https://arthena.com.

Composite

There are not enough publicly traded companies, mutual funds, ETFs or hedge funds dedicated to art investing to create a composite of art-related vehicles that is meaningful. Most art investments are done directly or via platforms and advisors or are organized as private equity funds which do not report their returns to the public.

What to Look For?

Direct investing in artwork is usually reserved for people who get some intrinsic value from viewing or displaying the work itself. Investors looking to add art to their portfolio need to consider the type of art, be it modern, classic, painting, sculpture, drawing and so forth. They also need to consider the artist, whether living or dead, their background story, school or style, number of works, among other things. Once a specific piece is desired, a buyer must research its history and chain of ownership and ensure it is authentic. Has it been damaged or restored? The source of the artwork is also critical. Does it come from an auction house, a reputable gallery or a dealer? Most serious investors will use an art advisor or a person knowledgeable in art collecting to start creating a portfolio.

Investing in art using a platform allows investors to obtain some economics of scale and reliance upon professionals with extensive experience and track records. Each platform should be evaluated based on its in-house staff, partnerships with galleries, art fairs and auction houses, as well as appraisers and insurers.

When considering an art investment fund, a few additional considerations are warranted. What is the experience of the fund manager? What is the focus of the portfolio—for example, Old Masters or Modern Art? How will the fund manager and the portfolio adapt to changing preferences and tastes in the art world? How long has the fund been in existence? What process does the fund manager follow to identify new investment opportunities? How long is the lock-up period or fund term? Will the fund employ any leverage? Like any investment, an investor needs to critically assess the fees being charged by the fund manager as well. Are the fund and the manager providing enough diversification and return to warrant the additional fees being charged?

Valuation of course is always a challenge with alternative investments. Art investing can be very volatile depending on the portfolio. At its most basic level, the value of any artwork is a pure function of supply and demand. An artist's name is part of the story. How many works of art were created? How many have been traded or sold in recent years? What is the subject being depicted? The condition and quality of the piece of art are also important. Any previous damage or restoration may have an adverse impact on value. Other factors that impact value are trends in global wealth and the value of all other asset classes, the degree of economic and political stability around the world and the changes in tastes and preferences among buyers.

Appraisers are one popular way to get a sense of value, along with recent sales of similar works. Global interest rates, inflation and exchange rates also impact the value of art as much or more than many other exotic asset classes. In the end, the valuation of an art portfolio can be highly subjective and subject to many unique risks as well as a wider range of values than many other alternative investments.

Investing in art-related loans can also provide an attractive opportunity for investors. This has less risk than investing and owning artwork. The due diligence focus is a bit different as well. The artwork is collateral and the investor has indirect exposure to changes in value. Exposure may be with or without recourse to the owner. Investor due diligence should include some basic research on the platform or manager or advisor who is originating loans. Some of the due diligence questions should cover the fees and charges of the advisor, platform or fund, areas of specialization, valuation methodology, loan to value ratios, default history, loan terms, insurance and storage requirements and whether loans are fixed or floating rates. Of course, strong references are always a good idea as well.

Unique Risks

Artwork, like many collectibles, has a unique set of risk factors. Taxes are certainly an issue. Art gains are taxed at 28% in the United States, which is higher than the capital gains tax on stocks and bonds. Artwork pays no dividend and earns no interest, so there is an opportunity cost associated with holding and storing art that eats into an investor's profits over time. Storage costs are expensive. Fire and water damage are also risks that are always present. Fraud, of course, is another major risk in the art world. Many of these risks can be mitigated but at a cost. Art is also not very liquid, so it may not be able to be sold when cash is needed. While it has been improving, access to information and transparency in this department still needs work and is insufficient in many cases. Finally, transaction fees and broker charges can also be very costly when art is purchased or sold.

Social, Legal and Ethical Considerations

Artists and their work can be controversial. An artist can be political, violate social norms or offend religious values. Investors buying artwork for investment purposes may need to be aware of the impact of the artist, whether positive or negative, on the value of the artwork.

Trends and Outlook

The Citi Private Bank Art Advisory and Finance Group 2019 report entitled *State of the Art Market* looked at the state-of-the-art market in 2018 and some trends for 2019 and beyond, including the increasing role of technology, consolidation, the use of artificial intelligence and the need for more transparency and oversight in the art world. This report is a valuable resource for those interested in this type of investment.[11]

---

11. Gyorgy et al., *State of the Art Market*.

Manager Perspective and Insights

Cynthia Sachs, YieldStreet.com

What is your general experience in finance or asset management and with esoteric types of alternative investments such as life settlements, litigation funding, tax liens, trade claims or art or artwork finance, Bitcoin, collectibles and the like?
I have over 20 years of high-yield corporate credit experience at major banking institutions like Morgan Stanley, Bank of America and others in debt origination, port-folio management and trading (par and distressed). My career took a major shift post the 2008 financial crisis, which led me to Bloomberg LP where I created and man-aged a global fixed income data analytics/pricing business, called BVAL, for five years. I then decided to return to credit investing and became a founding member and the chief investment officer of Athena Art Finance, a Carlyle portfolio company, which was acquired by YieldStreet in 2019.

What is your specific experience investing in art finance?
I'm the chief investment officer of Athena Art Finance, a specialty finance company that provides art collectors, art investors and art trusts with art-backed loans.

What is your opinion on the opportunity presented by investing in artwork or art finance? What is the expected return, liquidity and so on?
Investing in artworks can be an interesting portfolio diversification strategy as it's a phys-ical asset that is less correlated to the volatility in the global financial markets and therefore should perform well during inflationary times. However, artworks do not generate a cash flow such as interest income or dividend income and must also be properly stored and insured. In addition, it's important to choose signature artworks from top artists. Art is a relatively illiquid, long-term buy-and-hold asset class, which is important to consider when investing to achieve acceptable returns.

What are some of the risks associated with art finance?
Major art-related risks include authenticity, title and maintaining the long-term condition of the piece.

Where would you see art finance fitting into the asset allocation process? Is it a stand-alone asset class, part of a credit- or fixed-income portfolio or part of an alternative's allocation? And what type of investors are best suited for allocating to life settlements either as a discrete portfolio or part of a credit or alterna-tive investments allocation?
I see art as an alternative asset and as a minority portion of well-diversified equity and fixed income portfolio.

Academic Perspectives and Research

Articles related to artwork as an investment vehicle first appeared in the academic lit-erature during the 1980s and continue to be prominent today. According to Google Scholar, today there are over 77,000 academic articles that have been written about art as an investment vehicle, with 8,000 articles produced since the beginning of 2018 alone. Many articles with investment themes are focused on returns on art over various periods, return accruing to specific artists or specific mediums such as fine art or sculpture. Other articles detail the relative return of artwork to market benchmarks, holding periods and the collection of data on sales.

One article by University of Luxembourg researchers Roman Kräussl and Ali Nasser Eddine, titled "To Have and to Hold? The Optimal Holding Period of Art as an Investment," analyzed the optimal holding period for artwork as an investment. The researchers analyzed millions of public auction sales, using a standardized method to track changes in art prices over time. The researchers constructed repeat-sales data sets by evaluating whether or not the piece of art in question was previously sold at another auction. Data came from available auction sales from 60 different auction houses covering the period 1990–2014 and data included in the Blouin Art Sales Index (BASI) database for 2014 and 2015. The researchers also used Christie's and Sotheby's art libraries and data, specifically using data covering the fine art auctions at their London and New York locations for years between 1990 and 1998 and most other auctions for which there was data between 1980 and 1989. The final data set included 63,936 unique artworks, out of which 56,579 were sold twice, 6,057 thrice and 984 four times. The study created the largest up-to-date data set of the repeat sales of art ever constructed for academic research.[12] The researchers considered seven different holding periods. The researchers grouped all repeat-sales pairs that were traded within time frames of two years: 2–5 years, 5–10 years, 10–15 years, 15–20 years, 20–30 years and >30 years. They ran an Ordinary Least Squares regression to identify the association of holding periods with expected returns. The findings showed that there is a positive relationship between the holding period and return. They also noted that artwork traded over very short periods, for example, that of two years or less, generated the highest annual returns and had the highest volatility. This result was surprising, given the high transaction costs in the public art market and the fact that these costs are inversely related to the holding duration.[13]

A paper titled "Blockchain, Fractional Ownership and the Future of Creative Work" by researchers from New York University and the University of Luxembourg tested the hypothesis that artists could profit from retaining equity in their work more than from investing in financial markets over the same time frame. The researchers studied theoretical returns of artwork constructed under the premise that the artist would maintain fractional equity in their artwork upon its initial sale. The model would allow artists to receive a smaller percentage of the proceeds when their work is first sold and to retain a percentage of equity going forward, that is, profits from future sales. For example, instead of artists receiving the traditional 50–50 dealer–artist split,

12. Howarth, *International Directory of Corporate Art Collection*.
13. Roman Kräussl and Ali Nasser Eddine, "To Have and to Hold? The Optimal Holding Period of Art as an Investment," University of Luxembourg, Dec. 2018, https://papers.ssrn.com/sol3/papers.cfm?abstract_id=3304876.

the split instead becomes 50–40–10, with the artist taking 40% cash and keeping 10% equity. This model uses primary data from the initial sale, which is often difficult to find and even regarded as a trade secret. Their approach then combined the first-sale data with secondary market sales to determine returns over time. The researchers tracked artwork from two prominent artists, Jasper Johns and Robert Rauschenberg. They combined publicly available auction data with private sales information received from the Leo Castelli Gallery papers at the Archives of American Art for the period between 1958 and 1963.[14] The researchers utilized their proprietary database of over 3 million auction returns to generate 89 auction records for Jasper Johns paintings and 363 pieces by Robert Rauschenberg, with auction results that started in 1970 and went through 2016. They then matched these to the original sales data which contains records for 38 Johns sales and 61 Rauschenberg sales over the 1958–63 period.[15]

To test their hypothesis, the researchers analyzed the return on artwork from the perspectives of the works individually and the entire group of Johns' works and Rauschenberg's works, respectively, as if a hypothetical collector had bought each grouping. They also evaluated a portfolio representing 10% of each artist's group of works, as if each artist had retained 10% equity, and finally two portfolios that isolated the earliest works by each artist. They did this with the intention of observing the significance, if any, of buying the artists' work at the earliest opportunity. The researchers used value-weighted portfolios since an equal weighting would be strongly influenced by the variation of initial gallery sales price, from $150 to $12,000. The results demonstrate an enormous difference between the original sales prices, which start as low as $150, and the auction prices, which sometimes grew to millions of dollars. Some of the artists had annualized ROIs of 30%–40% over decades. They modeled the opportunity cost by assuming the artist invested the cash into the S&P 500 index, three-month US Treasury Bill or 10-year US Treasury bond. The article found that the retained equity model drastically outperforms these benchmarks in every case. The model tracked the worst-performing piece of art by each artist. Even the worst works by Rauschenberg and Johns outperformed the S&P 500 index by 3.6 and 21.2 times, respectively. The researchers concluded that retained ownership for these two artists would have resulted in a significantly higher return as opposed to not receiving ownership. Fractional ownership would allow creative workers to become co-investors alongside the parties that purchase their work, allowing them to share in what could be incredibly lucrative profits for the work they created. Another interesting finding from this research was the suggestion that tracking fractional ownership could be facilitated using blockchain technology. This would allow for the management of fractional shares and low transaction cost trading of such shares. The researchers stated

---

14. Bank of America Private Banking.
15. Amy Whitaker and Roman Kräussl, "Blockchain, Fractional Ownership and the Future of Creative Work," CFS Working Paper Series 594, Center for Financial Studies (CFS), June 2018, https://ideas.repec.org/p/zbw/cfswop/594.html.

that equity ownership can provide important optionality to artists, diversification to investors and liquidity options to both parties.[16]

Summary

Art investing and financing is an asset class that can provide investors with both portfolio diversification and attractive returns. It is unique in that supply is limited, acquisition of artwork can be costly and the investment often lacks liquidity. Platforms, services and the use of technology are improving transparency and access to this market for investors. Much of the investment in art, however, still comes from those who have a passion for the works themselves, in addition to wanting a solid financial return.

Useful Websites and Additional Reading

"Accounting for Taste: Art and the Financial Markets over Three Centuries," http:// www.jstor.org.avoserv2.library.fordham.edu/stable/2117568.

"Art as an Investment and Conspicuous Consumption Good," http://www.jstor.org. avoserv2.library.fordham.edu/stable/25592524.

"Art as an Investment: The Top 500 Artists," http://citeseerx.ist.psu.edu/viewdoc/dow nload?doi=10.1.1.308.6243&rep=rep1&type=pdf.

"Arts Managers as Liaisons between Finance and Art: A Qualitative Study Inspired by the Theory of Functional Differentiation," https://www.researchgate.net/pub- lication/249037351_Arts_Managers_as_Liaisons_between_Finance_and_Art_A_ Qualitative_Study_Inspired_by_the_Theory_of_Functional_Differentiation.

"Contemporary Art, Capitalization and the Blockchain: On the Autonomy and Automation of Art's Value," http://financeandsociety.ed.ac.uk/article/view/1724.

"Fine Art and High Finance: Expert Advice on the Economics of Ownership," https:// onlinelibrary.wiley.com/doi/book/10.1002/9781119204688.

"Glossary of Art Terms," https://www.artevolution.com/glossary.

"Investing in Creativity: A Study of the Support Structure for U.S. Artists," https:// www.tandfonline.com/doi/abs/10.3200/JAML.34.1.43-58?journalCode=vjam20.

"Investing in Fine Art," https://todaytrader.com/investing/fine-art/.

"The Sotheby's Mei Moses Indices," https://www.sothebys.com/en/the-sothebys-mei- moses-indices?cmp=ppc_mei-moses_google_20-mar-.

---

16. Whitaker and Kräussl, "Blockchain, Fractional Ownership and the Future of Creative Work."

Chapter Three

LIFE SETTLEMENTS

Introduction

Investing in mortality is another exotic alternative investment. Mortality is one of life's most certain events. Most people will own a life insurance policy to protect assets, pay taxes, provide for family members or to cover costs associated with death. During their lifetime a person will pay a premium, and after their death their beneficiary will receive a death benefit. In between the time a policy is purchased and a final benefit is paid, a policy will have a cash surrender value that the insurance company will pay out for early termination. This value is often quite low, so most people will hold their policy until it pays off. Typically, the owner and the insured are the same person, and the beneficiaries are the estate, children or other designees.

Insurance companies profit when the premiums collected over time, plus investment income, exceed the amount paid to those insured. There are many types of life insurance. Whole Life, Term Life and Universal Life are three popular types of life insurance products.

A life settlement is the sale of a life insurance policy to a third party that occurs without changing the insured, for an amount that exceeds the cash surrender value of the policy, but which is lower than its death benefit. A policyowner who is the seller receives a cash payment, while the purchaser or investor in the policy agrees to continue the premium payments. The buyer will receive the death benefit upon the death of the insured.

Life insurance policy sales came into fruition as a result of a landmark US court case in 1911. In the Grigsby versus Russel Supreme Court case in the United States, the court upheld a policyowner's right to assign a life insurance policy to an unrelated third party. The case eventually made its way to the US Supreme Court where it was affirmed.[1]

Many individuals faced with large or rising premiums in retirement will let their policy lapse or sell it back to the insurance company at a very low cash surrender value. Selling to a life settlement fund or investor is now another viable option. This is attractive to investors because the rate of return on the purchase relative to the expected mortality date can be quite high relative to any interest rate or credit risk. There is usually a significant risk premium that can be earned over risk-free rates or bonds, given that most

---

1. "Defining a Life Settlement," Life Insurance Settlement Association (LISA), accessed Sep. 2019, https://www.lisa.org/consumer-advisors/life-settlement-basics/defining-life-settlements.

contracts that are purchased will have a predictable payment date and will be paid off by a highly rated insurance company. Returns increase if mortality rates increase and returns fall if mortality rates decline. Since mortality rates are relatively stable and predictable, this product offers investors a highly rated and predictable cash flow at a relatively high discount rate or yield.

A Few Definitions and Key Terms

According to the SEC website (SEC.gov), a life settlement transaction occurs when a life insurance policyowner sells his/her policy to an investor in exchange for a lump-sum payment. The amount of the payment from the investor to the policyowner is generally less than the death benefit on the policy, but more than its cash surrender value.

The cash surrender value of a life insurance policy is the amount available in cash upon voluntary termination of a policy by its owner before it becomes payable by death or maturity. The amount is equivalent to the cash value stated in the policy minus a surrender charge and any outstanding loans and interest.

The face amount is the amount that will be paid in case of death or at the maturity of the policy. It does not include additional amounts acquired through the application of policy dividends.

Life expectancy is the probability of an individual living to a certain age. It usually comes from a mortality table prepared by an actuarial firm.

Mortality is the incidence of death at each age or the "frequency of death." Policy proceeds are the amount actually paid on a life insurance policy at death or when the policyowner receives payment at surrender or maturity.

A policyowner is the person who owns a life insurance policy. This is usually the insured person.

A premium is the payment that a policyowner makes in exchange for an insurance policy. Depending on the terms of the policy, the premium may be paid in one payment or a series of regular payments (e.g., annually, semi-annually, quarterly or monthly). The premium charged reflects the insurance provider's expectation of loss, expenses and profit contingencies related to the policy and the insured.

For more definitions and terms, please reference the New York Department of Financial Services Life Insurance Resource Center website using the following link: https://www.dfs.ny.gov/consumer/cli_gloss.htm.

Industry Associations and Best Practices

The Life Insurance Settlement Association was established in 1994. Membership includes brokers, providers, financing entities and industry service providers such as law firms, medical underwriters, consultants, investment funds, actuarial firms, trustees and escrow agents. For more information, visit the association's website at https://www.lisa.org/about.

Market Participants and Industry Players

There are several major players in this industry. Of course, we start with the insurance companies and underwriters who create these policies. Then we have the policyowners, particularly those who are age 65 and older and likely at or near retirement. The policyowners typically targeted for life settlements are those that hold life insurance policies with an average face value of $1.0 million.

Demand for cash comes from policyowners who need funds to manage expenses. This is an increasing concern for seniors who are retired and have limited options to increase income or raise cash. Many seniors will sell their home or use a reverse mortgage or home equity loan to raise cash in retirement. Selling a personal life insurance policy is another option. According to the US Bureau of Labor Statistics, individuals 65 years and older spend more than their income by almost 12%, and those 75 years and older spend over 21% more than what they earn. The majority of their income comes from Social Security and private and government retirement plans.[2] The demand for cash is increasing, while the supply of cash and liquid assets is extremely limited or decreasing in many cases. This imbalance in supply and demand therefore provides an opportunity for investors with cash who can offer liquidity. According to the Life Insurance Settlement Association, there were $143 billion in lapsed policies by policyowners age 65 and older in 2015.[3]

Investors here include institutional investors, accredited investors and fund managers advising private LPs. Institutional investors such as endowments, family offices and commercial banks are some of the major investors in life settlements. Individuals who are accredited investors also invest in life settlements via private funds or mutual funds. Due to the complexity of life settlement structure and the difficulty in pooling a large number of policies, both institutional investors and accredited investors invest in life settlements through collective investment vehicles.

Financial advisors to individual policyowners play a significant role in this market. The financial advisor is often in the best position to identify a policy and educate an owner about the use of life settlements to raise cash. Brokers also participate in this market. Brokers will identify and purchase portfolios and assume all administrative responsibilities for investors. Ashar Group, Welcome Funds, Windsor Life Settlements, Amrita Financial and Magna Life are examples of brokers who offer a pool of insurance policies to be purchased by investors and who charge brokerage fees. Brokerage fees are estimated to be approximately 10%–20% of the face value of a contract.

Estimates of Market Size

The primary market for life insurance exists between the insurance company and the insured, who is the initial buyer. This is the largest marketplace and is measured in

---

2. "Consumer Expenditure Survey," Washington, DC, US Bureau of Labor Statistics, Sept. 2018, https://www.bls.gov/cex/.
3. "Defining a Life Settlement," LISA.

tens of trillions of dollars. The secondary market is the market that exists between the insured and a third-party investor. This market is measured in billions. There is also a tertiary market that exits between the brokers and third parties looking for liquidity or to acquire previously purchased policies. All transactions are over the counter and there is no exchange or central clearing in place for life settlements today.

According to a 2017 article in *The Deal* entitled "Market Volume Continues to Surge; 2016 Busiest Year in Secondary Market Since 2009," the number of life settlement policy sales grew from 1,123 in 2015 to 1,650 in 2016, while the total face value of policies purchased increased to $2.14 billion, compared to $1.65 billion for the same period.[4] In 2018, the face value of settled life insurance policies was $3.4 billion and there were 2,722 policies settled for an average face value of $1.24 million according to the Magna Life Settlements report.[5]

The value of life settlements is relatively small compared to the total value of life insurance policies outstanding of approximately $12 trillion at the end of 2016, according to the *Life Insurers Fact Book*.[6] Based on this data, it appears that less than 1% of outstanding life insurance policies today have been sold or settled. Most people who are sellers in the United States are those who are of age 65 or older. There were approximately 50.9 million people aged 65 and older in the United States, which equates to approximately 15.6% of the total US population as of 2017. This compares to 13.1% of Americans aged 65 and older in 2010. This means that the target population of potential life insurance sellers is also expanding, although usage of the product and overall product awareness remains relatively low.[7] Not surprisingly, activity among firms specializing in investment in life insurance is also increasing as capital is raised to fill the gap between the supply and demand for money that is facilitated by life settlement sales.

Opportunities and Strategies

Opportunities exist to invest in policies related to several types of life insurance such as term, whole life, universal life or convertible term. Strategies can vary based on geography, size or health of the insured and the degree of diversification or concentration desired in a specific portfolio. Strategies can be based on traditional life policies owned by persons needing liquidity and standardized mortality tables or "viatical" policies of people with a terminal illness with less than two years of life expectancy.

4. Jon Kostakopoulos, "Market Volume Continues to Surge; 2016 Busiest Year in Secondary Market Since 2009," *PR Newswire*, 26 June 2018, www.prnewswire.com/news-releases/market-volume-continues-to-surge-2016-busiest-year-in-secondary-market-since-2009-300467074.html.

5. *Magna Life Settlement Industry Report 2018*, Magna Life Settlements, 2018, https://www.magnalifesettlements.com/wp-content/uploads/2018/10/Magna_2018IndustryReport.pdf.

6. Michele Alexander et al., *Life Insurers Fact Book* (American Counsel of Life Insurers, 2018), https://www.acli.com/Industry-Facts/Life-Insurers-Fact-Book.

7. *Annual Estimates of the Resident Population for Selected Age Groups*, Washington, DC, US Census Bureau, June 2016, https://data.census.gov/cedsci/.

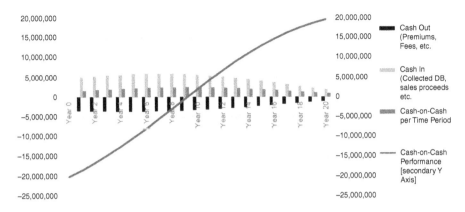

Figure 3.1. The effect of predicted cash flows on IRR over time.
Source: AAP, https://www.aa-partners.ch/about-aap/.

Investors in life settlements pay a premium above the cash surrender value of any individual contract as an inducement to the seller. The seller is motivated to sell the policy for a price that is higher than they would otherwise get from the insurance company. The purchase price of the life settlement therefore includes both the cash surrender value and a buyer's premium. The buyer is now responsible for all future premium payments on the policy. The premiums add to the investor's cost basis over time. The sum of the purchase price plus all paid premiums are deducted from the face value paid at death on a policy to determine the profit on a contract.

The performance of a life settlements portfolio is a function of several variables. There is cash that is paid out related to the initial purchase of a portfolio by an investor. There is also the annual cash out paid to cover premiums. Finally, there is the cash that comes in related to settlement events in the portfolio, that is, life insurance proceeds. A portfolio can generate attractive returns when all goes as anticipated and cash in exceeds cash out over the life of the portfolio, as is the case in Figure 3.1.

Alternatively, a portfolio can lose a great deal if the cash outflows occur longer than expected and cash inflows occur later than expected over the life of a portfolio, as is the case in Figure 3.2.

If a buyer can purchase a policy at a price that is lower than the current valuation model price, then the return on the policy will be higher, all else being equal. Policies that pay out later than expected will generate much lower returns. Policies that pay out earlier will generate much higher returns. The most important factors influencing the realized return on a policy are the buyer's initial cost and the time frame between the policy purchase date and payment dates (i.e., mortality and the ability of the insurance company to fully pay the face value of the contract). This means that estimates of mortality need to be obtained to assess the likely lifespan of the persons covered by each policy before investing. Investors also need to evaluate the creditworthiness of the insurance company that has written the policy to ensure it gets the default risk premium correct.

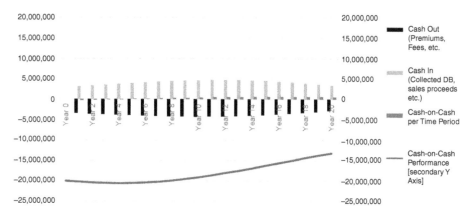

Figure 3.2. The effect of longer negative cash flows and latter cash inflows on IRR over time. *Source:* AAP, https://www.aa-partners.ch/about-aap/.

Investors can work backwards from the face value and time frame using a discount rate that reflects default risk and a risk-free rate to determine how much of a buyer's premium they are willing to pay. If the investor estimates for mortality are too low (i.e., the investor believes people covered by a policy will live longer), then the realized return will be lower than expected. If the investor estimates for mortality are too high (i.e., he/she believes people covered by the policy will live shorter lives), then the realized return will be higher than expected.

Assume an investor is willing to pay $27,000 for a face value of $1.0 million with a life expectancy of five years. The investor also will pay premiums at a flat rate of $50,000 per year during years one through five. The Internal Rate of Return (IRR) associated with these cash flows is approximately 18%. If, however, the policies terminate in just three years, the IRR jumps to 42%. Alternatively, if the policies don't pay for seven years, the IRR drops to under 10%.

Since most investments will be owned for a reasonable amount of time after the initial purchase date, valuation policies, best practices and assumptions are an important issue for life settlement investors.

Market data and transaction history can be used where available to value policies if available. Models and estimates are also common. The IRR obtained from similar transactions or using assumed inputs for the risk-free rate, default risk and liquidity premium are used to discount the face value of a policy for a given mortality assumption. Mortality assumptions are needed using probabilities and actuarial assumptions.

Any changes in interest rates, insurance company default rates or mortality assumptions will impact the futures' expected IRR and change the value of previously purchased policies that are market-to-market in a portfolio. Investors need to be careful that initial estimates are not too favorable and that the portfolio is being modeled for worst-case outcomes that could lead to substantial loss or lower-than-expected IRRs.

Who Invests?

Institutions and individuals invest in this asset class today using a variety of structures. According to a Life Settlement report issued by *The Deal*, Warren Buffett's Berkshire Hathaway Life Insurance Co. purchased a $300 million life settlement portfolio in 2014. Berkshire paid $60 million to acquire the 100 plus policies included in the portfolio from provider Coventry First. Berkshire has been active in the space since 2001 when Berkshire subsidiary Gen Re arranged a $400 million financing facility for Minnesota life settlement provider Living Benefits Financial Services. Bill Gates has also invested more than $500 million of his personal net worth in the asset class.[8]

How to Invest?

Investors can invest directly, they can invest using private funds, they can invest in mutual funds and/or they can invest in public companies offering exposure to life settlement assets. Due to the complexity of life settlement structure and difficulty with pooling a large number of policies, both institutional investors and accredited investors most often invest in a life settlement policy through collective investment vehicles or public companies.

Outside the United States, there are a handful of public companies and several closed-end funds and collective investment vehicles that offer exposure to life settlements.

Private funds are one way to invest in life settlements. According to private fund data from Preqin (https://www.preqin.com), there are many different commingled, insurance-linked funds that invest in life settlements. Preqin provides examples of private fund vehicles or hedge funds that invest in life settlements. Management fees range from zero to 2%, majorly at 1.5%. Performance fees range from 15% to 20%, majorly at 20%. Redemption periods range from one to three months. Many have hurdle rates that range from T-bills to 8%. There are also minimum investment sizes that range from $50,000 to $250,000. Vida Longevity Fund is the largest fund with more than $2.0 billion in fund assets under management.

Benchmarks and Indices

AAP Investable Index is an index that tracks the performance of open-end funds in the life settlement space. The returns come from the underlying fund performance data. According to information on the company's website, the AAP Investable Index outperformed the S&P 500 from December 2015 to June 2018. The index also exhibited significantly lower volatility and a higher Sharpe ratio than the S&P 500 during that period. For more information, visit the company's website at https://www.aa-partners. ch/aap-life-indices/aap-investable-life-settlement-index.

---

8. "Berkshire Hathaway Strikes Again," Reliant Life Shares LLC, 2014, https://reliantlifeshares. com/wp-content/uploads/2014/05/berkshire-hathaway-strikes-again.pdf.

Firms, Funds and Platforms

Global Insurance Settlements Funds PLC is a collective investment fund incorporated in Ireland. It is an umbrella investment company with segregated liability between sub-funds. The GIS General Fund is one of the products offered by Global Insurance Settlements Funds PLC. This structure is aimed at sophisticated institutional investors. The core activity of the fund is to actively manage a large and diverse portfolio of life insurance policies (life settlements) issued by companies in the United States. The fund's overall investment objective is to generate attractive risk-adjusted returns over time by actively managing a large and diversified portfolio of life insurance policies through life settlement transactions. For more information, visit the company's website at www.gisfunds.com.

Ress Life Investments is a private fund that invests in the secondary market for US life insurance policies, aiming to provide returns uncorrelated to stock and bond markets or other asset classes. The fund is managed by the Stockholm-based alternative investment fund manager Resscapital AB. The fund has a target annual return of 7% with no leverage and target volatility of less than 5%. The fund also offers a low correlation to traditional asset classes. For more information, visit the company's website at https://www.resscapital.com/fund.

Augury Hedge Fund is a specialist investment fund that aims to achieve long-term capital growth by investing in non-correlated asset classes with an emphasis on identifying short- to medium-term investment opportunities and a focus on risk mitigation and liquidity management. It offers an arbitrage share class that focuses on strategic short-term opportunities in the insurance marketplace including, but not limited to, the purchase and resale of traded life policies (TLPs) and insurance portfolios, short-term asset-backed financing arrangements and fee-based services to institutions. The fund offers a 2% management fee and a 20% performance fee structure and monthly liquidity. Since its inception in 2014, the fund has delivered a net annualized return of approximately 10% with 12% volatility, along with a Sharpe ratio of .59 using a 2% risk-free rate. All fund information and terms are as reported by preqin.com. For more information, visit the company's website at https://www.auguryhedgefund.com.

AIR US Life Fund I is a hedge fund that was created in July 2009. As of June 2019, it had an AUM (assets under management) of $22.69 million. The fund provides investors with exposure to life insurance policies bought from individuals who no longer have either a need or the desire to maintain their current policies. The manager, AIR Asset Management, charges a 2% management fee and a 20% performance fee with an 8% hurdle rate and a minimum investment of $250,000. All fund information and terms are as reported by preqin.com. For additional information see the company's website at https://www.airassetmanagement.com.

Leadenhall is a hedge fund that was created in October 2009. As of July 2019, it had $828 million of AUM. The fund provides investors with exposure to the insurance and reinsurance markets and focuses on cat (catastrophe) bonds, cat swamps and other insurance-linked investments. The fund is managed by Leadenhall Capital Partners, a London-based hedge fund manager which is exclusively focused on insurance-linked investment portfolios. Management fees range from 1% to 1.5% and performance fees range from 10% to 20%. All fund information and terms are as reported by preqin. com. For more information, visit the company's website at https://www.leadenhallcp. com.

BlackOak Investors is a UK-based hedge fund managed by SL Investment Management. As of May 2019, it had an AUM of $38.6 million. It seeks to provide investors with returns uncorrelated to other asset classes by investing in US senior life insurance settlements that are sold to them by individuals in their senior years who decided to sell their policies in the secondary market. It charges a 1.5% management fee, a 20% performance fee and has a $100,000 minimum investment threshold. The fund managers seek to meet and exceed the fund's hurdle rate of 8%. All fund information and terms are as reported by preqin.com. For more information, please see the company's website at https://www.blackoakinvestors.com/en/home/.

Laureola Investment Fund is a Bermuda-based hedge fund that was launched by Laureola Advisors in May 2013. It uses a bottom-up approach to identify pricing inefficiencies in the life settlement industry and identify high-quality life settlement policies for investment. As of August 2019, Laureola Investment Fund had an AUM of $54 million and has a minimum investment threshold of $100,000. All fund information and terms are as reported by preqin.com. For more information, visit the company's website at http://www.laureolaadvisors.com/about-us/.

Vida Longevity Fund is a US-based hedge fund created in May 2010 that focuses primarily on senior life insurance settlements in addition to other longevity-linked assets. The fund seeks to provide investors with net annualized returns in the 8%–12% range that are largely uncorrelated to other asset classes and macroeconomic trends. The fund has a minimum investment of $500,000 and had an AUM of $2,444 million as of August 2019. All fund information and terms are as reported by preqin.com. For more information, visit the company's website at http://www.vidacapitalinc.com.

Composite

A composite of life settlement investment vehicles, shown in Table 3.1, had a correlation to the S&P 500 of −0.13, an average annual return of 6.42%, a standard deviation of 3.67% and a Sharpe ratio of 1.75 for the period between January 2016 and December 2019. This compares to the return, standard deviation and Sharpe ratio for the S&P 500 of 14.33%, 11.56% and 1.24%, respectively. Despite the lower absolute return for the period, an investment in life settlements would have had a positive portfolio effect in terms of risk reduction and Sharpe ratio due to the low correlation and standard deviation relative to the S&P 500.

A $1,000 investment in a life settlement composite in January 2016, shown in Figure 3.3, would have grown to almost $1,300 by December 2019 compared to $1,708 for the S&P 500, although with much less volatility.

Table 3.1. The performance, risk and correlation of a composite of life settlement company investment vehicles versus the S&P 500 between January 2016 and December 2019.

	Life Settlements	S&P 500
Correlation	−0.13	NA
Standard Deviation	3.67%	11.56%
Average Annual Return	6.42%	14.33%
Simplified Sharpe	1.75	1.24

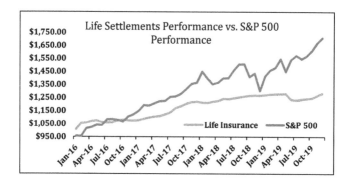

Figure 3.3. The growth of $1,000 invested in a composite of life settlement vehicles versus the $1,000 invested in the S&P 500 from January 2016 to December 2019.

What to Look For?

There are five major risks related to life settlement investments that investors must consider. These include operational risk, premium risk, longevity risk, liquidity risk and fraud risk.

Investors should understand how portfolio policies are administered. Who is servicing the policies, making payments, collecting payments and providing valuations impacts all investors. A portfolio of policies has inherent operational risk related to premium payments, legal claim documentation and validity, along with valuation risk. Life insurance policies have various forms of premiums to be paid. The policy is only in force when the premiums are paid on time. A lapse in premiums could result in a loss of benefits. The premiums become a liability for the investors or a fund when they purchase policies from the original owners.

What assumptions have been made about premium increase over time? Are they locked in and contractual or can they vary? Premium risk exists if the cost of owning a policy can increase over time without notice. The cost of most life insurance policies is determined by the age of the policyowner, along with gender, health and lifestyle. The cost is normally stated in the contract. The risk for the life settlement investor is any unanticipated premium growth. This growth is caused by the health of the insurance company, any catastrophic event and the interest rate of the market.

What are the mortality assumptions being used when policies are purchased or to value policies in the portfolio? How diversified is the portfolio? Longevity risk is the most immediate and inherent risk in a life settlement investment. Any increase in the probability of the policyowner outliving the expected policy term can significantly affect the overall return. However, the unpredictability of the mortality rate can be hedged by having a diversified portfolio.

How does the liquidity of the investment vehicle or fund compare to the liquidity of the portfolio of policies? Liquidity risk exists in the life settlement due to the limited secondary market for the settled policies. There is also a potential mismatch between fund terms for investor liquidity and the cash flows expected to accrue to the portfolio of policies over time. Most purchased policies have 10 or more years remaining before any gain can be realized. However, some funds may have a shorter investment and redemption period.

Who are the counterparties in the portfolio? What are their ratings and is there any concentration? There is a degree of counterparty risk with all insurance companies. There is a small possibility that an insurance company might fail to pay the death benefit or total cash amount at the termination of the policy. However, this risk is quite minimal given that most policies are purchased from highly rated insurers.

Are third party brokers used by the fund? How are the assignments and ownership of policies documented? There is a certain degree of fraud risk when policies are purchased via independent brokers. Because there are limited data related to fraudulent policy sales, the due diligence process followed by managers or investors related to documentation of all policies is critical. In one instance, a firm had sold participation in life insurance policies to individual investors and asset managers, but it was found by a federal jury that the company was guilty of deliberately under-estimating how long the insured people would live, leaving buyers with policies that were significantly overvalued.

Unique Risks

Life insurance policies purchased by third parties have a number of unique risks. First, there is a significant valuation risk in a life settlement portfolio. Transaction data is hard to find. Often, there will be no market price to use in valuation. Market risk may also exist if the portfolio needs to be sold and cannot be held to final maturity. There is no exchange or formal market for this product and the sale of a portfolio may need to be arranged privately or via a broker at a significant cost. There is also default risk and credit risk based on the quality of the insurance company from whom payment is expected in the future. Generally, the default risk of life settlement policies is very low due to the high credit ratings of most insurance companies. Life settlements bear the risk of rising premiums or changes in premiums as the policies age, lowering IRRs. Interest rate risk is also embedded in any portfolio. Of course, there is an operational risk due to the need for the premiums to be paid; death notices must be obtained and payments of policies must be applied for and processed on a timely basis. Finally, there is longevity risk. Longer life of the insured means lower returns to the investor. Actual experiences that differ from expectations built into the purchase price can both positively and negatively impact returns.

A Securities and Exchange Commission release on life settlements suggests investors take note of several important issues. The release explains that a return on a life settlement depends on the insured's life expectancy, the date of the insured's death and on the accuracy of life expectancy estimates. They suggest investors consider the risk associated with inaccurate or improper valuations and note that when life expectancy is miscalculated, additional premiums may need to be paid which increase cost and thus lower returns. They also noted the risk that insurance companies can fail to pay face amounts due upon the death of the insured due to insolvency. They also will not pay if they believe the policy was sold under fraudulent circumstances or if the heirs who would have received the death benefit challenge the payout to the investor. They also encourage investors to be wary of the fact that life expectancy underwriters may not be regulated by state insurance agencies and that purchasing life policies and any related data on the insured's individual medical history may also raise privacy issues.[9]

Valuation

Accounting rules in the United States require that most investment funds record their life settlement policy holdings' fair market value. Fair market value can be determined using comparable transactions and traded prices of similar policies or by using private model inputs to generate a model valuation.

Due to the nature of the market, policies tend to be illiquid. No two policies are truly the same or fungible due to varying terms and the unique medical conditions of each person insured. Some consultants and brokers or insurance companies can provide data on transactions that can be used to value policies in an investment fund. In this case, the policy value would come from the transaction price of a similarly aged individual with a similar type of policy.

Most often, policies in a fund are valued using a model based on unobservable model inputs with limited transparency. Fair market values using models provide values that are significantly different from the cash-on-cash performance of any policy. The fair market value based on a model takes into consideration the current interest rate projected timing estimates for cash flows in and out of the policy. Model valued investments are classified as level-three assets from a U.S. Generally Accepted Accounting Principles (GAAP) financial statement perspective.

There are several valuation models for life expectancy and mortality that can be used to model the fair value of a life insurance investment. A deterministic approach would assume that death occurs at a specific point in time based on an individual's age and average life expectancy. A statistical approach to the determination of an insured's average life expectancy could also be done using a simulation like a Monte Carlo model, sometimes referred to as a stochastic approach. Finally, a probabilistic approach can be used that relies on a mortality table and data related to an insured's age, gender and

---

9. "Investor Bulletin on Life Settlements," US Securities and Exchange Commission, Jan. 2011, https://www.sec.gov/investor/alerts/lifesettlements-bulletin.htm.

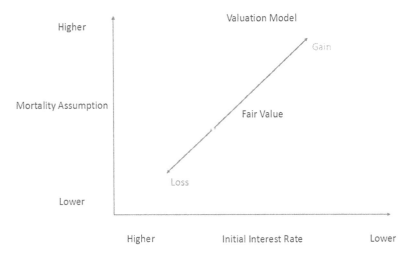

Figure 3.4. The relationship between mortality, interest rates and fair value of a life settlement contract.

health status rather than specific life expectancy. Inputs for a probabilistic model include a premium schedule, a discount rate, death benefits, survival and mortality probabilities for a specific insured person. The value of any policy today using a valuation model is the present value of the expected payouts—the present value of expected premiums up to a specific date in the future, less the present value of any expenses paid to service the policy.

A portfolio of life settlement policies would change in value as interest rates or credit spreads change and as assumptions for longevity or mortality are updated. Valuations are negatively related to both life expectancy and interest rates.

Assuming you owed a portfolio with an average age of 70 and a life expectancy of age 75 and when the current interest rate or discount rate is 15%. Any revaluation that increases the mortality assumption and lowers the life expectancy of the insured will increase the value of the portfolio. Any changes related to interest rates and risk premiums that lower the discount rate used to value policy payouts would result in market-to-market gains in the portfolio. Conversely, a revaluation that lowers the mortality, increases life expectancy or raises the interest rate assumption would result in market-to-market losses. The relationship between mortality, interest rates and valuation is shown in Figure 3.4.

Social, Legal and Ethical Considerations

The primary ethical conundrum that may exist for some is that profits are being made on the death of the insured. The counterargument here is that lives are being enhanced by the provision of liquidity. Let's consider an example where a person is terminally ill. They want to cash in a life insurance policy to travel the world with their spouse before death. The cash surrender value may be significantly less than an investor would pay to buy the policy. It is clear in this example that cashing in the policy is helping the patient and their family, while the investor can also make a profit. Once again, the perspective taken in this book is strictly a financial one, arguing that the returns and lack of correlation to the market justify the investment.

There is still some degree of regulatory risk associated with this asset class; however, it is improving. In 2010, for example, the government accountability office warned consumers about participating in life settlement transactions "due to a lack of clear, consistent state oversight." At the time, 12 states and the District of Columbia had no laws or regulations pertaining to life settlements. Today, 43 states and the territory of Puerto Rico regulate life settlements, providing approximately 90% of the US population protection under these consumer laws.[10]

In 2007, the National Conference of Insurance Legislators adopted the Life Settlements Model Act in an attempt to define and improve standards associated with many forms of direct settlements of life insurance or indirect sales of life insurance to investors through a sale of an interest in a trust or other entity. The National Association of Insurance Commissioners model establishes a five-year "lock-up" period on the settlement of policies, meaning insurance policyholders have to wait a minimum of five years before being able to settle their life insurance policy unless they acquire a terminal illness or other medical exceptions. Many states have eased the statutory waiting period needed before settling a policy, bringing the lock-up period to as low as two years in some states. The act also required life settlement brokers to disclose to policyowners important information about the life settlement transactions, such as commissions and other purchase offers.[11]

Unlike death benefits, portions of the proceeds of a life settlement sale are taxable to the insured. The Tax Cuts and Jobs Act of 2017 allowed policy sellers to receive up to their tax basis free of income tax. In other words, owners are not taxed on the value of the proceeds received equaling the monthly premium contributions being paid to maintain the insurance policy. There is also a special rate applied up to the proceeds received that extends up to the policy's cash surrender value. Normal tax rates apply to amounts in excess of the policy's cash surrender value.

Trends and Outlook

Improvements in technology related to data mining and policy evaluation plus the potential for reduced brokerage fees and market efficiency and perhaps some direct marketing to policyholders should allow the market to grow, become more efficient and channel more capital into this asset class without adversely impacting investor returns. Conning and Co. released an independent study of the market in November 2018 titled *Life Settlements: Continued Growth, Positive Outlook*. The report notes that "the volume of new

10. "Life Settlement Regulation," Life Insurance Settlement Association, accessed Sep. 2019, https://www.lisa.org/industry-resources/life-settlement-regulation.
11. Life Settlements Model Act, National Conference of Insurance Legislators, Nov. 2007, http://ncoil.org/wp-content/uploads/2016/04/AdoptedLifeSettlementsModel.pdf.

settlements continues to increase, a positive indicator for growth in the number of in-force life settlements."[12]

Manager Perspectives and Insights

Rajiv Rebello, FSA, CERA, Principal and Chief Actuary, Colva Actuarial Services

Rajiv helps investment groups structure investments in the life settlement space to minimize longevity risk and maximize returns. Prior to his work in the life settlement space, Rajiv was an actuary for New York Life where he worked on the pricing and design of New York Life's Universal and Variable Universal Life Products.

Which esoteric alternative investments (life settlements, litigation funding, tax liens, trade claims, artwork, Bitcoin, collectibles, etc.) have you had operational or investment experience in?
I've only worked in the life settlement space.

What is your specific experience, if any, investing or evaluating in life settlements?
I've worked in the life settlement space on the investment side helping investors structure funds and actively invest in the space, on the third-party valuation side and helping investors reduce the premiums they pay on the policies on the servicing side.

What is your opinion on the opportunity presented from investing life settlements? What is the expected return, liquidity and so on? How has it changed over time?
In an economic environment in which investors are worried about volatility in the equity markets and low yields in the bond markets, life settlements offer an uncorrelated alternative asset that can be properly managed and help mitigate risk in clients' portfolios. Life settlements is one of the few asset classes in which the underlying risk, mortality risk on life insurance policies, are uncorrelated to the state of the economy. While the cash flows of other alternative assets may experience significant setbacks if the economy sours, the underlying mortality-dependent cash flows of a diversified pool of life settlement policies will not. Whether the economy is in great shape or on a downturn will not affect when insureds on these policies will pass away. Furthermore, mortality and insurance risk are a lot easier to statistically manage and predict than market or interest rate risk with the right expertise.

From a technical standpoint, government regulation and improvements in the life expectancy underwriting have revolutionized the industry. Buyers and sellers have never been more protected and life expectancy underwriting has never been more accurate

---

12. Michael Warner, "Life Settlements Market Growth Continues into 2018," Conning Holdings Ltd., 6 Nov. 2018, https://www.conning.com/about-us/news/life-settlements-market-growth-continues-into-2018.

than they are now. The industry has become more sophisticated and respected than it was 10 years ago. But as more capital has come to the space, expected returns have dropped. So, whereas net returns in the life settlement space could be expected in the high teens 10 years ago, now investors should expect net returns in the 8%–14% range depending on the expertise of the fund managers.

In terms of liquidity, most funds typically require some sort of lock-up, generally around two years, and then they will offer quarterly redemptions after that.

What are some of the risks associated with life settlements today?

There are a few main risks to consider. Mortality risk is the risk that insureds on the pool of policies live longer than expected. This can be mitigated by investing in a diversified pool of polices. Insurance risk is the risk that the premiums on the policy are higher than expected. This can be mitigated by ensuring that funds have the proper insurance expertise to project premium costs on a policy before it is acquired into the fund. Liquidity and market-to-market risk. While the underlying cash flows of life settlements are uncorrelated to the state of the economy, the liquidity value of the portfolio is correlated. So, if the economy tanks and capital decides to exit alternative assets, then the market value of life settlements will drop even if the underlying intrinsic value has not changed. Funds that mark their port-folio to market prices may see a temporary drop in value in such circumstances even if there hasn't been a real loss. It's important for funds to mitigate this temporary book loss by limiting liquidity and "run-on-the-bank" events in such scenarios.

Where would you see life settlements fitting into the asset allocation process? Is it a stand-alone asset class, part of a credit portfolio or part of an alternative's allocation, and what type of investors are best suited for allocating to life settlements either as a discrete portfolio or part of a credit or alternatives allocation?

While life settlements can be part of a stand-alone allocation, doing so requires that significant due diligence be made on the expertise of the particular fund or funds that the client is considering investing in. There are immense amounts of tech-nical expertise and relationships involved in acquiring and managing a portfolio and there is a large disparity in the level of expertise of varying life settlement funds. Life settlements, in general, should be part of an alternative asset allo-cation in order to mitigate risk in clients' portfolios, particularly those who are looking to shift away from a heavy equity portfolio to a heavy bond portfolio allocation.

Academic Perspectives and Research

Academic articles on life settlements became very prominent amidst the AIDS/HIV epi-demic in the late 1990s. Many people who contracted the disease were given life expec-tancy predictions of less than two years at the time of diagnosis. Life settlement financiers used this epidemic to offer liquidity to life insurance holders who needed costly surgeries or treatments.

Unanticipated medical advances, aggressive sales practices and inaccuracies in estimating policyholder lifetime led to the market shifting from viatical customers near death to senior citizens looking for cash in retirement where most of the business and research is focused today. Academic articles on life settlements have historically focused on the ethics, benefits and some of the negative consequences or risks associated with this sort of investment.

An article published by researchers at the Cass Business School set out to determine whether or not it is ethical to profit from life settlements. Several ethical dilemmas have emerged in the life settlements industry, stemming from regulatory issues, privacy concerns and the vulnerability of policyowners. One concern with life settlements is the lack of oversight and regulation by the government. Today, regulation is very inconsistent, as the life settlement market is regulated by state governments rather than at the federal level. Currently, the market is undergoing review and reform in many cases. However, not all states regulate the market and those that do tend not to adopt common rules. Regulators and investors in life settlements might also be concerned that overly optimistic mortality assumptions, which would inflate the cash sums paid to policyholders, would reduce the potential return on life settlement portfolios and funds.

Another concern of regulators is the potential market distortions associated with "stranger-originated life insurance" practices. This practice occurs when seniors are persuaded to take out insurance through a "premium-financing" arrangement, which occurs when an investor provides a loan or pays cash to cover the cost of premiums, with the intention of buying the policy in the future. Life insurance companies are concerned that such practices would distort the primary purpose of life insurance. Life insurance is supposed to be originated to pay for funeral costs or provide liquidity to estates. It is not intended for arbitrage or purely speculative investment opportunities where origination is done with the intention of resale only. Stranger-originated life insurance (STOLI) cases are risky for investors as they could be contested and the benefits could then be paid to a family rather than the investor. [13]

Another paper from the *Journal of Derivatives* suggests how to construct a pool of life settlements that also mitigates the longevity risk of the portfolio. The researchers suggest two classes of securities whose duration is altered from the duration of the underlying pool of insurance contracts. According to the authors, creating a class with a stable duration requires the creation of a class with an exceptionally unstable duration. By creating these two classes, the longevity risk embedded in the pool of life settlement contracts is stripped out of one class and reallocated to the other class. The Planned Duration Class is structured to address the needs of investors looking for investments with fairly certain durations. In exchange for assuming the

---

13. David Blake and Debbie Harrison, *And Death Shall Have No Dominion*, Cass Business School, Pensions Institute, July 2008, https://papers.ssrn.com/sol3/papers.cfm?abstract_id=1344332.

longevity risk of the pool, investors in the second class would be offered a higher yield.[14]

An article advocating that life settlements are a viable option for life insurance holders was written by Harold G. Ingraham Jr. and Sergio S. Salani. It is entitled "Life Settlements as a Viable Option." According to the article, there was only one market participant that was able to buy the policyholder's insurance contract, that is, the insurance company that originally sold it. By opening up the market, policyholders could receive much more in times of need, such as to cover surgeries or large medical expenses. Situations where policyholders benefit from life settlements include when the policy premiums become cost-prohibitive, when the level term period is about to expire and renewal premiums will become significantly higher, situations in which there are changes in the insured's estate or if the insured outlived the intended beneficiaries. The article goes on to analyze the current market participants in the life settlement market. In their sample of approved life settlements, 48% were on male insureds, 22% on female insureds and 30% involved second-to-die policies on the lives of male/female insured combinations. The average policy size studied was $1.75 million. For the single life policies, the average age of the male insureds was 78.3 years. The average age of the female insureds was 80.6 years. For the second-to-die policies, the average ages of the male/female combinations were 80.4 and 79.9 years, respectively. The average life expectancy for the male insureds, as determined by the life settlement company underwriters, was 6.15 years. The corresponding life expectancy for the female insureds was 5.79 years. For the second-to-die policies, the average life expectancy of the male/female combinations was determined to be 7.32 years.[15]

Summary

The market for life settlements has a major imbalance in supply and demand and an improving regulatory framework. The number of individuals who need cash and liquidity and who hold policies eligible for sale at values higher than those offered by insurance companies will continue to drive demand. The education of financial advisors and intermediaries regarding who can benefit from policy sales is still ongoing. This is likely to lead to more turnover and opportunities for investors. The relatively small amount of capital in the market today means that, when it comes to this type of exotic investments, investors should benefit from higher yields, but must also be mindful of the potentially significant downside risks. The primary benefit of this asset class is its low correlation and volatility relative to traditional investments. The primary risk is that the

---

14. Carlos Ortiz and Anne Zissu, "Securitization of Senior Life Settlements: Managing Interest Rate Risk with a Planned Duration Class," *Journal of Derivatives*, Spring 2016, https://jod.pm-research.com/content/13/3/66.

15. Harold G. Ingraham Jr. and Sergio S. Salani, "Life Settlements as a Viable Option," *Society of Financial Service Professional*, Sept. 2004, http://www.sandorcapital.ca/press/articles/article08.pdf.

projected IRR may not be equal to the realized IRRs due to longevity and other risks embedded in a life settlements portfolio.

Useful Websites and Additional Reading

AAP Life Settlement Valuation Manual, https://www.aa-partners.ch/fileadmin/files/ Valuation/AAP Life Settlement Valuation - Manual V6.0.pdf.
"Buying Out Life Insurance Policies Is a Bad Investment when People Keep Living," https://consumerist.com/2015/06/03/buying-out-life-insurance-policies-is-a-bad-investment-when-people-keep-living/.
"Death-Services in the U.S.", https://www.statista.com/study/56094/death-services-in-the-us/.
"EY's Global Insurance Trends Analysis 2018," https://www.ey.com/Publication/ vwLUAssets/ey-global-insurance-trends-analysis-2018/$File/ey-global-insurance-trends-analysis-2018.pdf,
"Grim Risks of Reaping Death's Rewards,"
www.wsj.com/articles/SB10001424052748704094304575029581062228168.
"Life Settlement Funds: Current Valuation Practices and Areas for Improvement," https://www.elsa-sls.org/wp-content/uploads/pdf/current-valuation-practices.pdf.
Life Settlements Task Force Report, July 2010,
https://www.sec.gov/files/lifesettlements-report.pdf
"The Morbid Niche of Life Settlement Funds,"
https://money.usnews.com/investing/funds/articles/2017-10-17/ the-morbid-niche-of-life-settlement-funds.
"Statista Dossier on Life Insurance in the US," https://www.statista.com/study/40774/ life-insurance-in-the-us-statista-dossier/.
"World Development Indicators: Population, Total," http://data.worldbank.org/indi- cator/SP.POP.TOTL
"World Development Indicators: Death Rate, Crude (per 1,000 people)," http://data. worldbank.org/indicator/SP.DYN.CDRT.IN.

Chapter Four

LITIGATION FINANCE

Introduction

This focus of this chapter will be to explain and illustrate some of the key terms and basic economics of litigation financing investment strategies. Strategies and opportunities in litigation finance vary a great deal. Lawsuits can be related to consumer or commercial disputes, intellectual property and patent disputes or infringements, malpractice, accidents, contracts, employment disputes, tort law, commercial code violations, class action suits and negligence, to name just a few. Litigation funding is about getting a return. Investors should be dispassionate about the principles or politics underlying any suit. It is not about moral victories, but rather financial ones.

In this chapter, we will discuss the value proposition, review examples of transactions, discuss some of the current players in the marketplace, provide information about the ways that investors can invest in litigation finance opportunities and evaluate some of the risks. We will also discuss some of the pros and cons of direct investments in specific cases compared with commingled investments in litigation funding firms, mutual funds or ETFs and using the ownership of shares in public companies engaged in litigation finance activity.

In litigation finance, an investor can provide pre-settlement funding to a plaintiff, law firm or corporation in exchange for a percentage of any future judgment or settlement. The investor bears the risk of loss if the case is lost. An investor can also buy a claim that has already been awarded in a class action lawsuit to a specific class of plaintiffs. In a class action lawsuit, it may take months or years after the initial judgment for the members of the plaintiff class to be finalized. Investors can buy any qualifying plaintiff's right to participate in the class action settlement at a discount. The investor will be paid any future award due to the plaintiff when the class is finalized. Finally, an investor can also buy a structured settlement from a plaintiff related to a past judgment or settlement that is being paid to the plaintiff by a defendant or their insurance company over time, typically over many years in periodic installments.

Litigation finance provides investors with an opportunity to profit from successful litigation outcomes, while hopefully minimizing losses from unsuccessful outcomes or unpaid judgments or losses due to the defendant's credit risk. The primary effect of litigation finance in its various forms is to shift some or all of the risk and rewards associated with legal action from the plaintiffs and law firms to third-party investors. It allows less-capitalized plaintiffs to pursue better-capitalized defendants, for law firms to free up capital and for corporations to manage or hedge legal risk and improve return on equity (ROE), and it allows those who have won awards to get access to immediate cash flow.

Litigation finance also provides investors with opportunity to generate liquidity for a plaintiff in a tort case or in a structured settlement. In addition, law firms who work for contingency fees will seek litigation financing sources to manage cash flow, lower capital costs, reduce their own risk or improve their firm's liquidity.

One reason that there is a demand for funding of litigation claims and judgments is that the financial capacity of those making claims or seeking to litigate disputes may be limited relative to the resources of those against whom claims are being pursued or against whom judgments have been awarded. In addition, even when there has been a settlement or judgment in the plaintiff's favor, there may be a significant delay between the date of the judgment or settlement and the timing of when funds are released or paid to those involved in the action. In certain cases, a class of individuals that has been harmed may need funds right away to pay expenses or to make up for lost income or profits. Those who have done the harm may have the funds to defend themselves or have insurance to pay for any judgments. This increases the demand for litigation finance capital or loans and creates an opportunity for litigation finance investors.

Lawsuits and actions that get funded are typically those brought against firms who have the capacity to pay or access to insurance coverage by individuals or firms that do not have the financial capacity to pursue their case. Lawsuits against large, well-funded or insured defendants brought by those who lack funds or have incurred a large loss and have significant projected expenses make the most attractive cases for investors. These situations will have the highest returns and the least counterparty credit risk.

In the United States, the size and volume of all legitimate claims and settled cases in favor of plaintiffs at any point in time can far exceed the financial resources and liquidity of those individuals who are seeking action or who are due an award. Litigation is expensive. Plaintiffs usually have incurred financial hardship or loss. Judgments and damages are difficult to estimate. Settlements in favor of the aggrieved party can take time to be paid. Plaintiffs may lack deep enough pockets to make their claims or wait for settlements or judgments to be paid out. Law firms may have limited capacity and not want to work solely on contingency fees. There may be significant imbalances between the financial resources of those being accused of contractual breaches or wrongdoing and those pursuing claims, litigating them or getting favorable judgments. This situation creates opportunities for financially strong players not engaged in the litigation to act as a source of capital for those who are involved in the litigation, in exchange for very attractive risk-adjusted returns. There is simply more demand for litigation finance than there is supply of available third-party funds, making the market attractive for growth.

Investors in litigation finance have no involvement in a case's decision making or any recourse. Investors can demand a high return for the risk they are taking given that they have little to no control over the decision making in the case or structure of a settlement payout. In some cases, the litigation finance provider will receive nothing and must write off the cost of any funds given to a firm or plaintiff. Therefore, investors need to cash in on the winners to compensate themselves for any losers. In this regard, the use of litigation finance portfolios and diversification principles is one of the main value-added services offered by portfolio managers who are experts in this area. Managers who can minimize write-offs and losses while generating attractive fees on the winners will produce superior portfolio returns.

The return on a claim or on funds for a settled, but unpaid judgment, provides compensation for the uncertainty associated with the outcome of a lawsuit, the time value of money and any default or credit risk or other illiquidity associated with the judgment or settlement. This means that an investor can earn a return on their investment that includes some optionality, some risk of loss, some riskless yield and a credit spread.

A Few Definitions, Key Terms or Phrases

Before going any further, it is important to review some of the nomenclatural and vocabulary needed to understand litigation finance.

A claim represents a creditor's assertion of a right to payment from a debtor or the debtor's property.

A judgment, on the other hand, is the official decision of a court finally resolving the dispute between the parties to the lawsuit.

A plaintiff is a person or business that files a formal complaint with the court whereas a defendant is an individual or business against whom a lawsuit is filed or against whom the claim is being asserted.

A bilateral action is between two parties, as opposed to a class action lawsuit, in which one or more members of a large group or class of individuals or other entities sue on behalf of the entire class. In class action litigation, a district court must find that the claims of the class members contain questions of law or fact in common before the lawsuit can proceed as a class action.

More definitions and key terms and phrases can be found at: http://www.uscourts. gov/glossary.

Market Participants and Industry Players

The litigation finance industry is growing rapidly and is attracting more capital as knowledge and experience with this type of funding and the related investment opportunities become more widely known and accepted. It is a global business with large domestic markets in the United States, the United Kingdom and Australia.

The primary players in the litigation finance industry are independent law firms, in-house legal counsel, special purpose finance companies, third-party aggregators and brokers of claims, litigation funders and plaintiffs. The demand for litigation finance capital currently exceeds its supply and is growing rapidly.

Law firms and in-house legal counsel are among the consumers of funding along with the plaintiff community. Knowledge of the market and first-hand experience among law firms and in-house counsel are growing. According to a 2019 survey by Lake Whillans, approximately 50% of large law firms with 500 or more attorneys and 41% of all law firms regardless of size had first-hand experience using litigation funding. According to the report, law firms were motivated by a lack of cash flow or funds to pursue contingency arrangements. In-house counsel cited hedging of legal risk and expenses as the primary motivation. In-house counsel and their business partners need to consider the return on litigation just like any other investment. In certain cases, it is better to sell the claim and use the proceeds to invest in its operating business than fund the claim internally. Economic terms and flexibility of deal structures were considered the most important factors in choosing a litigation funding provider. Over 75% of law firms surveyed indicated that the industry would continue to grow. A small number of survey respondents who had never used litigation finance cited ethical concerns. Law firms seeking litigation funding sources generally do so via referrals or from industry sources, according to the same Lake Whillans study.[1]

Alex Javelly provides an overview of the litigation funding brokerage market in an article entitled "How Brokers Work 101." The article describes third-party aggregators or brokers as organizations that source plaintiffs for law firms, finance companies and funders, particularly in consumer-related cases. Brokers are the main point of contact with the law firms and plaintiffs and work as agents for the litigation funders who will ultimately provide loans, capital or buy claims. Brokers charge fees for sourcing deals that can be quite significant. It is very difficult to identify the number of litigation brokers operating today. The primary services of a broker are finding plaintiffs, contacting law firms, preparing term sheets and negotiating fees. The broker will also apprise the investor of the status of the lawsuit and provide updates on decisions that are made along the way. Fees vary with each broker and can be front- or back-end-loaded.[2]

The primary litigation funders are special purpose private funding corporations, public funding corporations, hedge funds or private equity funds. An independent research firm named Chambers and Partners that typically ranks law firms recently started ranking litigation funding firms. The research breaks the funding market into three tiers. It found that the largest and most experienced funders were Burford Capital and Bentham IMF, based in New York. Bentham IMF is owned by IMF Bentham Limited, which is publicly listed on the Australian Securities Exchange. The large public companies can afford to fund commercial claims with large upfront fees, binary outcomes and large settlements. The second tier included Lake Whillans Litigation Finance and Longford Capital Management. Lake Whillans closed a $125 million round of funding at the end of 2017. Longford closed its second fund in August at $500 million in 2017. The last tier included private companies and hedge funds such as Vannin Capital and Woodsford Litigation Funding. Other names in the litigation funding market include companies such as Law Cash and Oasis. These firms aggregate individual consumer claims and create portfolios that can be sold or offered to investors. Some of these firms will exclusively fund consumer actions with

1. Lake Whillans and *Above the Law, 2019 Litigation Finance Survey*, 2019, https://lakewhillans.com/research/2019-litigation-finance-survey-report/.
2. Alex Javelly, "How to Work with Brokers 101," *Mighty*, Oct. 2017, https://www.mighty.com/blog/legal-funding-brokers.

more certain settlement histories and predictable awards and terms. A firm like J. G. Wentworth is an example of an organization that provides funding for structured settlements.[3]

Industry Associations and Best Practices

The American Legal Finance Association (ALFA) is the trade association that represents the leading consumer legal funding companies across the country. Formed in 2004, ALFA is dedicated to ensuring fair, ethical and transparent funding standards within the consumer legal funding industry. The association is governed by a board of directors and includes over 30 of the estimated 50 firms globally who actively provide litigation funding and are dedicated to this business. The industry association website, including the Code of Conduct, is located at https://americanlegalfin.com.

The Association of Litigation Funders is a UK-based industry association dedicated to this market. Its Code of Conduct addresses issues related to capital adequacy of funders, termination and approval procedures and guidelines related to control of cases. The industry association website, including its Code of Conduct, is located at http://associationoflitigationfunders.com.

The Australian Association of Litigation Funders (AALF) is an industry group that seeks to assure that those in need of litigation funding will find organizations that meet high-quality standards. All AALF members have regard to the Best Practice Guidelines which provides a framework to guide members in developing their own standards, policies and procedures. The industry association website is located at https://www.associationoflitigationfunders.com.au/about-us.html.

Estimates of Market Size

The US market is a litigious one. While much of the market is well documented as a matter of public record, the ability of investors to gather and analyze market data can be a challenge. Much of the information resides in federal courts and local municipalities with limited automation and search tools that can be easily used by investors. Boutique consulting firms and industry specialists do periodically evaluate the aggregate size of the market. According to BTI Consulting, beginning in 2020, spending on litigation in the United States will rise across all types of litigation. Commercial litigation spending is estimated to be the largest spending segment, followed by spending on employment, intellectual property violations, class action, product liability and securities-related litigation.[4]

---

3. Litigation Support Rankings: Litigation Funding in USA, Chambers and Partners, accessed Dec. 2019, https://chambers.com/guide/usa?publicationTypeId=58&practiceAreaId=2816&subsectionTypeId=1&locationId=12788#23030748_editorial.

4. "BTI Litigation Outlook 2019," BTI Consulting, 2019, https://www.bticonsulting.com/litigation-outlook-reports-highlights/.

Total Revenue in 2018	Annual Growth 2013–2018	Annual Growth 2018–2023	Profit Margin in 2018	Wages as a share of Revenue in 2018	Number of Businesses 2013–2018
$971.2 m	5.3%	1.9%	21.4%	10.1%	−4.7%

Figure 4.1. IBISWorld statistics related to the personal litigation funding industry at the end of 2018.

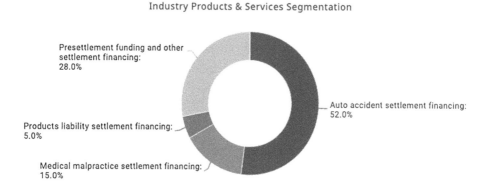

Figure 4.2. IBISWorld breakdown of personal injury litigation funding segments for 2018.

The global litigation finance market was estimated to be valued at $11 billion in 2018. The market is expected to grow to $22.4 billion by 2027, which represents a compound annual growth rate (CAGR) of 8.3%. One reason for positive growth is that the litigation finance industry may be inversely correlated to financial markets, given that insolvencies increase during times of recession.[5]

The US personal injury litigation funding market data from IBISWorld in Figure 4.1 shows that industry revenue was approximately $971.2 million and the profit margin was 21.4% for the year ending 2018. Growth is expected to slow between 2019 and 2024.[6]

Within the personal injury segment shown in Figure 4.2, auto accident and medical malpractice claims contributed the most to annual revenues. The remaining revenue came from product liability and pre-settlement funding.[7]

---

5. Shreyas Tanna, "Global Litigation Funding Investment Market," *Absolute Market Insights*, Feb. 2020, https://www.prnewswire.com/news-releases/global-litigation-funding-investment-market-was-valued-at-us-10-916-3-mn-in-2018-and-is-expected-to-reach-us-22-373-3-mn-by-2027-growing-at-a-cagr-of-8-3-over-the-forecast-period-owing-to-litigation-funding-investments-being-un-301005840.html.

6. Victor Adeleke, "Settlement Funding Companies," IBISWorld, Dec. 2018, https://my.ibisworld.com/us/en/iexpert-risk-specialized/od5740/iexpert-risk.

7. Ibid.

Opportunities and Strategies

Litigation typically involves several steps or stages. It starts with pleadings, proceeds to pre-trial and trial stages, moves to settlement, acquittal, retrial or appeal and finally ends with enforcement. In the pleading stage, a complaint is filed and a motion to dismiss can be made by the defendant. The pre-trial stage involves the mutual discovery process between the plaintiff and the defendant's legal teams. The trial stage is where the case is heard by a judge, jury or arbitrator and where a ruling or acquittal may occur. The post-trial stage can include the process of an appeal or a motion for a new trial. The enforcement stage is where a plaintiff is waiting for payment or taking steps to streamline, negotiate terms or accelerate a payment. A claim can end quickly or drag on for many years as it passes through each phase of the legal process. Investing in any type of litigation involves evaluating cases during each of its phases of origination, underwriting and structuring.

One common strategy is investing in commercial disputes that have been initiated but not yet ruled upon by the courts. This typically involves commercial disputes between contractual counterparties seeking financial damages. In this strategy, value is created by investing in cases with a high probability of successful outcomes and where there is some ability to estimate awards. Funding can be provided directly to law firms or to the plaintiffs initiating a claim.

Another common strategy is providing loans or purchasing outright the judgments in tort cases that have already been settled via class action lawsuits or other consumer actions against a plaintiff, such as product manufacturers or insurance companies in a product liability case. In this strategy, value is created by estimating the likely time to value period and by providing liquidity against known settlements subject to structural delays or a significant time between the judgment and the payment of claims to plaintiffs.

A third strategy is funding structured settlements between insurance companies and plaintiffs. In this case, a defendant will have purchased an annuity to offset the judgment owed to the plaintiff as part of the settlement. The plaintiff will receive payments from the insurance company or directly from the annuity provider. In this strategy, a finance provider is able to purchase a stream of payment in whole or in part at a discount rate that is significantly higher than the risk. A funder may discount an annuity at 7%–10% even though it is from an AA/AAA-rated insurance company. This means an investor can buy a dollar of cash flow for less than its present value, based on its risk alone.

A key difference between these strategies is that the first strategy involves unknown cash flows and a substantial risk of loss, whereas the second and third strategies involve known cash flows and much less risk. Both require a discount rate that considers time value, opportunity cost, liquidity and default risk associated with a case. Claims with uncertain cash flows will generally earn a higher multiple or rate of return than those where there is a known payoff from a lump sum or structured settlement. Firms will tend to specialize in one strategy or the other or offer a combination of strategies in a single vehicle.

Litigation financing can be opportunistic or can focus on specific types of litigation, such as consumer or commercial. Within consumer lawsuits, there are separate categories related to automobile accidents, slip and fall cases, rent- and premises-related suits, medical malpractice and labor disputes. Within the commercial litigation space, disputes can be related to patents and intellectual property, breach of contract, copyright infringement, patent infringement, breach of fiduciary duty, product liability and the theft of trade secrets. Well-documented, valid, consumer claims generally will have some payout based on the injury, jurisdiction and representation. The investors in consumer actions will generally get paid something, usually in excess of the cost of the litigation itself. Commercial claims are more binary in nature and more expensive, harder to aggregate into portfolios and will be won or lost based on the facts of the case.

Funders can purchase deals for special purpose companies or brokers or do deals with a law firm who represents multiple plaintiffs. Plaintiffs can be individuals, business owners or companies seeking damages. Defendants are generally business partners, competitors, distributors, landlords or tenants or another corporation, municipalities or government entity that is a party to an action. Law firms can free up capital to pursue other opportunities.

The specialty finance companies or brokers who fund and aggregate individual cases will maintain loan files and statistics on settlement histories and payouts and perform all the administration associated with each lawsuit on behalf of the investor.

Consider a commercial litigation case involving a patent infringement where the plaintiff—a software developer, for example—asserts a claim against a commercial competitor or user of what is believed to be a proprietary and patent-protected technology, process or business application. The plaintiff would seek to prevent the defendant from using the software or applying the process it believes is protected and will also seek damages for past infringements. The defendant may try to show evidence and assert that the patents are not valid or their process is somehow different and ask that the case be dismissed. If the case moves forward, the plaintiff may be facing a significant legal bill of an unknown size with an unknown outcome.

The plaintiff will need to provide evidence that the covered technology was used by the defendant without compensation and will need to assert damages. This may involve the use of expert witnesses or testimony from witnesses for the plaintiff. The firm representing the plaintiff may incur significant legal costs, third-party fees to expert witnesses and its own hourly billings to represent the plaintiff from the pre-trial phase to the ultimate disposition of the case. If the firm is operating on a contingency basis, it will need enough in-house cash flow to support a team on the case during the litigation, appeal or enforcement process. If the defendant prevails, the law firm will incur a substantial loss. Either the plaintiff or its lawyers may wish to consider using a litigation finance firm to pay for some or all of the cost of litigation in exchange for a percentage of any recovery.

The litigation finance provider will enter into a purchase and sale agreement related to this claim if it meets its underwriting standards and expected return parameters. The purchase and sale agreement will specify the amount, any conditions or limitations, any discounts on attorney billing rates that have been negotiated, a cost multiple for pricing or a percentage of any settlement or judgment and the order of payments as between the plaintiff, the funding entity and the law firm representing the plaintiff. The agreement should include language confirming the sale is a nonrecourse sale. The agreement should set out the eligible expenses and the timing of payments by the purchaser. The agreement will normally not transfer any control over this litigation or any decision making relative to the case to the buyer.

Investing in active ongoing litigation requires specialized skills and risk management to generate value. It requires an ability to source and identify cases with a high probability of success at reasonable payoffs. Funding cases requires investors or raising funds to pay all or substantially all of the upfront litigation costs in exchange for a percentage of the settlement if successful. Research skills are necessary to estimate claims and payoff probabilities for specific cases and require an ability to extract information from court records and relationships with law firms who are originating cases. Data from court records can identify trends related to specific judges or district courts and are important factors to consider when trying to estimate both payoffs and the probability of judgments in favor of a plaintiff. Law firms can often identify situations where there are significant upfront costs, financial constraints on the commercial or individual plaintiff or limitations on the amount of contingency fee exposure a particular law firm is willing to take on a specific case.

A fund can also profit by funding law firms directly. An investor can pay a law firm to cover its pre-trial research and trial-related expenses in return for an assignment of a portion of any contingency fee the law firm would collect in a favorable settlement. Many law firms place a limit on the amount of contingency cases they can have on the books at any point in time due to the adverse cash flow it creates for the law firm or partnership. This drain on resources can be reduced by the use of litigation funding sources by the law firm.

In class action tort cases, such as a product liability lawsuit that has been settled, a litigation finance provider can enter into an assignment arrangement or outright purchase. In this case, the buyer stands in the shoes of the plaintiff who is the seller and receives payment from the defendant or their insurance company pursuant to a settlement or judgment agreement. The buyer will offer the seller a dollar amount that is the discounted value of the judgment at an annual rate that compensates the buyer for illiquidity and any residual credit risk in exchange for an upfront payment to the seller or injured party. Typical discount rates can run as high as 50% in some cases. In some cases, a claim may result in more than 100% being paid out to those who file if some members of the original claim do not file for their fair share. In these cases, the IRR of the portfolio with excess recovery on purchased claims will be much higher. Fees paid to collect or aggregate claims would serve to lower returns.

The factors that determine the value of any investment for an investor are complex. Value realization is based on both an unknown cash flow and an unknown time horizon. This makes it necessary to estimate settlement probabilities, time horizons and potential judgments and to choose a payoff multiple that reflects the illiquidity of the action and pending claim and that will satisfy investors' expectations.

Who Invests?

Investing in litigation finance has historically been the domain of high-net-worth individuals, family offices and hedge funds. More recently, institutional investors such as endowments and pensions have become active as well.

According to a recent article in *Pension and Investment Age*, in 2017 the University of Michigan committed $50 million to Lake Whillans Fund I, managed by Lake Whillans Capital Partners, as part of the university's $10.5 billion long-term endowment portfolio.[8]

As the infrastructure supporting the market matures and the number of investment vehicles increases, more institutional investment will naturally follow. There is currently an imbalance in claims needing financing and the pool of funds available for financing. This of course is one of the reasons there are outsized returns and a healthy risk premium associated with litigation funding. Investors are getting paid for the illiquidity of litigation funding and the seeming complexity of the asset class. As investors better understand the asset class, more investment will follow and returns will compress; however, that may take a significant amount of time to occur. In the meantime, the risk-adjusted, non-correlated returns of the investment will remain attractive.

How to Invest?

Investing in litigation finance can be done directly by individuals using a search engine or platform to source deals, as well as by investing in private LPs and publicly traded stocks. Not surprisingly, due to the illiquid nature of litigation funding, there are very few mutual funds or ETFs currently available for this asset class. Returns are asymmetrical with losses limited to the amount of the funded legal cost or purchased claim. Gains can be a multiple of funded legal costs or exceed the estimated value of a purchased claim. Duration is relatively short. Diversification can be obtained within the asset class by creating portfolios from different industry groups, courts, sizes and geographies.

Direct investments in individual cases offer one avenue to gain exposure to litigation finance. Several platforms offering exposure to individual investors have recently been launched. Direct investment opportunities can be obtained using one of several platforms for accredited investors to participate directly in litigation funding. Two of the more interesting platforms are YieldStreet and LexShares. Both offer participation in litigation finance to individual investors who qualify for their platform. Investors are buying into individual loans and creating their own portfolios. They get paid back as soon as a case settles and the judgment is enforced.

Investing in public companies listed on major stock exchanges is one way to get exposure to litigation finance opportunities. Unfortunately, there are only a few listed companies offering litigation funding services. Public companies who specialize in litigation

---

8. "University of Michigan Slates $50 Million for Litigation Finance Fund, Building SBIC Program," https://www.pionline.com/article/20170217/ONLINE/170219875/university-of-michigan-slates-50-million-for-litigation-finance-fund-building-sbic-program.

finance will carry claims or other litigation assets on their balance sheets and investors in their publicly traded shares get a dividend and an attractive ROE. In these cases, assets and claims may also be carried at cost and may not have value released to income until realized. Public companies can offer leveraged exposure, may offer attractive price to earnings ratios and multiples due to their complexity and may earn fees from managing funds.

Private LPs offered by independent fund managers to a collection of investors using a private equity or hedge fund structure is another route. In this case, an investor is generally buying a fractional share in a portfolio of cases or loans. The fund will generally last a specific period such as five years, before repaying all of its capital to its investors. There are many expert fund managers who have launched private funds that invest in litigation funding. Private investment funds are available that specialize in legal funding using both private equity and hedge fund style structures. Investors in private funds will pay both a management fee and an incentive fee in many cases and will not realize returns until cases are settled or judgments awarded. This means there will be a sizable J-curve for investors. In addition, the fund and expected returns may be difficult to model in advance or during interim periods. This may present a challenge if investors want interim valuations during the life of the fund. To do so would require expert judgment and estimates of potential awards based on probabilities applied to potential judgments. Many funds will choose to carry all litigating investments at cost and only recognize gains when realized, that is, upon payment. A fund will use investor assets and perhaps some leverage to invest in individual claims and create portfolios.

Benchmarks and Indices

There are limited benchmarks or indices that track the performance of the litigation finance business at this time. Performance analysis is limited to evaluating data provided by individual firms or consultants and is subject to self-reporting bias and other data integrity issues. An anecdotal review of offering documents and private surveys indicates the market is using a return expectation of between 25% and 35% as a benchmark for expected returns from litigation finance portfolios.

Firms, Funds and Platforms

Burford Capital Inc. is the largest publicly traded company engaged in litigation funding. Burford Capital trades under NYSE symbol BRFRY. It was founded in 2009 and today is one of the leading funding sources for law firms and plaintiffs alike. The firm operates globally with offices in New York, Chicago, London and Singapore. It has a large staff of experts in legal and regulatory risk and a robust origination platform. The firm makes principal on balance sheet investments in litigation claims and also earns fees for managing funds related to litigation funding. According to the firm's annual report, the firm managed $2.5 billion in assets related to litigation finance at the end of 2018. The trailing 12-month ROE was approximately 30% at the end of the first quarter of 2019 and the firm traded at a trailing price to earnings ratio of 12x with a market capitalization of more than $4 billion. Investors can obtain exposure to a diversified legal funding business by simply buying shares of the company or investing in any of the private fund vehicles they may offer. For more information, visit the company's website at https:// www.burfordcapital.com.

YieldStreet.com is a platform that connects accredited investors to asset-based alternative investments, including litigation finance opportunities. The firm targets 8%–15% returns for investors in litigation finance opportunities. They help businesses involved in a lawsuit raise capital quickly by streamlining fundraising and connecting them directly to accredited investors. They believe in the power of technology to drive equality and transparency in alternative investing and have endeavored to build a platform designed to provide easy access to institutional quality investments. The firm professes to put all investment opportunities through a strict due diligence process to determine if they meet their investment philosophy and return targets. Investments are targeted that can provide short duration and low correlation to traditional and other alternatives markets. They also focus on investments managed by experienced teams that have a long-standing history in their industry and domain expertise in the associated asset class. Investors in Yield Street offerings are buying into shares of an LLC or other special purpose vehicles that are registered with the Securities and Exchange Commission. The investment is a purchase of a private placement security. Deals offered on the platform normally offer a net return in excess of 10%. For more information, visit the company's website at https:// www.yieldstreet.com.

LexShares is a platform focused on accredited investors that offers the opportunity to invest in the outcome of many types of litigation. Plaintiffs can use LexShares to raise $100,000 to $1 million in financing to fund their litigation expenses. Investors can participate in a case for as little as $2,500. The amount invested in any one case is generally no more than 10% of the expected settlement or judgment value of the case. Investors receive a return if and when the plaintiff wins or the case settles. Investors receive a membership interest in a special purpose investment vehicle created for the specific claim. LexShares doesn't charge any upfront fee, but does collect carried interest and charges various administration and management fees. LexShares makes no assertion as to the probability of success or the ultimate outcome of the litigation. It provides investors with a suite of documents about each case so that investors can perform their own due diligence on each deal. Deals offered on the platform also normally offer a net return in excess of 10%. For more information, visit the company's website at https://www. lexshares.com.

Legalist Inc. is one of the more interesting fund managers offering private fund products in the litigation funding space. The firm is located in San Francisco, California. Legalist manages and offers private funds that invest in legal claims based on the use of proprietary algorithms and analytics. They use cutting edge technology to evaluate court records and to originate claims that have a high probability of settlement of verdict in favor of the plaintiff. Legalist considers itself a technology company. It has also raised venture capital funding for the management company to fund its operations. The firm's goal is to make life easier for plaintiffs and law firms. For more information, visit the company's website at https://legalist.com.

Burford Alternative Income Fund LP is a private fund focused on post-settlement financing. The fund charges a 1.5% management fee and a 10% incentive fee after a 5% hurdle rate. The product is designed to meet the needs of law firms waiting for their fee and for clients eager to obtain cash associated with a favorable settlement. The product is primarily marketed and sold to institutional investors. For more information, visit the company's website at https://www.burfordcapital.com/media-room/media-room-container/burford-capital-closes-new-300-million-post-settlement-investment-fund/.

Curiam Capital LLC is a hedge fund that provides financing for high-value litigation. Per the firm's website, Curiam focuses on providing flexible solutions that allow parties to hire lawyers they otherwise would not be able to. This allows parties to pursue strong legal claims without having to organize contingent-fee arrangements that often misalign incentives. Curiam typically only gets a return on its money if the litigation is successful. According to data collected by Preqin, the firm was established in 2018 with $100 million of committed capital. For more information, visit the company's website at http://www.curiam.com.

Pravati Capital is a hedge fund focused on providing collateralized bridge funding to US-based law firms and plaintiffs. The fund provides financing mostly to mature cases where there is established liability of the defendant as well as precedent regarding a favorable settlement. Pravati differentiates itself by having industry expertise that allows the fund to provide industry-specific support in addition to the capital. According to Preqin data, Pravati Credit Fund III was established in 2017 and, as of September 2019, has an AUM of $50.27 million. The fund charges a 2% management fee and a 20% performance fee. For more information, visit the company's website at http://www.pravaticapital.com.

IMF Bentham Ltd. is an Australia-based litigation funding company focused on providing funding to plaintiffs, law firms and corporations around the world. Its principal activities include the investigation, management and funding of litigation. According to the firm's website, Bentham's portfolio has a total claim's estimated recoverable amount of $2.63 billion as of June 30th, 2019. The firm has 14 offices throughout the United States, the United Kingdom, Australia, Canada and Asia. Since its establishment in 2001, The firm's success rate is 89%, and clients, on average, retain 63% of case proceeds. For more information, visit the company's website at https://www.imf.com.au.

AxiaFunder is a London-based crowdfunding platform that connects investors with high-quality commercial litigation opportunities that the company has identified as having strong potential to generate attractive returns. AxiaFunder differentiates itself by focusing on the lower market of litigation finance in geographies that have a shortage of capital and clearly attractive cases. For more information, visit the company's website at https://www.axiafunder.com.

Composite

A composite of litigation finance vehicles, shown in Table 4.1, had an average annual return of 62.78%, a standard deviation of 25.67%, a Sharpe ratio of 2.45 and a correlation to the S&P 500 of 2.45, between January 2016 and December 2019. This compares

Table 4.1. The performance, risk and correlation of a composite of litigation finance company investment vehicles versus the S&P 500 between January 2016 and December 2019.

	Litigation Finance	S&P 500
Correlation	0.12	NA
Standard Deviation	25.67%	11.56%
Average Annual Return	62.78%	14.33%
Simplified Sharpe	2.45	1.24

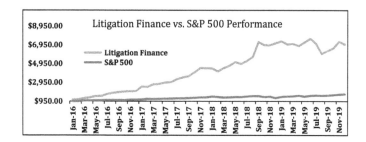

Figure 4.3. The growth of $1,000 invested in a litigation finance vehicle composite versus the $1,000 invested in the S&P 500 from January 2016 to December 2019.

to the return, standard deviation and simplified Sharpe ratio for the S&P 500 of 14.33%, 11.46% and 1.24.

During this period, an investment in litigation finance would have had a positive portfolio impact due to the low correlation to stocks and the higher Sharpe ratio.

A $1,000 investment in a litigation finance composite in January 2016, as shown in Figure 4.3, would have grown to over $7,000 by December 2019 compared to just $1,708 for the S&P 500.

What to Look For?

Of course, there are many unique factors that need to be evaluated or considered before investing in any litigation finance strategy, even where a professional manager is involved.

Investors in a fund using an expert fund manager or a platform that provides direct access to cases should ask about their experience evaluating deals, how claims are being researched and sourced, the specific terms of any structure involved and what fees and third-party brokerage or other charges exist. Investors need to ensure the investment process is aligned with the investment vehicle's structure and terms and their own expectations.

Understanding how a manager and fund identify, source, vet and aggregate cases or claims is critical. Deciding what will make a good loan or claim purchase takes time and occurs months before any loan or purchase against a claim is finalized. In a 2018 study, Cardozo Law School and the University of Texas researchers looked at a single nationwide firm investing in litigation funding that evaluated some 200,000 applications over a 10-year period and found that the firm rejected 52% of applications for funding and lost some or all of the investment on 12% of those cases accepted. As a comparison, the report noted that charge-off rates for commercial bank credit cards that charge 15%–20% interest are historically between 3% and 5%. Since losses on litigation funding portfolios tend to be higher than other forms of lending, investors naturally will require a higher return. Firms that can mitigate litigation by funding write-offs and negotiating higher multiples or loan rates will provide investors with attractive risk-adjusted returns [9]

Similar to private equity funds, a litigation funding manager needs working capital and capital commitments for funding in place to evaluate deals and to provide certainty that they can execute on a new investment as they are reviewed and approved. This often necessitates the use of a private equity style structure with capital commitments made in advance of portfolio loans or purchases and fees charged in both committed and invested capital. Managers who lack dry powder may be at a disadvantage to those who do. Managers using hedge fund style structures that are funded upfront may sit on cash for extended periods while sourcing opportunities, thereby diluting returns.

Investors should consider carefully the liquidity of the portfolio compared with the term structure of the fund. The ability to match investor terms related to initial lock-up, notice, redemption and gates with the likely terms and liquidity of a portfolio of loans or claims is critically important to avoid asset–liability mismatches within the structure. Since cases take many years to go to trial and given the fact that even settled cases or judgments may take months or years to be paid, a fund may impose a minimum three- to five-year term and/or a structure. The structure should have a defined waterfall for allocating payments to investors as they are received from day one and until the fund winds down.

We must also consider the question of whether the firm is set up with the right type of people and organizational model and if it is being run like an investment business. Finding investment professionals with the necessary legal and finance backgrounds who are managing money in this space can be a challenge. Early investors in this space have sometimes had difficulty with the integrity of some managers, so there is definitely a high degree of reputational risk. Providing financing for litigation should not be a source of funding for frivolous claims, and a manager needs a process to ensure that any pre-trial claim financing is focused on legitimate actions with highly likely outcomes that favor the investors. Verifying the manager's background, competency, reputation and outlook is obviously critical.

Investors in this asset class, like many alternative investments, most often will use a professional manager dedicated to this litigation finance and invest in a portfolio of deals via a commingled fund structure. Investing directly in cases is time-consuming, logistically complex and beyond the capacity and skill of most individual and institutional investors. Given the lack of available funding sources to meet market demand and the

---

9. Ronen Avraham and Anthony J. Sebok, "An Empirical Investigation of Third Party Consumer Litigation Funding," *Cornell Law Review*, Mar. 2018, https://papers.ssrn.com/sol3/papers.cfm?abstract_id=3137247.

complexity of the sourcing, underwriting and monitoring process, it is no surprise that there is a growing market of professional fund managers who are seeking to raise capital and employ professional investment techniques to create diversified portfolios of cases.

Both managers of funds and platforms offering access to litigation funding need to have strong relationships with law firms to originate the best deals. Law firms want to deal with funding sources that are easy to use and that can consistently provide funding for their cases. Pricing must be reasonable and easy to understand. Firms offering litigation funding need to think of the legal community as their partner and may need to offer education and incentives to get deals approved by a law firm.

Strong relationships with sourcing law firms are also critical as they can often help determine the likelihood that a case will be settled and the potential amount of a judgment. They may be in the best situation to know specific judges and past rulings on similar cases.

Not all law firms are aware of the availability and general terms involved in funding a lawsuit. Some do not support the use of litigation finance and will not introduce cases to funding firms or recommend funding options to their clients.

Investors in public companies participating in this asset class will be concerned with many of the same things as those who invest in funds, plus the additional concerns that come with investing in any public company, whether it be governance, liquidity or institutional shareholders of outstanding or short interest.

Other research or due diligence questions might include questions about fees and charges, brokers, success rates, technology, typical deal terms, time frames and valuation methods.

Unique Risks

Some of the unique risks associated with litigation finance include the risk of an adverse judgment and credit risk due to the potential difficulty with the enforcement and collection of judgments in favor of plaintiff judgments. There is also illiquidity risk and interest rate risk related to the time it will take to get your money and the impact of changes in interest rates. Litigation finance loans are also exposed to rising interest rates.

Valuation

Valuation of a litigation funding portfolio is a function of several factors related to the cash flows associated with any claims or settlements. Many if not all claims are unique, so it may be difficult to find comparable transactions to use to value a portfolio of claims. In this case, a model valuation is most appropriate. The fair value model for a portfolio of litigation claims will be a function of its assumptions related to the amount and timing of any claim changes and the appropriate interest rates and risk premium used to value the estimated cash flows. The value of the portfolio will be inversely related to time, positively related to estimates of settlement values or payouts and inversely related to interest rates and risk premiums used to discount the estimated payouts for the claims in the portfolio.

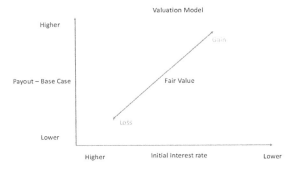

Figure 4.4. The relationship between payouts, interest rates and fair value for a litigation finance claim.

Assume a claim was estimated or known to be worth $1.0 million, with a 25% participation by the litigation funder and a 24-month estimated time remaining to any judgment or settlement. What is the value of this claim to a funder and how much should a litigation funder be willing to pay? If the case is won and the estimated judgment was correct, the value of this claim using a hurdle or discount rate of 25 is $160,000. A purchase at that price would generate a 25% return per annum. The value of the claim would of course change over time as probabilities of success and time to recover are updated or if interest rates or risk premiums rise or fall. The relationship between payouts, interest rates and valuations are shown in Figure 4.4.

Social, Legal and Ethical Considerations

A few states do not allow litigation funding. Historically there were, and in some states there are still, prohibitions against offering funding to initiate a lawsuit. Some will argue that third-party funding increases the likelihood of litigation and is a negative for society. According to the Burford Capital 2018 report, the issue of whether litigation finance will lead to frivolous lawsuits is losing momentum, with only 10% of those surveyed finding this to be the case, compared to 81% in 2012. Among all respondents, ethical concerns ranked last among obstacles, at only 9%. Finally, there is no standard or unified law that requires disclosure of litigation funding relationships.[10]

Trends and Outlook

The year-end 2018 survey by Burford Capital also highlighted several trends facing the litigation finance industry. The survey showed that litigation finance is growing rapidly, increasingly being used by law firms and plaintiffs alike. The survey found that 32% of US law firms had used litigation finance products or services, compared to less than

---

10. *2018 Litigation Finance Survey*, Burford Capital, 2018, https://www.burfordcapital.com/insights/insights-container/2018-litigation-finance-survey/.

10% in 2012. Law firm clients cited the use of litigation finance to fund favorable yet unpaid judgments as increasingly important. Respondents also cited the use of litigation finance as most important in high-risk commercial cases, such as those involving intellectual property violations and patents. A strong majority of 77% of all respondents agreed that litigation finance is a growing and increasingly important area of the business of law. Some 70% of US companies reported having forgone claims due to the high cost of litigation. According to the survey, the majority of litigation funding is used to finance individual cases, although increased use of funding for entire portfolios of claims appears to be rising. The primary concerns raised in the survey among those using litigation finance were related to the perceived high cost of litigation funding, concerns over control, concerns over the time required to negotiate a deal, concerns over the lack of awareness regarding specifics about this process works and lastly, ethical concerns.[11]

A recent article in a trade publication called *Above the Law* found that awareness is expanding rapidly. It also found that there are more questions today about how firms will differentiate themselves as capital and competition increase. However, it also highlighted concerns over a lack of uniform disclosure and some potential concerns over a New York Bar Association finding in 2018 that noted that litigation funding, and particularly portfolio financing deals with law firms, may violate fee-sharing arrangement prohibitions.[12] An earlier article in *Bloomberg Markets* in 2016 that included several interviews with some of the most active players in the market noted that returns from litigation funding significantly exceed those of the S&P 500 from 2011 to 2016.[13] This type of investment continues to attract investor attention and is growing as an asset class globally.

Manager Perspectives and Insights

Eva Shang, Chief Executive Officer, Legalist Inc.

Eva Shang is the co-founder and CEO of Legalist. Legalist is an algorithmic litigation finance firm that helps businesses pay for their lawsuits. Headquartered in San Francisco, Legalist uses technology to source and underwrite litigation investments

Why do you believe litigation finance is an attractive investment?
Litigation finance is an attractive investment for three main reasons: the asset is uncorrelated, has a high yield and is underappreciated.
Uncorrelated returns are one reason. Litigation finance is an investment in a legal claim and whether that claim succeeds is completely unrelated to how the overall equity market is performing. Thus, litigation finance returns are not only uncorrelated to each other, but also to the market as a whole. This makes litigation funding attractive

---

11. *2018 Litigation Finance Survey*, Burford Capital, 2018.
12. David Lat, "Current and Future Issues in Litigation Finance," *Above the Law*, Mar. 2019, https://abovethelaw.com/2019/03/current-and-future-issues-in-litigation-finance/.
13. Kit Chellel, "In Pursuit of a 10,000% Return," *Bloomberg*, Nov. 22, 2016, https://www.bloomberg.com/news/features/2016-11-22/big-bets-on-vw-lawsuit-could-yield-10-000-or-nothing.

for investors looking to hedge risk from the rest of their portfolio, especially if the stock and real estate markets take a hit in the next recession.

High yield is another. The rapid growth of the litigation finance market can be attributed primarily to double-digit returns in early funds. Because litigation is a contingent asset and funding deals are structured as nonrecourse in the event of a loss, successful cases often pay out multiples on the initial investment. Even factoring in losses in every portfolio, the winners more than pay for the losers.

It is also an underappreciated emerging asset. Even assuming that markets eventually reach some lower-yield, steady state, the current state of litigation finance is that it's still an underappreciated, emerging asset class. Although disputes between people are as old as time itself, the idea that litigation finance can unlock value in disputed assets is a relatively new one. At least for now, investors can expect to see higher returns as befitting a youthful emerging asset.

What are the risks associated with litigation finance as an investment?

I would sum up the pitfalls of any individual litigation finance investment as loss, long duration and misaligned incentives.

Risk of loss: At the risk of stating the obvious, litigations do not always succeed. The average litigation starts off with a complaint, at which point the claimant may not have all relevant information regarding the case. Information that can negatively impact the case frequently surfaces in discovery, at which point cases can be dismissed on summary judgment. Finally, even if a case survives all the way to trial, juries can be unpredictable in their verdicts. A lawyer we know frequently says, "If a jury likes your client, they will drape the law over them in order to give them money." The opposite is also true, hence there is a significant risk of loss, even in the most meritorious claims. The only way to hedge against a significant idiosyncratic risk of loss is diversification. Assembling a portfolio of investments, some of which will fail randomly, is the only sensible way to invest in litigation.

Duration risk: The average case in the federal trial system lasts just over two years, but many cases last longer. Long durations often occur in cases of greater complexity and higher stakes, which frequently happen to be the cases that funders invest in. To exacerbate the problem, most litigation funding agreements cap returns after a certain period, so long durations can destroy returns on an otherwise solid investment. To hedge against duration risk, litigation funders will try to incentivize plaintiffs to settle, but even this is an imperfect solution that relies on a willing defendant.

Misaligned incentives: Not every litigation is funded, and the ones that are frequently experience adverse selection and moral hazard problems. To start, the most obviously culpable defendants may settle cases early on before the need for funding arises, leading to an adverse selection problem in the cases that are left. The meritorious cases that are left may refuse otherwise reasonable settlement offers if a litigation funder is footing the bill, thereby unnaturally distorting the progression of the case and leading more funded cases to go to trial. Thus, although a tiny fraction of filed cases every year go to trial, the proportion of tried cases is overrepresented in the portfolios of litigation funders. When millions of dollars are owed to a litigation funder, the plaintiff's threshold for settlement is correspondingly higher. Some measure of misaligned incentives is par for the course as a result of injection of capital, but combating adverse selection and moral hazard is a very real challenge for many funders. Requiring attorneys to take some portion of the case on contingency, ensuring that plaintiffs retain some "skin in the game," and capping legal fees are all ways of guarding against the misaligned incentive problem.

What are some of the more significant due diligence or research efforts that should be considered before investing in litigation claims or providing funding that can improve returns and mitigate risk?
Litigation funders look for cases with strong liability, damages and collectability.
The first question our underwriters ask of any case is the obvious: will it win? The quickest way for a case to fail is through a Motion to Dismiss or Motion for Summary Judgment. Due diligence requires our lawyers to determine whether facts line up to existing law and whether any glaring vulnerabilities exist for which the judge could dismiss the case. Even if a case is successful, a litigation funder may find themselves disappointed with the outcome if the damages are too low. If the funder has invested more money than the court awards, for instance, the victory can be a hollow one. The realistic damages frequently differ from the optimistic, speculative damages that the plaintiff and attorney tell the funder they are seeking when they apply for funding. A big part of due diligence is figuring out the difference. Let's assume that the case wins at trial and it wins big. If the defendant does not have sufficient assets to pay the judgment, the victory is still in name only. That's why assessing collectability is the important final step in any litigation funder's due diligence process.

Where does or should litigation finance investing fit into an investor's portfolio construction and asset allocation?
Institutional investors who are interested in alternative, uncorrelated assets, especially in an emerging field, may find litigation finance an interesting complement to more traditional holdings in their portfolio. The best litigation funds have a track record, a strong team of legal and financial experts and often, some technical or proprietary edge that allows them access to a specialized part of the market.

Academic Perspectives and Research

Academic articles focused on litigation financing became prominent during the late 1990s and the first decade of the 2000s following a series of British and Australian court rulings which found that external financing of legitimate grievances was legal. Academic articles mostly focus on the ethics of litigation financing wherein authors argue whether or not it should be legal. Other articles examine the impact of the outcome of court cases where litigation financing was utilized.

One article by Susan Lorde Martin, published in the *Fordham Journal of Corporate and Financial Law*, argues that litigation financing should be tamed, not abolished. The author argues that litigation financing allows for plaintiffs with good cases and little financial resources to have the option to see their case to the end. Martin argues that this group of plaintiffs with little financial resources is put at a severe disadvantage relative to many defendants, such as a large corporation, which has much deeper pockets and could afford to draw out the lawsuit. Meanwhile, an aggrieved party may suffer ongoing financial losses while waiting for the settlement. One such example is that of a small business that cannot operate until the lawsuit is finished or an individual who has been injured and cannot work. Martin also argues that the industry should be regulated more, but not to the extent to inhibit the industry entirely. Martin suggests a disclosure requirement wherein litigation financing firms would disclose easily comparable rates to help plaintiffs choose the litigation financing firm that offers the best deal. Additionally, she recommends expanding the Truth in Lending Act (TILA) to cover the litigation financing industry, which strengthens competition by enabling their customers to easily compare credit terms available. Protection under TILA would provide plaintiffs and borrowers disclosure of finance charges and annual percentage rates calculated uniformly. [14]

A paper by the RAND Corp. debates the ethics and laws of litigation financing. Author Steven Garber argues that litigation financing conflicts with professional rules prohibiting lawyers from splitting fees with nonlawyers, which exist in all states except for Washington, DC. Additionally, litigation financing could exacerbate the conflict of interest between contingency fee-based lawyers and clients. Garber argues that lawyers might be more likely to advise clients to see the trial to the end, which would lead to declining settlement offers, a greater potential for a larger payout and the possibility of nothing at all. Thirdly, there are concerns with due diligence processes involved in litigation financing, which might result in inadvertent waivers of lawyer–client and work–product privileges. This may occur because litigation financiers generally ask to evaluate confidential, and possibly privileged, information belonging to the plaintiff. If the plaintiff elects to provide the information to the financing company, any privilege protecting it likely would be waived. Garber also brings up moral considerations of litigation financing. One consideration is that litigation financing can allow access to justice, which is socially desirable and a positive outcome. Garber considers both the plaintiff and defendant perspectives. He states that those who believe that plaintiffs are much more disadvantaged in civil litigation than defendants, and that additional litigation as a result of litigation financing will be legally rewarding, will believe that litigation financing is desirable from a moral perspective. In contrast, litigation financing is likely to be viewed as morally suspect by those who believe that defendants are most often disadvantaged in civil litigation. Examples would be defendants forced to defend themselves against and pay damages on legally unmeritorious claims. In sum, additional access to the courts does not necessarily involve improved access to justice in this case. [15]

Finally, a paper in the *American Economic Review* describes the effect of litigation financing on the plaintiff's settlement prospects. The authors evaluate the terms of the

---

14. Susan Lorde Martin, "The Litigation Financing Industry: The Wild West of Finance Should Be Tamed Not Outlawed," *Fordham Journal of Corporate and Financial Law*, 2004, https://ir.lawnet.fordham.edu/cgi/viewcontent.cgi?article=1185&context=jcfl.
15. Steven Garber, "Different Meanings of Ethics and Implications for ALF Activity," RAND Corp., 2010, https://www.jstor.org/stable/10.7249/op306lfcmp.11?seq=1#metadata_info_tab_contents.

nonrecourse loans offered by litigation financiers and their impact on settlement nego-tiations, the attorney–client relationship and other factors. The researcher found that the effect of a nonrecourse loan on a settlement is substantial. The research shows that an optimal loan, which is one that maximizes the joint expected payoff to the litigation funder and the plaintiff, induces full settlement. The author believes that this is a remarkable result because settlement bargaining under asymmetric infor-mation generally results in bargaining breakdown, leading to trial. In the case of no loan (or a traditional loan that must be repaid), it is a variation in the expected recovery from the trial that allows a plaintiff to reveal her damages through her set-tlement demand. A plaintiff with higher damages is willing to make a higher settle-ment demand and face a higher likelihood of rejection by the defendant because her expected net recovery from trial is also higher. But if her expected net recovery from trial does not vary with her type, then no revelation is possible and pooling is the equilibrium outcome; this will happen with a nonrecourse loan if it is an optimal structure.

The researchers also found that plaintiffs' attorneys benefit from litigation financing, as it eliminates the need to take the case to trial due to bargaining breakdown, which reduces the costs of a trial. This will also result in a reduction in the attorneys' contin-gent fees, creating an additional surplus that will be captured by the litigation funding industry (if it is concentrated) or by plaintiffs (if litigation funding is competitive). Another effect of litigation is that it will make the plaintiff less likely to settle, even for a reasonable amount, due to the nonrecourse character of the arrangement. A rational plaintiff will not settle for any amount offered by the defendant that is less than the aggregate of the principal amount advanced to her and the current interest accrued, which is often immense due to the staggering rates charged by many litigation finance companies. Overall, the nonrecourse loans offered by litigation financiers will lead to increased failure of settlement negotiations and interfere with the attorney–client relationship.[16]

Summary

Investors can realize attractive returns that are not correlated to the broad equity and bond markets by investing in litigation funding products and companies. Realizing attractive returns comes from mitigating losses and realizing significant upside or pre-ferred yields. There is a scarcity of funds available and increasing demand for litigation funding by law firms and plaintiffs. The fact that there are both public and private investment options makes this section attractive for both institutional and individual investors.

---

16. Andrew F. Daughety and Jennifer F. Reinganum, "The Effect of Third-Party Funding of Plaintiffs on Settlement," *American Economic Association*, Aug. 2014, https://www.jstor.org/stable/42920899?seq=1#metadata_info_tab_contents.

Useful Websites, References and Additional Reading

2019 Litigation Finance Survey Report, https://lakewhillans.com/research/2019-litigation-finance-survey-report/

"Alternative Litigation Financing in the United States: Issues, Knowns and Unknowns," https://www.rand.org/pubs/occasional_papers/OP306.html.

"Alternative Litigation Financing: Perils and Opportunities," https://heinonline.org/HOL/LandingPage?handle=hein.journals/ucdbulj12&div=6&id=&page=.

"Association of Litigation Funders' Membership Directory." http://associationoflitigationfunders.com/membership/membership-directory/.

"For the World's Super Rich, Litigation Funding Is the New Black," https://www.bloomberg.com/news/articles/2018-08-27/for-the-world-s-super-rich-litigation-funding-is-the-new-black.

"The History and Evolution of Litigation Finance," https://abovethelaw.com/2017/01/the-history-and-evolution-of-litigation-finance/?rf=1.

"In Low-Yield Environment, Litigation Finance Booms," https://www.marketwatch.com/story/in-low-yield-environment-litigation-finance-booms-2018-08-17.

"The Litigation Financing Industry: Regulation to Protect and Inform Consumers," https://heinonline.org/HOL/LandingPage?handle=hein.journals/ucollr84&div=21&id=&page=.

"Litigation Finance: How Wall Street Invests in Justice," https://money.usnews.com/investing/stock-market-news/articles/2018-01-22/litigation-finance-how-wall-street-invests-in-justice.

White Paper on Alternative Litigation Finance, https://www.americanbar.org/content/dam/aba/administrative/ethics_2020/20111019_draft_alf_white_paper_posting.authcheckdam.pdf.

Chapter Five

INTELLECTUAL PROPERTY

Introduction

Some investments are tangible while others are not. Tangible assets include factories, plants and equipment, inventory, hard assets and commodities and claims against them, such as stocks or bonds. Intangible assets are those that are not physical, but rather are evidence of an idea, business process, brand, a particular right to a restricted activity and so on. Patents, copyrights and licenses document unique ideas or access and limit others from reproducing or using the same idea or accessing the same resource or space upon which a license was granted. Intellectual property, much like physical property, can be owned and traded, may have a limited supply and often can be leased or rented to others, thereby creating value for those who own it. Some intangible assets last forever, such as a brand or image, while others may have a limited life or term, for example, a patent on a drug.

Owners of intellectual property can profit from exclusive use or from either the outright sale, rental or lease of their rights to the idea, invention or business process. Investors can profit from investing in intellectual property rights by receiving royalty or leasing income.

At the outset, sellers of intellectual property can obtain the value of the cash flow stream created by the royalty or rent and use the proceeds to reinvest in new research and development or fund their business or lifestyle. More often than not, the owner will license the use of the protected property to another trade or business for production and manufacturing, for incorporation into their product or for distribution to end users in exchange for a royalty. The use of the protected property and the royalty stream payments can be for a specific term or for the entire life of the protected asset.

Intellectual property can be used to generate royalties in the music, mining and exploration, technology, entertainment, healthcare and pharmaceutical industries, among many others. Mineral rights and land rights can be licensed to those who wish to develop the land or use its by-products, such as timber or coal. Music royalties can be collected by artists each time their music is performed or when it is used in a movie or game. A patent owner of a piece of technology can license it in whole or in part to manufacturers who wish to incorporate the technology in their product. An inventor of a game can sell the idea to a toy company that will produce, market and distribute the game to consumers.

Those who own the protected property will generally receive a percentage of the revenue associated with the use of the protected resource in a trade, business or other commercial application. The rates or fees for use of the various forms of intellectual property vary widely across industries. The royalties are generally a function of the cost to generate the protected asset, supply and demand for use of the protected property, the competitive advantage gained from the property, and the exclusivity, geography and term. Royalty rates can be less than a percentage point or as high as 50% of the revenue derived from the use of the protected right or property. Intellectual property rights can also be leased for a fixed annual fee, sold for a lump sum or exchanged for equity in a business or venture that will develop a product or service based on the protected property.

Royalty cash flows and payment streams from intellectual property can also be securitized and used to support equity and rated debt issued by a special purpose vehicle created by a financial sponsor, such as a bank. In this case the resource owner would sell the rights to the cash flows on the property to a trust that in turn issues equity and debt, in exchange for a lump-sum payment.

A Few Definitions and Key Terms

A patent is a protection given by a regulatory authority, government or the courts with a specific jurisdiction that limits the use of a specific technology, invention or process for a specific timeframe. In the United States, patents can be obtained via an application filed with the United States Patent and Trademark Office.

A trademark is a protection given to a picture, logo or word associated with a product or service. The Nike swoosh or the image of NBA star Michael Jordan jumping through the air are examples of trademarks. You can visit the US Patent and Trademark Office website at https://www.uspto.gov/ for more information about patents and trademarks.

A copyright is a protection given to an original song, sound, artistic work, dance or design. A songwriter can obtain copyright protection for his or her lyrics and get paid when others perform copyrighted songs. You can visit the US Copyright Office at https://www.copyright.gov/ for more information about copyrights.

A royalty is a payment from one person or party to another associated with the use of intellectual property.

A licensee is the party that pays a royalty and the licensor or owner of the protected asset is the individual that receives such payment. A license agreement outlines the rights, responsibilities and terms between an owner and the licensee of intellectual property.

A patent or copyright infringement occurs when one party is accused of using a protected asset without permission or without paying for it. The patent or copyright infringement by one party may result in litigation between the owner and the unauthorized user. The owner of the asset would sue for damages associated with loss of revenue, market share or other losses as a result of the unauthorized use of the licensed property by another.

Market Participants and Industry Players

The market can be segmented into content or product creators and innovators, owners of intellectual property, distributors, exchangers and service providers (responsible for facilitating the transfer of risk and tracking and collecting monies due to intellectual property owners).

Inventors and owners can be individuals, firms or universities. Inventors who cannot distribute the product they invent will license the invention to a distributor who is able to do so. A toy inventor, for example, can license his or her idea to Mattel or Hasbro. A drug patent can be licensed to big pharmaceutical companies like Merck or Pfizer. There are even some special purpose entities that exist solely to accumulate patents or to buy them for resale at low cost or via auction to the highest bidder.

In some industries, intermediaries and intellectual property service organizations play an important role in the collection and disbursement of royalties. Performing rights organizations (PROs) collect fees from businesses that use certain intellectual property, such as songs or videos, in their place of business, in a public or commercial setting or for resale. Broadcast Music Inc. (BMI), the American Society of Composers, Authors and Publishers (ASCAP) and the Society of European Stage Authors and Composers (SESAC) are three of the biggest players in the music and entertainment business. Each represents and assists artists with registered copyrights in their efforts to collect royalties from businesses that use the intellectual property. BMI has a library of nearly 13 million musical works including those by Mariah Carey, Lady Gaga, Taylor Swift, Eminem, Rihanna, Maroon 5, Sam Cooke, Dolly Parton and Shakira. ASCAP's mission is to ensure its members get paid promptly and fairly when their compositions are performed publicly or used in a business. ASCAP artists include Justin Timberlake, Vampire Weekend, Duke Ellington, Dave Matthews, George Gershwin, Stevie Wonder, Beyoncé and Marc Anthony. Most PROs are privately owned or organized as not-for-profit organizations on behalf of the artists. SESAC is an invitation-only, for-profit platform owned by the Blackstone Group. Its composers include Bob Dylan, Neil Diamond, Young Love, Rapture and Adele. SESAC was acquired by Blackstone's Core Equity Partners Fund in 2017.[1]

Industry Associations and Best Practices

The Intellectual Property Owners Association is a trade association that serves the intellectual property community. The organization was established in 1972. Its members benefit from updates on legislative trends, educational services, networking and the dissemination of key information to the public. More information about the association can be found on their website: https://www.ipo.org/index.php/about/.

The Association of Intellectual Property Firms is an industry association whose mission is to provide an international forum for firms who practice patent, copyright and trademark law. The association helps members improve their business, develop global relationships and engage with industry representatives on important issues. More information about the association can be found on their website: https://aipf.com/about-us/.

---

1. Lianne Starr, "The Guide to PROs," Songtrust, May 2018, https://blog.songtrust.com/songwriting-tips/pros-whats-the-difference

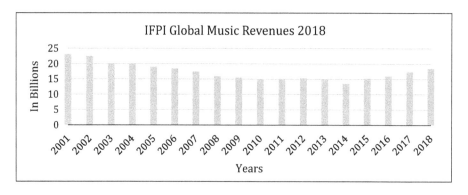

Figure 5.1. Changes in music industry royalties from 2001 to 2018.
Source: IFPI

Market Size and Scope

In 2016, the Economics and Statistics Administration and the US Patent and Trademark Office produced a joint report titled *Intellectual Property and the U.S. Economy: 2016 Update.* The main conclusions of the report were that intellectual property intensive industries are a significant part of the US economy and that they will continue to grow. Patent, trademark and copyright-related employment accounted for over 50 million jobs at the end of 2010. Almost 40% of US GDP was derived from industries associated with intellectual property in 2014. Revenue in 2014 from the licensing of intellectual property rights from all sources was reported to exceed $115.2 billion.[2]

Music industry revenues, shown in Figure 5.1, have been rising since 2015, according to data collected by the International Federation of the Phonographic Industry (IFPI). Revenues include physical sales, performance rights and digital, streaming and other sources. Royalties from music licensing was estimated at almost $20 billion in 2018.[3]

According to the 2019 IBISWorld data in Figure 5.2, revenue for the U.S. intellectual property rights licensing industry was estimated at $48.7 billion as of August 2019. Revenues have grown 3.2% annually from the period 2014 to 2019 and are expected to grow 1.8% annually from 2019 to 2024. Important drivers for further revenue increases include increasing corporate profits, higher advertising spending, higher consumer purchases, higher per capita disposable income and a higher percentage of services conducted online.[4]

2. *Intellectual Property and the U.S. Economy*, U.S. Patent and Trademark Office, Sep. 2016, https://www.uspto.gov/sites/default/files/documents/IPandtheUSEconomySept2016.pdf.
3. Frances Moore et al., *Global Music Report 2017*, IFPI, 2017, https://www.ifpi.org/downloads/GMR2017.pdf.
4. Ryan Roth, "Intellectual Property Rights Licensing in the US," IBISWorld, Aug. 2019, https://www.ibisworld.com/united-states/market-research-reports/intellectual-property-licensing-industry/.

Total Revenue in 2019	Annual Growth 2014–2019	Annual Growth 2019–2024	Profit Margin in 2019	Wages as a share of Revenue in 2019	Number of Businesses 2014–2019
$48.7 bn	3.2%	1.8%	24.2%	9.0%	2.9%

Figure 5.2. IBISWorld statistics related to the intellectual property industry as of August 2019.

Industry Products & Services Segmentation

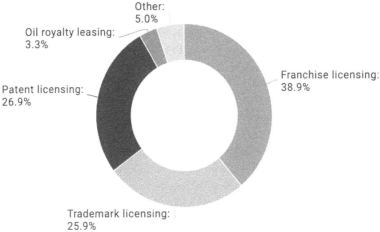

Other: 5.0%
Oil royalty leasing: 3.3%
Patent licensing: 26.9%
Franchise licensing: 38.9%
Trademark licensing: 25.9%

Figure 5.3. IBISWorld breakdown of the intellectual property industry's $50.3 billion in 2019.

According to the IBISWorld analysis in Figure 5.3, 38.9% of revenues were from franchise licensing, 26.9% from patent licensing, 25.9% from trademark licensing, 3.3% from oil and gas royalty licensing and 5% from other sources. The report was based on data provided by 6,283 intellectual property rights licensing businesses that reported their revenue in 2019.[5]

Opportunities and Strategies

Healthcare royalty investing allows investors to earn a percentage of sales for a wide range of healthcare products, including both medical devices and drugs. Small firms or universities that invent a drug or a device often lack the capability to manufacture and sell the product and need to sell some or all of their product rights to larger pharmaceutical companies or device manufacturers. Healthcare royalties for products developed by

---

5. Roth, "Intellectual Property Rights Licensing in the US."

larger, more established firms with distribution track records can be also used to create structured products, such as royalty-backed bonds and equity.

Equity capital can be provided to fund research and development. These deals carry more risk, as the underlying drug may not get approved. Other strategies for investors include extending loans or buying debt issued by firms with drugs or devices that are patent-protected but that may lack the working capital or access to bank loans due to a lack of profits. These smaller, less-capitalized firms for approved medicines and devices may prefer issuing debt over issuing new equity.

Firms can also sell patents and licenses on drugs or equipment to a special purpose vehicle created by a financial sponsor such as a bank. The sponsor underwrites bonds and equity to raise capital to pay for the patents and licenses transferred to the trust. The cash flow on the revenue stream from the patents and trusts are income to the trust, and the interest on the debt and equity issued by the trust are expenses. Bond holders get a higher-than-normal return on the investment-grade bonds issued by the trust, while the equity holder gets any residual or windfall profit if revenue on the royalties exceeds the interest paid on the bond, adjusted for expenses. Equity owners, of course, also bear the risk that the royalty revenue stream dries up or is insufficient to pay off the bonds.

In the music industry, the top 10 highest earning songs in history are "Candle in the Wind" by Elton John and Bernie Taupin, "The Christmas Song" by Mel Torme and Bob Wells, "Pretty Woman" by Roy Orbison and Bill Dees, "Every Breath You Take" by Sting, "Santa Claus Is Coming to Town" by Haven Gillespie and Fred J. Coots, "Stand by Me" by Ben E. King, Jerry Leiber and Mike Stoller, "Unchained Melody" by Alex North and Hy Zaret, "Yesterday" by John Lennon and Paul McCartney, "You've Lost That Feeling" by Barry Mann, Cynthia Weil and Phil Spector and "White Christmas" by Irving Berlin, according to an article published in 2017 in the *Income Investors* magazine.[6]

Music royalties can be purchased on several private and public exchanges today. The investment can generate cash flows that last 70 years beyond the selling artist's life. Royalty streams can increase or decrease over time as a function of the artist or specific song's popularity. An investment in the royalties of a song used in a movie soundtrack or performed by another artist could see royalties rapidly rise. The death of the original recording artist may also cause sales and royalty payments to rise. Streaming services and fee income on songs will also mean higher royalties in the future. Music royalties are typically purchased for a multiple of the current year's royalty cash flow stream. A revenue stream of $10,000 might be sold for a low multiple of its current cash flow, say one or two times, or between $10,000 and $20,000. In other cases, it might sell for as high as 10 or 20 times or between $100,000 and $200,000. This depends on the outlook for sales growth. The key to success is finding either rapidly growing artists with increasing sales or, alternatively, very mature artists with large stables of songs that have demonstrated consistent sales over many years. Consider this as similar to investing in growth stocks or value stocks.

---

6. Susan Lassiter-Lyons, "How to Invest in Royalties," *Income Investors*, Sept. 2017, https://theincomeinvestors.com/how-to-invest-in-royalties/

Some notable music industry icons have also securitized their royalties by issuing bonds collateralized by future royalties. "Bowie Bonds" were securities backed by royalties from the 25 albums that the artist recorded prior to 1990. The bonds were issued in 1997 and generated $55 million for David Bowie. The bonds had a yield-to-maturity of approximately 8% and were issued as investment-grade bonds with a spread of approximately 150 basis points over treasuries at the time. Royalties from the 25 albums provided the cash flow to make the bond interest payments. The artist gave away 10 years of expected royalties in exchange for the upfront payment. The bonds matured in 2007 as planned, without default, and the rights to the income from the songs reverted to Bowie.[7]

Many well-known performing artists do not collect any royalties when their performances are played on the radio. This is the case if they did not write the song and do not own the copyright. Generally, it is only the songwriter and composer who own the copyright and who can collect royalties when the music is played on the radio or performed by other artists.

Movies and television shows are unique products that can also be protected by copyright. The owners of the copyrights are entitled to charge royalties when their products are used or viewed by others. A movie or television show copyright is usually owned by the producer of the film or program. Everyone else involved in creating the program will normally be asked to sign contracts, as part of which they either give up any rights to the work or which stipulate a percentage of individual participation or ownership in the work. Performers may demand royalties as a condition of participation in a production and have royalty rates included in their contracts. Other members of the crew, such as writers and directors, may not have as much leverage to do so. Unions representing these groups will often seek to negotiate rates for their members. "Residuals" is the term used in this segment of the industry to refer to the royalties made upon the rebroadcasting of an original movie or show. In television, residuals begin once a show starts airing reruns or is released to DVD, subscription television, broadcast television, basic cable or new media. In films, residuals begin once the movie appears on DVD, basic cable and free or subscription television or new media. Residuals are typically paid quarterly. As long as the films and television programs are being broadcast, the performers continue to receive payments.

Actors, directors, writers, producers and recording artists can auction the future payments for large lump sums of cash. Investors receive consistent cash flow and a higher yielding asset than traditional investments. The sellers do not lose any rights to the residuals. For example, on the Allegany royalty exchange, only specific payments are assigned to the residual buyers. Sellers choose how many years of residuals to sell. At the end of the term, the assignment expires and the performer will continue receiving payments or can sell additional residuals.[8] Streaming services are having a positive impact

7. Max Hartley, "Royalty-Backed Securities: The Future of Asset-Backed Securities," Seeking Alpha, Dec. 2017, https://seekingalpha.com/instablog/48941456-max-hartley/5082217-royalty-backed-securities-future-asset-backed-securities

8. "Alternative Investment Marketplace," Allegheny Exchange, accessed Oct. 2019, http://alleghenyexchange.com/.

on movie and television show royalties. As more programming is purchased by Netflix and Amazon, the anticipated number of views and revenues paid to the royalty owner will rise. Increased competition among streaming services is also likely to lead to price competition for content and higher royalty rates. Investors in residuals would benefit from both of these trends.

In the mining and oil and gas industries, there are several ways for investors to be paid a royalty based on a percentage of sales or production. These royalty stakes allow investors to own a stake in oil production without having to provide the upfront capital associated with exploration and drilling or distribution. Some oil and gas trusts also offer tax advantages, such as pass-through taxation and lower capital gain rates on distributions. Mining companies in the gold and silver industries and many others also sell royalties to generate cash flow. Investors who own mineral rights on a property are able to collect royalties each time a mining company extracts gold or silver from a mine. Investors can once again participate in the upside of the revenue stream from an asset that is hard to extract without providing the capital cost associated with mining and exploration. These royalty trusts offer high yields, tax advantages, pass-through treatment and commodity exposures.

Minerals rights are valued based on the demand for a particular type of mineral in the market. Minerals prices are driven by supply and demand imbalances between producers and consumers, barriers to entry, regulation and speculation. Investors outside of direct market participants and producers or consumers are not readily able to invest in individual or even groups of rare minerals per se. There are, however, a significant number of private equity funds, mutual funds and ETFs that offer diversified exposure to many types of minerals, either directly or via stakes in market participants or from the direct ownership of mineral rights. There are several unique risks related to this type of investing, including extremes in price volatility, natural disasters, regulation or nationalization. Investment in mineral and oil and gas rights may be less sensitive to changes in the spot price of the underlying commodity in the short run. The immediate price risk is taken by the companies who are buying the rights to develop and sell the underlying commodity. When the value of the commodity declines for an extended time, then the value of the rights to mine that commodity will also fall.

Who Invests?

Many pension funds, hedge funds, family offices and scores of individual investors participate in the royalty market today. Institutional investors typically invest in royalty-backed bonds as part of a fixed income or credit portfolio.

Individual investors can invest in royalties via exchange-traded products or mutual funds. Fidelity offers several mineral and mining funds that provide retail investors some exposure to the sector.

According to a recent *Wall Street Journal* article, there is currently a total of about $3.2 billion invested in funds focused on music royalties alone. Investors are attracted to these products since royalties' earnings historically have not been correlated to the equity or bond market.[9] Investors with long-term time horizons, such as pensions, endowments and foundations, may find commingled funds attractive. Round Hill Music Royalty Fund, for example, owns the rights to more than 4,000 songs, including Chris Kenner's "Land of a Thousand Dances," which appears in the movie *Forrest Gump*.[10] Warren Buffett has even compared owning royalties to owning a toll road! Once you build the road, you can collect cash forever as you control who is able to use it.[11]

How to Invest?

Investors today can invest directly and trade existing patents or royalties on several exchanges. They can usually invest quickly using standard documentation and terms provided by the exchange. Exchanges allow investors to bid on intellectual property, sell or auction property or obtain prices for similar assets. Investors use exchanges and platforms to buy existing intellectual property rights either for relicensing or to invest and receive future royalty streams. Investors can create their own bespoke portfolios of royalties and diversify their holdings on their own. Like other exotic alternatives, direct investing, portfolio construction and diversification takes more time and due diligence than investing in commingled products or funds.

Investors can invest in commingled private funds that provide capital to inventors or businesses that are in the process of developing new intellectual property, such as fintech applications or a drug, in exchange for revenues from future royalties. An individual making investments or a manager running a fund that provides capital for research and development to fund new ideas or drugs or in search of minerals will need robust resources and a suitable due diligence process to identify and select investments. Venture capitalists, scientists, academics and others often collaborate to source capital for a new drug from investment funds with an expertise in healthcare. These players can go to a variety of exchanges and platforms to buy existing intellectual property rights either for relicensing or to invest and receive future royalty streams. Like other exotic alternatives, direct investing takes more time and due diligence than investing in commingled products or funds. Investors can also invest in private credit funds that originate loans or buy bonds secured by royalties.

There are also several public companies and publicly listed trusts or funds can be used to get exposure to a growing number of intellectual properties-backed securities in the healthcare, mineral and mining and entertainment spaces.

---

9. Mischa Frankl-Duval, "Investors in Search of Yield Turn to Music-Royalty Funds," *Wall Street Journal*, Sept. 2019, https://www.wsj.com/articles/investors-in-search-of-yield-turn-to-music-royalty-funds-11569204301.

10. Anthony Greco, "Music Royalty Funds Charm Investors," Private Wealth, Sept. 2013, https://www.fa-mag.com/news/music-royalty-funds-charm-investors-15473.html.

11. Simon Black, "Royalties—Warren Buffett's 'Tollbooth' Investment Strategy," *Early To Rise*, Sept. 2017, https://www.earlytorise.com/warren-buffetts-tollbooth-investment-strategy/.

Benchmarks and Indices

Benchmarks for intellectual property and royalty returns are hard to find. However, there are private research companies who can perform studies and provide information on specific portfolios owned by their clients. This would be a reasonable source of information to use to benchmark individual portfolios owned by investors.

One example is the Royalty Exchange's study of the royalties sold over its platform in 2019. The study found that the royalty assets acquired on the Royalty Exchange marketplace delivered a 12.14% return on investment in 2019. For more information about returns from royalty investing, including the methodology used to calculated annualized returns for 2019, visit the Royalty Exchange website at https://www.royaltyexchange.com/blog/music-royalties-deliver-12-14-yield-in-2019#sthash.E7Qaz0xN.dpbs.

Firms, Funds and Platforms

Hipgnosis Songs Fund Ltd. is a public company listed on the London Stock Exchange. The company operates as an investment company. It offers exposure to songs and associated musical intellectual property rights in the form of royalty payments. For more information, please visit the company's website at www.hipgnosissongs.com.

San Juan Royalty Trust was established in November 1980 by a trust indenture between Southland Royalty and the Fort Worth National Bank. It owns a royalty interest in Southland Royalty's oil and gas leasehold and royalty interest in the San Juan Basin of northwestern New Mexico. This royalty interest is the principal asset of the trust. Distributions are made to provide trust owners with dividends and a return of principal. For more information, visit the company's website at http://www.sjbrt.com/Annual-Qtrly-Reports/default.aspx.

Ligand Royalty is one of the largest and most diverse portfolios in the biotech and pharmaceutical industry. Its portfolio includes approved drugs that treat cancer, osteoporosis, fungal infections and low blood platelets, among others. For more information, visit the firm's website at https://www.ligand.com.

Xoma is a biotech royalty aggregator with over 65 assets in its current portfolio. XOMA purchases future royalty payments from pre-commercial clinical drug candidates, thus allowing firms to fund the development. For more information, visit the firm's website at https://www.xoma.com.

PDL BioPharma is a publicly traded holding company that manages commercial stage pharmaceutical assets and late-stage clinical pharmaceutical products in which the company has royalty interests. PDL BioPharma provides royalty sellers with a combination of debt/equity funding to support drug development and commercialization. For more information, visit the firm's website at https://www.pdl.com.

Royalty Pharma is a private firm that is an industry leader in investing in marketed and late-stage biopharmaceutical products. The firm holds over $15 billion in royalty assets. Royalty Pharma not only acquires existing royalty interests from the original developers but also co-develops and co-funds products in late-stage clinical trials. The company's portfolio includes royalty interests in over 40 approved products including

AbbVie's Humira, AbbVie and J&J's Imbruvica, Biogen's Tecfidera and Tysabri, Vertex's Kalydeco and Orkambi, J&J's Remicade, Merck's Januvia, Gilead's Atripla and Truvada, Pfizer's Lyrica and Astellas and Pfizer's Xtandi. Royalty Pharma has committed over $850 million to direct R&D funding in exchange for royalties. For more information, visit the firm's website at https://www.royaltypharma.com.

HealthCare Royalty Partners is an investment firm that buys commercial- or near-commercial-stage biopharmaceutical royalties. The firm raised a $1.8 billion fund in January 2020. For more information, visit the firm's website at https://www.healthcareroyalty.com.

Oberland Capital Management is a private fund founded in 2012 that invests in healthcare royalties. It specializes in structured financing in the global healthcare industry. Since inception, the firm has raised over $1.2 billion. Its financing solutions include monetization of royalty streams, acquisition of future product revenues, creation of project-based financing structures and investment in debt and equity securities. The company seeks to invest $20 million to $150 million at a time and has the ability to handle larger transactions. For more information, visit the fund's website at https://www.oberlandcapital.com.

Allegheny Exchange is an online marketplace for alternative investments. Actors, producers, recording artists, publishers, directors and songwriters use the platform to raise cash by auctioning their residuals and royalties. High-net-worth and institutional investors are able to purchase an asset class which provides superior and uncorrelated returns to traditional investments. In addition to intellectual property royalties, the exchange also sells tax liens and trade claims to qualifying investors. For more information, visit the company's website at https://www.alleghanycc.com.

The Royalty Exchange is an online marketplace where investors can bid on royalties, including those related to music, film, television, books, solar energy, pharmaceutical, intellectual property, oil, gas and more. Clients pay a 2.5% premium when purchased and another 2.5% for the management and payout of the royalty stream over time. For more information, visit the exchange's website at http://www.theroyaltyexchange.com.

Lyric Financial is an online royalty platform. It was created to assist musicians that need money early in their careers. The platform helps musicians monetize and collect short-term advances on their royalties. The company's royalty advances were developed specifically for artists, songwriters, composers, producers, distributors and independent labels who earn at least $5,000 per year from royalties, streaming revenue or sales of their music. For more information, visit the company's website at http://www.lyricfinancial.com.

SongVest is a platform that allows users to buy or sell royalties. It allows investors to finance albums that are being made today using a crowdfunding model. Investors then share in a percentage of the royalties. The money raised allows the musicians to create and market the albums and investors get a quasi-equity stake in the artist. For more information, visit the company's website at https://www.songvest.com.

Techquity is a platform through which individuals can monetize their intellectual property. Techquity seeks to acquire high-quality patents related to the communications,

Table 5.1. The performance, risk and correlation of a composite of healthcare and pharmaceutical investment vehicles versus the S&P 500 between January 2016 and December 2019.

	Pharma Royalties	S&P 500
Correlation	0.30	NA
Standard Deviation	44.93%	11.56%
Average Annual Return	11.13%	14.33%
Simplified Sharpe	0.25	1.24

Table 5.2. The performance, risk and correlation of a composite of mineral and mining royalty investment vehicles versus the S&P 500 between January 2016 and December 2019.

	Mining Royalties	S&P 500
Correlation	−0.0003	NA
Standard Deviation	25.39%	11.56%
Average Annual Return	25.32%	14.33%
Simplified Sharpe	1.00	1.24

media and computing industries. For more information, visit http://www.techquitycap.com/patent-owners/.

Patent Auction is an online auction platform where individuals buy and sell patents. Patent Auction lists hundreds of inventions protected by patent rights for sale or license by their owners. For more information, visit the company's website at https://www.patentauction.com.

IP Marketplace is an online platform that allows individuals to put their patents, patent applications, utility models, design and trademarks up for sale or out-licensing. IP Marketplace is owned, run and updated by the Danish Patent and Trademark Office. It is free of charge for both buyer and seller. For more information, visit the company's website at https://www.ip-marketplace.org.

Composite

Investing in a pharmaceutical and healthcare composite between January 2016 and December 2019, shown in Table 5.1, produced an 11.13% return versus 14.33% for the S&P 500. The composite had very low correlation to the S&P 500 of .30. It also had significantly more risk and an unattractive Sharpe ratio of just 0.25.

Investing in a mining and oil and gas royalty composite between January 2016 and December 2019, shown in Table 5.2, produced a 25.32% return versus 14.33% for the S&P 500, with a lower Sharpe ratio of 1.0 versus 1.24. The composite had virtually no correlation to the S&P 500, with a coefficient of approximately zero.

Investing in a combined composite including all the pharmaceutical, healthcare, mining, oil and gas vehicles between January 2016 and December 2019, shown in

Table 5.3. The performance, risk and correlation of a composite of all the intellectual property investment vehicles versus the S&P 500 between January 2016 and December 2019.

	IP Composite	S&P 500
Correlation	0.23	NA
Standard Deviation	25.15%	11.56%
Average Annual Return	25.10%	14.33%
Simplified Sharpe	0.88	1.24

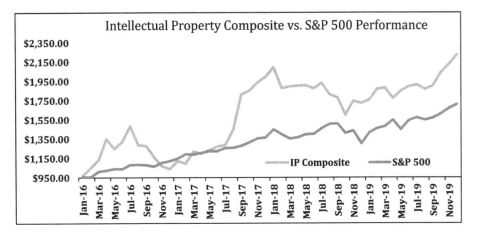

Figure 5.4. The growth of $1,000 invested in an intellectual property composite versus the $1,000 invested in the S&P 500 from January 2016 to December 2019.

Table 5.3, produced a 22.1% return versus 14.33% for the S&P 500, with significantly higher risk and a lower Sharpe ratio. The composite's correlation to the S&P 500 was a very low 0.23.

A $1,000 investment in an intellectual property composite in January 2016, shown in Figure 5.4, would have grown to over $2,200 by December 2019 compared to just $1,708 for the S&P 500.

Valuation

Intellectual property can be valued similar to other financial assets. Common approaches include a discounted cash flow model or a comparable transaction analysis. One of the unique twists in valuing intellectual property is that an income stream may have a negative growth rate. In addition, since the royalty stream is generally reliant on a unique work or process, finding a truly comparable or identical sale may be impossible.

Let's look at an example in the pharmaceutical industry. Assume a drug patent has 10 years remaining before its date of expiration. At the point of expiration, anyone can produce the drug without a royalty payment or risk of litigation. The royalty stream in this example is expected to provide $100,000 in the first year and last for 10 years.

Assume that the royalties peak in the first year and will decline by 10% annually over the duration of the term, until expiration. If investors want a 12% return or hurdle rate on their royalty investment, then the value of the cumulative cash flow of $651,321, using a 12% discount rate, would be $403,516 today.

A perpetual royalty stream, for example in a music royalty, would be valued using a model similar to a perpetual growth annuity or a common stock with an increasing dividend. Assuming the same initial cash flow, discount rate and decay as the example above, one would make this type of calculation by simply dividing the initial cash flow by the discount rate less the growth rate. Since the growth rate is negative, the cash flow would be divided by the sum of the discount rate and the absolute value of the decay in cash flow. In our example, $100,000 is divided by 12% plus negative 10% or 22%, to get a valuation of $454,545.

The comparable transaction approach would try to evaluate recent deals for similar drugs paying similar royalties. Transaction prices would be accumulated and averaged until a reasonable proxy was found for valuation purposes. If we assume, for example, a distribution of observed values with a mean of $425,000, a high of $475,000, a low of $375,000 and a normal distribution, then a valuation of $425,000 would seem reasonable.

What to Look For?

Each type of intellectual property investment requires a slightly different form of due diligence. Music royalties require an understanding of pop culture and entertainment trends. Healthcare royalties involve a deep understanding of specific drugs and their life cycles. The question of who is paying the royalty stream to the investor also matters. Is there credit risk and how strong is the identification and collection process associated with a particular form of intellectual property? Are infringements and litigation common? A good intellectual property attorney will be necessary for firms that invest in more complex deals. Each patent license agreement will need to document the specific rights being sold and the term, the payment to be received, the records that are required to be maintained, the periodic reports to be issued, the way in which infringements get handled and how liabilities that may arise from the use of the property will be treated.

Unique Risks

Many forms of intellectual property investments are depleting assets. Direct investments may have no value after a certain number of years. This means that the revenue stream eventually ends. Distributions can also be very volatile from period to period. The ability of the user of the royalty license to pay fees to the owner is a form of credit risk. License fee agreements are often established between small biotech companies and large pharmaceutical companies who can distribute the drug or treatment. The royalty stream from these fees can be purchased by investors. The investor will have credit exposure to the pharmaceutical company who is paying the fees. Royalty streams may also be illiquid and difficult to value. Structured products that issue bonds back by cash flows from royalties owned by special purpose vehicles or issued by healthcare companies themselves can be used to mitigate the risk of the royalties suddenly becoming worthless.

Trends and Outlook

Trends and outlook are favorable for this type of investing in intellectual property. The rise of fintech, healthcare and the changes in the music and entertainment industry all support expanding revenue from the use of protected intellectual property. It is unclear how the COVID-19 crisis will impact the industry in the long term.

Today, there are several exchanges and platforms that allow direct investment in both public and private funds that own royalties. Investors can also buy individual royalty streams on many of these platforms.

Manager Perspectives and Insights

Dr. Evan Bedil, Managing Director, Marathon Asset Management

Dr. Evan Bedil is a managing director and has led Marathon Asset Management's Healthcare Structured Credit and Royalty Monetization investment program since 2017. Dr. Bedil previously worked at Marathon as a vice president and the senior health-care investment analyst investing in drug royalties and loans from 2005 to 2008. Prior to rejoining Marathon, he was a partner at Healthcare Capital Solutions/Crown Sterling LLC. From 2011 to 2015, he spearheaded PDL BioPharma's investments in drug roy-alties and structured credit that invested over $750 million. He has applicable experi-ence working as a business development consultant at Defined Health between his initial tenure at Marathon and PDL. Following his business school studies, he spent two years at Morgan Stanley in biotechnology equity research. He holds an MBA from the Ross School of Business at the University of Michigan and received his MBBCh (MD equiv-alent) from the University of the Witwatersrand Medical School in Johannesburg, South Africa. Dr. Bedil sits on the Medical Advisory Board of the R Baby Foundation.

In general, what is your experience with investing in more esoteric types of alternative investments such as life settlements, intellectual property and royalties, litigation funding, tax liens, trade claims or things like artwork, Bitcoin or collectibles?

I have trained as a medical doctor and graduated from business school. Over the past 15 years, I have invested over $2 billion across 20 deals in healthcare royalties and secured debt.

What is your specific experience investing in intellectual properties and royalties? Perhaps you can mention or give an example of some structures, instruments or strategies you have found the most interesting over time and those you avoid.

All of my deals have had significant IP [intellectual property] and royalty value. The best structures provide significant downside protection as anything that can go wrong often will and it's important to keep the counterparty properly incentivized. Despite deals that have gone sideways at times, almost all our deals have realized profits in the end.

An interesting structure which is becoming more common on the marketplace is a royalty-backed note whereby a note is paid off by royalties from the sales of approved drugs. We avoid pre-approved drugs because FDA approval is a binary outcome and by betting on it we would be taking equity risk. Any rejection by the FDA would be a disaster for a financial instrument which is paid off by royalty flow. We also avoid undifferentiated drugs with weak intellectual property and weak marketing companies behind them.

What is your opinion on the opportunity presented from investing in intellectual property assets going forward? What is the expected return, liquidity premium and so on?
By nature, intellectual property assets are illiquid and thus command a higher expected return. In healthcare, there will always be innovation with new treatments. Given the tremendous cost to bring a drug to market and then commercialize it, the vast majority of drugs have associated out-licensing arrangements and royalties attached which can be monetized. Given that these are debt-like instruments, they will typically be cheaper than equity so we expect there to be continued interest from counterparties looking to monetize their intellectual property.

What are some of the major risks associated with investing in intellectual property-backed instruments?
The obvious risk is that the intellectual property is worthless or unenforceable or that it expires within the tenor of the royalty. Additionally, if a competing drug loses patent protection and goes generic, pricing throughout the market will suffer as generics enter. Another major risk is that the drug gets pulled from the market for a particular manufacturing or safety issue. That would be devastating. Usually we need to balance expected growth through a financial forecast versus valuation discounting at a certain rate; in other words, we have to make assumptions about the value of an asset in order to price it.

Where would you see intellectual property- or royalty-backed investments fitting into the asset allocation process? Is it a stand-alone asset class, part of credit or fixed income portfolios or part of an alternative's allocation? What type of investors are best suited for allocating to this space?
Intellectual property- and royalty-backed investments are uncorrelated from standard asset classes. It would be best to allocate for those seeking high risk-adjusted returns and have exposure to other asset classes. Investors who are able to stay locked in for three plus years would benefit most from the space.

Academic Perspectives and Research

Academic articles relating to intellectual property date back to the nineteenth century wherein scholars discussed the emergence of intellectual property laws in American industries. More recently, academic articles have discussed the legal aspects of intellectual property ownership, the flaws in the intellectual property system and suggestions for how to fix it.

One article published by the *University of Chicago Law Review* evaluated the patent system in the United States. The author claimed that despite having a unitary patent system, the process of obtaining a patent differs widely across technologies and industries. The authors measured the differences in the patents by analyzing patent litigation outcomes. The way the authors went about collecting the data was utilizing the Lex Machina database, which pulled information from the Public Access to Court Electronic Record (PACER) website. From there they classified the cases between the technology and the related industries. The technologies include mechanical, electrical, chemical, biotechnology, software and optics patents. The industries include pharmaceutical, semiconductor, medical devices and others. The researchers first looked at results filtered by technology patents. They found that 26% of technology cases that went to a definitive outcome were won by the patentees, which includes a large variation among categories. Chemical patents won 52% of the cases that went to a final decision, while software patents prevailed in only 13.5% of cases. That difference is consistent with the received wisdom in the literature that patents are stronger and more valuable in disciplines like chemistry than in software. When the data was separated into business method and non-business method patents, they found that business method patents fared substantially better than software patents, which tended to cover more technical software inventions. Patent owners won 17% of the business-method patents in cases that went to a final decision, compared to 12% of the non-business method patents. The results suggest that the low win rate for software patents cannot be attributed solely to business method patents. They also found that just 5.6% of biotechnology patent cases that went to final decision prevailed. The paper breaks down patent cases by industry. In the biotechnology industry, patentees only won 8.3% of the cases. Patentees also fared poorly in communications (14.8% win rate), consumer goods and services (15.1% win rate), construction (15.0% win rate) and computer and electronics (17.1% win rate). By contrast, patentees won a majority of cases in the pharmaceutical industry (51.6%) and a significant number in the energy industry (40%). The research continues to analyze the cases based on invalidity and infringement cases wherein the team breaks down each industry by the type of case. The paper concluded that while there is a unitary patent system, the system affects industries very differently. Because of the drastic differences between industries, the authors suggest patent legislation and policy changes in the future.[12]

Another article by the University of Missouri's Mary LaFrance examines royalty and copyright laws in the music streaming industry. LaFrance examines the flow of revenue from the music streaming services to the rights holders, the flaws that rights holders have identified in that infrastructure and the extent to which the flaws are addressed in Congress's latest reform. The article discusses a significant form of legislation called the Music Modernization Act (MMA), which was created to update the music regulatory

---

12. John R. Allison, Mark A. Lemley and David L. Schwartz, "One Divided Patent System," *University of Chicago Law Review*, 2015, https://www.jstor.org/stable/43575197?seq=1#metadata_info_tab_contents.

landscape given the rise of streaming services. The purpose of the act is to establish a nonprofit governing agency to construct a single, publicly accessible database that would link recordings to their underlying musical works and to all the creative participants who may be entitled to share in the proceeds of those works. By doing this, it would establish a system to properly identify the owner of the license and allow the proper payment of royalties. Another impact of the MMA was changing the payout structure to license holders. Instead of basing the royalty on the revenues of the streaming service from 2018 to 2022, the royalty will be based on the greater of a percentage of the service's revenues or a percentage of its "total cost of content," which refers to the amounts paid to record labels for the right to stream the recordings. Another aspect of the MMA is the CLASSICS Act (Compensating Legacy Artists for their Songs, Service and Important Contributions to Society Act), which provides copyright protection to songs created prior to 1972. One significant problem that the MMA has failed to address is the role of hosting sites in the music streaming industry. YouTube, the largest music streaming service in the world, pays little or nothing to artists in fees to music rights holders, even though it generates millions in advertisements from their videos. LaFrance stated that while no legislation to address this issue has been, the music industry will continue to pressure Congress to cover this issue. Another issue involves the CLASSICS Act, which introduced unnecessary ambiguity by relying on state law to determine the identity of the rights owner. Additionally, by subjecting pre-1972 recordings to the same royalty scheme as copyrighted recordings, and by not giving the recording artists any termination rights, the Act ensures that the majority of the financial rewards from the newly recognized right will go to the record labels rather than the artists.[13]

Finally, David Karp and Parker Milender address the oil and gas industry in their article entitled "Investing in Oil and Gas Royalties: Distressed Counterparty Risk Considerations." The article discusses some issues and things to consider when investing in oil and gas royalties. According to the authors, as oil and gas prices decline, exploration and production companies tend to refinance into more traditional term loans or divest royalties in an effort to raise cash. Due to this process, investors who own carved-out royalty interests need to be aware of counterparty risk associated with these investments and how these positions will be treated in a bankruptcy, including the potential risks of contract recharacterization or rejection and claw backs of payments already received. In the past, carved-out interests would be treated by bankruptcy courts as "true sales" of real property. But recent cases suggest that while the transaction may have been labeled as a sale, a court might instead recharacterize the carved-out interest transactions as financings or debt investments. Therefore, investors must be aware of the different types of royalty agreements in the oil and gas industry. In a recent case involving ATP Oil and Gas Corp.'s bankruptcy, the court denied a carved-out interest and instead ruled the

---

13. Mary LaFrance, "Music Modernization and the Labyrinth of Streaming," *Business, Entrepreneurship and Tax Law Review*, vol. 2, issue 2, 2018, https://scholarship.law.missouri.edu/betr/vol2/iss2/5/?utm_source=scholarship.law.missouri.edu%2Fbetr%2Fvol2%2Fiss2%2F5&utm_medium=PDF&utm_campaign=PDFCoverPages.

carve out as a financing agreement. Investors must be aware of the different types of royalty payments and the varying laws state by state. This article goes on to describe how different types of royalties are treated in each state.[14]

Summary

Intellectual property investments can take many shapes and forms. Investors can benefit from the use of protected property in a wide range of industries, including oil and gas, entertainment and healthcare. Infrastructure to support the industry appears stable, and there are a wide range of options to consider. The emergence of millennials and new technology are positive trends supporting music royalties. The search for yield in a low interest rate environment is supportive of healthcare royalties and many others. This type of investment has very high relative returns and very low correlation to traditional equity investments and is likely to have very positive portfolio effects despite a high degree of stand-alone volatility associated with some of the specific types of intellectual property investment vehicles.

Useful Websites and Additional Reading

"Fees Versus Royalties and the Private Value of a Patent," https://academic.oup.com/qje/article-abstract/101/3/471/1899629.

"The Healthcare Royalties Market Most Alts Investors Are Missing," https://citywireselector.com/news/the-healthcare-royalties-market-most-alts-investors-are-missing/a1213137.

"The Hidden Risk of Royalty Exchange Investing," https://theconservativeincomeinvestor.com/the-hidden-risk-of-royalty-exchange-music-investing/.

"How to Buy Oil and Gas Royalties—The 6 Step Process," https://blackbearddata.com/royalty-buying-101/how-to-buy-oil-and-gas-royalties-the-6-step-process.

"Investing in Oil and Gas Royalties: Distressed Counterparty Risk Considerations," https://www.srz.com/images/content/6/9/v2/69772/Investing-in-Oil-and-Gas-Royalties-Distressed-Counterparty-Risk.pdf.

"Investing in Mineral Rights and Royalties," https://mineralrightspodcast.com/mrp-26-investing-in-mineral-rights-and-royalties/.

"Investors in Search of Yield Turn to Music-Royalty Funds," https://www.wsj.com/articles/investors-in-search-of-yield-turn-to-music-royalty-funds-11569204301.

"A Primer on Healthcare Royalty & Credit Investing," https://www.icapitalnetwork.com/insights/education/a-primer-on-healthcare-royalty-credit-investing/.

---

14. David J. Karp and Parker J. Milender, "Investing in Oil and Gas Royalties: Distressed Counterparty Risk Considerations," Schulte Roth and Zabel, Mar. 2015, https://www.srz.com/images/content/6/9/v2/69772/Investing-in-Oil-and-Gas-Royalties-Distressed-Counterparty-Risk.pdf.

"Web Helps Musicians Sell Shares of Royalties," https://www.nytimes.com/2013/04/22/business/royalty-exchange-lets-musicians-sell-royalty-income-to-investors.html.

"The Whole Story Behind David Bowie's $55 Million Wall Street Trailblaze," https://www.billboard.com/articles/business/6843009/david-bowies-bowie-bonds-55-million-wall-street-prudential.

Chapter Six

INSURANCE-LINKED SECURITIES AND WEATHER DERIVATIVES

Introduction

Insurance-linked securities and weather derivatives are financial instruments whose performance has very little, if anything, to do with a normal business cycle. As such, they should provide a great opportunity for investors to get returns that are not correlated to the normal business cycle and provide some hedging value to traditional portfolios of stocks and bonds. Many insurance-linked securities and weather-related derivatives, while not exposed to the normal business cycle, are exposed to event risks such as natural disasters, storms and extreme weather patterns.

Insurance-linked securities transfer some of the risk and return related to insuring specific types of disasters from the insurance companies to the investors.

Normally, it is the insurance company that loses money if payouts on policies exceed premiums collected based on expectations for specific types of events in any given year. Policyowners are protected from the risk via their insurance and get a payout based on their policy terms, among other things. If an insurance company has excessive payouts in any specific year, it will need to fund those losses using its own capital. Large losses in a given year could cause an insurance company to have a reduction in its capital below the minimum considered prudent by the rating agencies or set by their respective insurance regulators. In extreme cases, this can lead to a credit downgrade or the need to recapitalize to meet regulatory standards. Insurance companies can issue bonds that convert to equity in whole or in part to offset losses related to various natural disasters. These bonds are referred to as catastrophic loss bonds.

Catastrophic loss bonds are issued by insurance companies to investors. Catastrophic loss bonds are a cheap way for insurance companies to raise equity capital during periods of financial loss. The bond's principal and interest payments are linked to specific insurance events. Normally, some of the value of the outstanding bonds can be included as a form of equity by the insurance company. This helps ensure that they have equity capital above or at least equal to the amounts required by rating agencies or regulators during a financial crisis.

Investors in catastrophic loss bonds provide capital to insurance companies during periods of increased insurance company losses and will lose money if there are an excessive number of unanticipated natural disasters in any given period. However, investors will profit if there are fewer natural disasters than expected due to the higher than normal coupon and yield on the bonds. This is one relatively simple way to get exposure to high yields and have potential upside if actual insurance disasters and losses are less than initial expectations when the bonds were issued. Of course, if covered losses exceed expectations, then an investor might lose all the income and some or all of the principal form of this sort of investment. Investors who hold bonds to maturity and have no covered losses will get all of their principal returns and earn a high yield from the coupons that were priced to include some natural disasters or impairment of the bond.

Catastrophic loss bonds come in a variety of shapes and sizes. Bonds are typically issued by insurance companies and are linked to specific events. Events can be related to geography, for example, events such as earthquakes in Japan, hurricanes in the United States or wildfires in California. These events can be linked to a wide range of "multi-peril" covering more than one type of disaster to which an insurance company has exposure. The covered events can be limited to specific geographies and time frames.

The need for catastrophic loss bonds became apparent in the later 1990s following massive insurance company losses in Florida related to Hurricane Andrew. In 1997, Residential Re issued what is considered the first catastrophic loss bond sold in the US capital markets.[1] Since then it has issued 34 additional catastrophic loss bonds.[2] With these types of bonds, issuers have to pay a premium to attractive investors. The yield or initial coupon must compensate investors for interest rate risk, credit risk and event risk related to the specific disaster. Generic catastrophic loss bonds have historically offered a yield spread to treasuries of as low as 400 to a high of over 1,000 basis points.[3] Spreads will vary based on the loss expectation for each of the covered events against which the bond was issued.

Investors can also profit from abnormal or excessive weather patterns by buying or short-selling weather derivatives such as futures contracts and options that have a payoff related to the average daily temperature in specific locations over a specific time frame. Weather derivatives were first approved by the Commodities and Futures Trading Commission in August 1999. The initial futures contract was on heating days. It began trading in September 1999 on the Chicago Mercantile Exchange (CME). Cooling day contracts were introduced in January 2000. Options on both heating day and cooling day futures can also be traded on the CME.[4] The futures and options contracts listed on the CME are all based on the difference between the actual average daily temperature realized in a particular month and a benchmark temperature of 65°F. The initial price of each month will be based on historical average daily temperature for that month,

1. J. Treaster, "High Yield and Big Risk with Catastrophe Bonds," *New York Times*, 1997, https://www.nytimes.com/1997/08/06/business/high-yield-and-big-risk-with-catastrophe-bonds.html.
2. "Catastrophe Bonds, ILS, Reinsurance, Risk Transfer," Artemis, accessed Apr. 2020, https://www.artemis.bm.
3. "Insurance Linked Securities Market Update", Swiss Re, Feb. 2019, https://www.swissre.com/dam/jcr:7467c134-2803-42f3-8a2f-cc2e9e156c34/ils-market-yearend-february-2019.pdf.
4. "CME Group Weather Products," CME Group, accessed Apr. 2020, https://www.cmegroup.com/trading/weather/.

using market intelligence related to weather measurements at specific times and in specific locations across the United States. During the month, the contract value will change along with the weather.

An investor who owns a contract can earn a profit if the actual temperature exceeds or falls below the benchmark temperature associated with a specific contract month. Companies whose business models are exposed to temperature fluctuations are often interested in selling some of this risk to an investor. Think of the exposure that a ski resort might have to excess warmth in the winter or the exposure of a beach resort in the case of abnormally cool summers. Investors who believe it will be a hotter summer than usual can buy contracts that have a positive payoff if temperatures are above normal. Perhaps a farmer who is worried about a very hot summer may want to buy some contracts that pay a profit if there are an excessive number of cooling days in July and August. Investors who believe it will be a colder winter than usual can buy contracts that have a positive payoff if temperatures are below normal. A municipality may incur increased snow removal costs during a cold winter and could buy contracts that pay off if there are an excessive number of heating days. Companies who buy or sell contracts to speculators or investors using futures markets may incur losses on those hedges, but they can make it up by having windfall profits in their core weather-related business or activity. A beach resort may have natural exposure to hot weather in their business, so they would sell a cooling day contract. A ski resort naturally expects long winters with cold weather, so it would short heating day contracts. If the weather pattern hurts their business, then companies will earn a profit on the futures hedges to offset some of the losses in their core weather-related business or activity. If the weather is favorable, then they will have to pay back some of the gains in their core business to pay for the cost of hedging.

A longevity bond is another type of insurance-linked security. A longevity bond is linked to life expectancies instead of natural disasters. In this case, an investor will also receive less than the par amount of the bond at maturity or less than the promised coupons if the actual average lifespan of a specific group of people observed over a specified time frame is higher than an agreed-upon level. Companies that sell lifetime annuities are the typical issuers because they incur larger losses when the people they have sold an annuity to live longer than the life expectancy at the time the annuity was sold. They pay out more in annual income than they anticipated when the policy was sold, thus incurring losses. They of course profit when people live shorter lives and receive less annuity payments since they will pocket all of the initial purchase price paid for the lifetime annuity. Companies can protect themselves by issuing bonds where the investor loses some of all of their coupon and principal if the life expectancy of a certain group of people that have been sold annuities exceeds a specific time frame. Pension plans and other organizations that have made fixed promises to pay income to a group of individuals "for life" are also natural issuers of longevity bonds. They too do better when people live shorter lives than originally expected.

Mortality bonds provide that investors will receive less than the bond's par amount at maturity if the mortality rate of a group of people observed over a specified time frame is higher than a prespecified level (for example, if they die sooner than expected). This is attractive for companies that lose money when mortality is high. Life insurers will lose money if people die sooner than expected. They have a fixed payout but will receive less premium than originally expected. Life insurers profit the most when people live longer and pay more premiums into the policy for the same fixed amount of insurance.

The use of the capital markets by issuers to raise capital and reduce event risk has been a positive development. Most companies use a combination of reinsurance and capital markets solutions to manage the risks they originate. The capital markets offer many advantages to simply reinsuring the origination of risk with another insurance company. Reinsurance has the advantage of being provided by another insurance company that fully understands and can model the risks being assumed. The downside is premium sharing and the fact that coverage may need to be renegotiated each year. Coverage can also be customized between parties. Capital market solutions may be more expensive due to the use of third parties and investment banks to model and underwrite the securities sold to investors. However, these solutions have the potential advantage of obtaining multi-year risk sharing and the ability to lock in rates.

One of the primary benefits of investing in either issuance-linked or weather-related strategies is their ability to generate higher than average risk-adjusted returns and income while having a low correlation to traditional investments. According to the Mann Institute, the correlation of insurance-linked portfolios to traditional stocks and bonds from the period from 2006 to 2018 was approximately 0.18 and 0.10 for passively managed catastrophic loss bond portfolios and 0.10 and 0.14 for hedge fund-managed, insurance-linked securities portfolios.[5]

Definitions and Key Terms

Insurance is simply an agreement by one party to pay another a fixed amount if a specific event occurs during a particular period in exchange for a periodic payment or premium. The seller bears all the risk of paying out against a claim if a certain trigger event occurs. The buyer bears only the risk or cost of the premium paid. Insurance companies write policies covering a wide range of risks related to health, life, property and casualties. The insurance company bears all of the event risk if someone dies or if property is damaged. Insurance companies profit when insured events occur infrequently and lose money when they occur more frequently.

Reinsurance is the process by which one insurance or reinsurance company sells or "shares" risk with another in order to limit the total loss that the originating or selling insurer or reinsurer would experience in case of a natural disaster or another insurable event. The company seeking to reduce risk is the selling party and the party accepting the risk is the reinsurer. Insurance companies who collect premiums reinsure risk by sharing premiums with the reinsurer in exchange for a reduction in its liability.

Event-linked bonds are debt instruments that are linked to specific insurance activities underwritten by an insurance company. A buyer of the bond provides capital to the

---

5. "Catastrophic Bonds: Investing with Impact," Mann Institute, Feb. 2018, https://www.man.com/maninstitute/catastrophe-bonds-investing-with-impact.

insurance company and shares in the event risk in exchange for a higher than normal interest rate or coupon. Event-linked bonds are not typically investment grade rated. The most common event-linked bond is called a catastrophic loss bond or CAT bond.

Trigger events are events that result in risk sharing between the buyer and the seller of an insurance-linked security. Trigger events may include hurricanes, earthquakes, plane crashes, pandemics and other natural disasters or business disruptions that would result in a significant economic loss to those providing individual life, property and casualty insurance or other forms of insurance to affected individuals and businesses. There are several ways to compute a trigger event in an event related to an event-linked security. The trigger events can be tied to the specific losses of a particular issuer or more broadly to losses at an industry-wide level or even based upon hypothetical losses resulting from a modeled event that could be either issuer-specific or industry-wide.

A weather hedge is a security or product that allows a buyer to reduce or eliminate weather or climate risk.

Industry Associations

The National Association of Insurance Commissioners (NAIC) is a great source of information related to the insurance industry and insurance-linked securities. According to its website, the National Association of Insurance Commissioners is the US standard-setting and regulatory support organization created and governed by the chief insurance regulators from the 50 states, the District of Columbia and five US territories. Information can be obtained by going to their website: https://content.naic.org.

Market Size

The outstanding market for catastrophic bonds and other insurance-linked securities was approximately $42.3 billion at the end of 2019.[6]

The catastrophic bond market alone had an outstanding value of $28.7 billion in 2018, up from the reported $25.2 billion of outstanding value in 2017. There were $9.1 billion of new issuances in 2018, down from $10.3 billion in 2017.[7]

Opportunities and Strategies

Investing directly in insurance- and weather-related products can be achieved by buying bonds or trading futures. In most cases, the research and attention to markets and liquidity constraints make this difficult for the average investor.

Buying a catastrophic loss bond is the equivalent of selling puts or going short the catastrophe. A rising number of catastrophes and increases in insurance company losses

---

6. "Catastrophe Bonds, ILS, Reinsurance, Risk Transfer," Artemis.
7. "Facts + Statistics: Catastrophe Bonds," Insurance Information Institute, accessed Apr. 2020, https://www.iii.org/fact-statistic/facts-statistics-catastrophe-bonds.

will incur losses in an investor's portfolio whereas a falling number of disasters and few-to-no financial losses by insurance companies will lead to financial gains in an investor's portfolio and excess returns.

Let's look at an example where a hypothetical investor believes there will be less hurricanes over the next few years than in the past. Assume the investor can buy a catastrophe loss bond from a broker issued by AA+ rated ABC Insurance Co. for PAR or $1,000 with a three-year maturity and a 6% coupon. The bond indenture also says that the coupon payments and up to 50% of the principal value must be forgiven by the investor in the event of a qualifying or covered disaster. If nothing happens, the bond investor gets 6% per year or $50 for three years for a total return of 18%. If there is a covered disaster and the bond holder participates in covered losses up to the amount of the coupon only, then the investor may in fact have a 0% return. In this case, at least the investor gets back their principal. If losses are big enough, the bond holder may lose all coupons and up to 50% of principal via mandatory forgiveness. In this case, the investor has the potential to earn a 50% holding period loss, assuming no default by the issuer.

If, at the time of issuance, three-year risk-free bonds were yielding 1% and traditional bonds issued by AA+ insurance companies were yielding 2%, then the event risk premium priced into this bond would be 3% or $30 per year. The investor is getting an extra $30 per year or $90 over the life of the bond as compensation for expected losses. If the investor believes there would in fact be less hurricanes, and therefore less than $90 per bond of allocated losses over the life of the bond, then buying this bond would be attractive on a risk-adjusted basis. In cases where the actual event occurrence is less than the expected event occurrence, the investor profits. If the bond actually had more than $90 in allocated losses, then the investor would earn less than their initial expectations. Investors in catastrophic loss bonds need to be able to compute the required risk premium to cover themselves for both the expected loss given a disaster and any credit risk associated with the issuer.

Managing credit and event risk is not practical for most individual investors. It is very practical for professional credit and event risk managers who manage insurance-linked portfolios. It is the reason that the manager gets paid his fee and why most individuals interested in this type of investment use external managers rather than work with a broker to invest themselves.

Now let's assume an investor wants to speculate that it will be a very hot summer in New York. The investor could open an account with a futures commission merchant and open a long weather futures contract position on the CME. This contract would pay off a set dollar amount for each degree and day that the average daily temperature exceeds 65°F. This is the standardized temperature used by the CME futures contracts. It was selected as baseline by the utility industry since furnaces and air conditioners are most often turned on above and below this benchmark. If the investor wanted to profit from a very cool summer, the investor would simply go short this contract. Each day during the contract period, the contracts would be settled in cash by the CME, the futures commission merchant and the investor. Many individual investors would not qualify to open a futures contract with a futures commission merchant due to the leverage and active trading embedded in weather derivative contracts. Use of a dedicated futures fund or commodity pool that trades weather-related futures contracts either exclusively or as part of a macro or trend-following strategy is normally the best way for an individual to obtain exposure.

Another type of investment in the insurance-linked space is to buy bonds that are based upon life expectancy and mortality. If longevity is higher than expected, the longevity bond will not pay interest and can return less than its par amount at maturity or no principal at all. Investors profit from shorter lives for a specified population. If there is no trigger event, they get to keep the higher than normal coupon plus all of the invested principal. Investors in mortality bonds, on the other hand, will receive less than the bond's par amount at maturity and lose coupon income if the mortality rate of a group of people observed over a specified time frame is higher than a prespecified level. From the investor's perspective, longevity bonds are betting that people will live shorter lives than expected and mortality bonds are bets that they will live longer than expected. Each of these types of bonds will most often pay a floating rate of interest to investors.

How to Invest?

Some institutions with a robust credit research infrastructure and futures trading operation may manage their own portfolios. Of course, only the biggest and most sophisticated pensions, sovereign wealth funds and hedge funds would be able to do so given the need for scale and dedicated expertise. Large institutions would more often use the services of dedicated institutional fund managers like Credit Suisse who have products and capabilities to create bespoke or customized insurance-linked or weather-related portfolios.

Most individuals and smaller institutions lack resources to perform in-depth credit research and do not have access to the derivatives and futures markets. They are not able to perform the unconventional research on natural disasters and weather patterns needed to be successful. In almost all cases, individual investors and smaller institutions would need to use professional external managers with dedicated strategies and commingled funds to obtain exposures to insurance-linked bonds or weather derivatives.

Today, commingled credit, insurance-linked or weather derivative structures such as mutual funds, closed-end funds or private funds offer investors diversification and professional management. Exposure can be obtained using some traditional mutual funds, closed-end funds or private hedge funds whose offerings include these securities and strategies in their funds either exclusively or as part of a broader insurance or energy strategy.

Investors must choose whether they want exclusive exposure to a particular segment of the insurance-linked market such as catastrophic loss bonds or a particular weather derivatives strategy via a narrowly constructed fund offering or whether they would prefer partial exposure as part of a diversified credit, insurance fund or energy-related fund.

Who Invests?

The investor base in the catastrophic loss bond market for the year ending June 30, 2019, was made up of approximately 59% dedicated catastrophic loss and insurance-linked funds, 16% institutions, 11% reinsurers, 7% mutual funds, 5% hedge funds and 2% other.[8]

Many institutional investors participate in the insurance-linked securities markets. According to data on the Artemis.bm website, a number of the world's largest pension and sovereign wealth funds are active and have experience in investing in insurance-linked securities. Allocations to the sector are generally limited to a relatively small percentage of an institution's portfolio. Investments can be made directly or via the use of third-party portfolio managers with dedicated resources and experience in this space or in a specific combination. Large institutional investors or fund managers can participate directly in new issues and secondary market opportunities related to a wide range of deals and offerings only if they have the appropriate size and scale.

Individual investors, high-net-worth investors, family offices and smaller institutions tend to invest in mutual funds and hedge funds that offer exposure to insurance-linked securities. Firms such as PIMCO and Pioneer offer commingled fund exposure to various types of insurance-linked securities, as do a number of private funds such as hedge funds. Many times, exposure to issuance-linked securities is part of a diversified high yield or opportunistic credit portfolio that includes insurance-linked securities such as catastrophic loss bonds. Pure play weather funds are very hard to come by on a stand-alone basis. Most investors will need to use energy funds with active hedging programs rather than individual hedge funds trading weather derivatives alone.

Benchmarks and Indices

The Eureka Hedge Insurance-Linked Security Advisors Index, shown in Figure 6.1, is an index of private funds in the insurance-linked investment space. It tracks the performance of funds managing insurance-linked securities, reinsurance and catastrophe bond portfolios. The index includes funds that allocate at least 70% of their assets to non-life risk related assets. It also allows for the comparison of funds and managers in the insurance-linked securities fund, reinsurance and catastrophe bond investment space. The index website can be found at https://www.eurekahedge.com.

Analysis of the Eureka Hedge Insurance-Linked Security Index of hedge fund vehicles from 2005 to 2019 versus the S&P 500 shows that the index delivered an annualized return of approximately 4.31% and a standard deviation of 3.31% for the period from 2006 to 2019. The S&P 500 delivered returns and risk of approximately 9.01% and 14.2% for the same period. The index had a significantly higher Sharpe ratio and a very low correlation to the S&P 500 of just 0.077. It would therefore have a positive portfolio impact when added to a traditional portfolio of stocks and bonds.

The Swiss Re Global Cat Bond Total Return Index is an index of catastrophic loss bonds produced by Swiss Re. The index tracks the performance of BB-rated bonds with

---

8. Paul Schultz, "Insurance Linked Securities Report 2019," AON, 2019, http://thoughtleadership. aonbenfield.com//Documents/20190905-ils-annual.pdf?utm_source=slipcase&utm_ medium=affiliate&utm_campaign=slipcase.

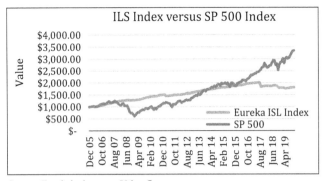

Source: Eurekahedge.com, Yahoofinance.com

Figure 6.1. The growth of $1,000 invested in the Eureka Hedge Insurance Linked Security Index of hedge fund vehicles from 2005 to 2019 compared to the S&P 500.
Source: Eurekahedge.com, Yahoofinance.com

exposure to various natural disasters. The index can be found on Bloomberg using the symbol SRGLTRR.

S&P Insurance Select Industry index is a broad insurance industry measure that tracks the performance of companies in the S&P 500 that are classified as insurance brokers, life and health insurance, multi-line insurance, property and casualty insurance and reinsurance providers. More information can be found at https://www.spindices.com.

Firms, Funds and Platforms

Nephila Capital Limited is a Bermuda-based fund manager who offers insurance-linked and weather-related securities to investors via a range of products and services, including private funds. The firm has been active in this space since 1998. The group manages the Nimbus Weather Fund, a hedge fund with approximately $60 million in assets under management that invests in weather-related instruments. For more information, visit the company's website at https://www.nephila.com/main/.

Nimbus Weather Fund Ltd is a Bermuda-based fund that is managed by Nephila Capital. According to Preqin, the fund invests long and short across the natural catastrophe insurance-linked security (ILS) sector. The fund seeks to provide investors with returns with minimal correlation to other markets, including equities and other traditional alternatives. For more information, visit the manager's website at https://www.nephila.com.

Swiss Re Alternative Capital Partners combines the resources and capabilities of the Swiss Re Capital Markets ILS team and the Retro and Syndication team into a unified center of expertise that offers its clients comprehensive alternative capital solutions tailored to their unique risk hedging and financing needs. Alternative Capital Partners serves a wide variety of sponsors, including reinsurers, governments and corporations, with expertise in both the Property & Casualty and Life & Health risk markets. As a registered broker-dealer, Alternative Capital Partners also offers ILS trading support via Swiss

Re Capital Markets. For more information, visit the company's website at https://www. swissre.com/our-business/alternative-capital-partners.html.

Citadel Investments is a diversified multi-strategy hedge fund. In 2018 it acquired the majority of the team of individuals managing the Cumulus Fahrenheit Fund and the Cumulus Energy fund. The funds had been founded by Peter Brewer, one of the early pioneers in weather trading. According to an interview done by Jacqueline Davalos, Citadel would be integrating the acquired team members into their existing energy organization and not acquiring the funds themselves. According to the article, Citadel hired 20 individuals to join their energy team. The energy team is one of several products or strategy-based teams that invests on behalf of the firm's over $28 billion multi-strategy flagship hedge fund.[9]

Stone Ridge Asset Management offers a range of structures and funds investing a variety of alternative investment products, including insurance-linked securities. The company offers closed-end interval funds and other vehicles that buy insurance-linked securities and other reinsurance products. As of December 31, 2019, the firm managed approximately $14 billion. For more information, visit the company's website at https:// www.stoneridgeam.com or visit https://www.stoneridgefunds.com.

GAM FCM Cat Bond is a British Virgin Islands fund that focuses on the catastrophe insurance market. According to Preqin, the fund, which was created in 2012, invests based on the probability of loss, credit risk, pricing and other criteria. For more information, visit the company's website at https://www.fcm.com.

Securis Non-Life Fund is a Cayman Islands fund that is managed by Securis Investment Partners. According to Preqin, the fund primarily focuses on insurance-linked securities connected to Europe, the United States and Japan. For more information, visit the company's website at https://securisinvestments.com.

Swiss Re Ltd. is a provider of insurance-based risk transfer, including reinsurance services. Its reinsurance arm covers both property and casualty as well as life and health. It is based in Zurich, Switzerland, and was founded in 1863. Swiss Re recently acquired GE Insurance Solutions and is now the world's second largest reinsurer. For more information, visit the firm's website at https://www.swissre.com.

Everest Re Group Ltd. is a Bermuda-based reinsurance company. The firm primarily focuses on property reinsurance but also has a presence in casualty insurance and reinsurance. Everest also sells catastrophe bonds through some of its subsidiaries. For more information, visit the firm's website at https://www.everestre.com.

PartnerRe Ltd. is a Bermuda-based reinsurance company that offers solutions in a variety of industries including agriculture, life and health and energy. The firm was founded in 1993, has 14 branches globally and has operated in approximately 150 countries. For more information, visit the company's website at https://partnerre.com.

---

9. Jacqueline Davalos, "Citadel Hires (Cumulus) Fund Team in Commodities Push," Press Release, *Citywire*, Apr. 2018, https://citywireusa.com/professional-buyer/news/citadel-hires-hedge-fund-team-in-commodities-push/a1115355.

Table 6.1. The performance, risk and correlation of a composite of an insurance-linked composite versus the S&P 500 between January 2016 and December 2019.

	Insurance-Linked Securities	S&P 500
Correlation	0.17	NA
Standard Deviation	5.06%	11.56%
Average Annual Return	5.61%	14.33%
Simplified Sharpe	1.11	1.24

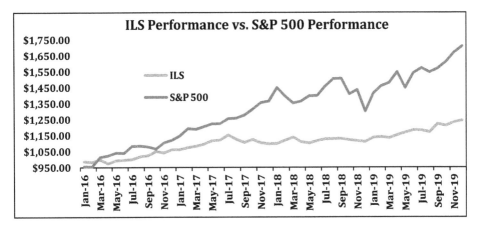

Figure 6.2. The growth of $1,000 invested in an insurance-linked securities composite versus the $1,000 invested in the S&P 500 from January 2016 to December 2019.

Composite

The insurance-linked composite in Table 6.1 significantly unperformed the S&P 500 between January 2016 and December 2019 with a return of just 5.61%. However, it also had a much lower volatility of 5.06% and, as such, only a slightly lower Sharpe ratio of 1.11 compared to 1.24.

A $1,000 investment in an insurance-linked composite in January 2016, shown in Figure 6.2, would have grown to $1,244 by December 2019 compared to $1,708 for the S&P 500.

What Do Investors Look For?

Due diligence needs to be performed on both individual bonds and on the impact of each bond added to a portfolio. All of the normal due diligence associated with bond investing will apply to catastrophic risk bonds. In addition, due diligence will include a careful and complex evaluation of the embedded probability of event occurrence over the life of the bond relative to investor expectation. Bonds where the market estimates higher event risk than investors will appear cheap. Those where the market estimates are for lower event risk will appear too expensive.

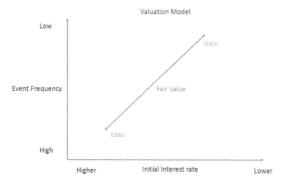

Figure 6.3. The relationship between covered event frequency, interest rates and fair value for a catastrophic loss bond.

The correlation of events within a portfolio is also critical. The goal is to have a portfolio of unrelated events across issuer, trigger, event category and geography. A portfolio of earthquakes in Asia, wildfires in California and hurricanes in Florida will have lower correlations than a portfolio made up of only hurricane events in the United States. Portfolios with similar yields and lower pairwise correlations will have a higher risk-adjusted return over time.

In all cases, whether buying bonds or trading derivatives, investors should only deal with top rated counterparties with strong credit ratings. Investors should also understand and manage the liquidity of the portfolio and the redemption terms of any funds that hold insurance-linked securities or that trade weather derivatives.

Valuation

The value of catastrophic loss and mortality bonds are each subject to interest rate risk, credit risk and event risk. In some cases, exchange prices or dealer transactions will be available to value a portfolio of bonds. In other cases, a model price must be used for valuation. If the number of covered events increases, then a portfolio of insurance-linked bonds will decline in value. If interest rates or credit spreads increase, then the value of the portfolio will decrease. The change in the value of the portfolio will be inversely related to the number of covered events and the discount rate used to value the bond cash flow. Rising events and discount rates will cause market-to-market losses and falling event frequency and discount rates will cause mark to market gains in the portfolio. The relationship between event frequency, interest rates and valuation is shown in Figure 6.3.

The valuation of weather derivatives that are exchange traded, such as listed futures contracts on heating or cooling days, is relatively simple. In most cases, there will be a last trade or settlement price available from the CME to mark to market a position in a portfolio. In the case of customized OTC weather derivatives, it is a bit more complex. A dealer price or model price may be the only source of valuation that is appropriate.

Unique Risks

Investors may incur significant losses when investing in insurance-linked securities. The most unique risk in this sector is event risk. Investors may lose all or a portion of their investment in insurance-linked securities if covered disasters, catastrophes, longevity rates or mortality rates trigger a loss of coupons or principal payment. Investors need to critically evaluate the assumptions embedded in each security about the cover events and decide if the estimates and the related premiums are adequate to cover that risk. Model risk exits to the extent triggers are set based on industry models for losses given an event or using other parameters besides the actual losses of the specific issuer. The uncertainty around models and risk projections is one reason that catastrophic loss bonds are rated below investment grade.

Most insurance-linked securities such as catastrophic loss, longevity or mortality bonds are of course subject to some liquidity, credit, extension, recall and interest rate risk. In some cases, the bonds can be redeemed early, at a lower coupon rate. In other cases, the maturity of bonds can also be extended without the prior consent of the investor. Issuers can become involved for reasons other than covered disasters. Rating agencies can downgrade the issuer. The bonds may not have recourse to any assets of the issuer in the event of issuer default without a trigger event. Investments may be subject to additional adverse tax consequences depending on the specific deal and terms. The market for any insurance-linked bond may be very illiquid. Finally, these bonds, like all fixed income instruments, are also subject to interest rate risk.

The issuer credit risk that exists between the insurance company paying the annual coupon and responsible for principal repayment and the investor in any bond can be mitigated by only investing in bonds issued by highly rated companies. This risk can be further mitigated using specialized structures and trusts that segregate bond proceeds and insurance company payments from general creditors of the firm issuing the bonds. Funds held in trusts may be subject to additional risk based on how the trust funds are reinvested during the life of the bond.

Investors in insurance-linked debt also run the risk of simply paying too much and accepting yields that are too low relative to the risks. An excess of global capital looking for yield could have the effect of making many insurance-linked securities appear attractive even though they may be overpriced relative to their risk. This might lead to returns that are too low and larger than expected losses or underperformance on a relative basis over time.

Strategies as to trading a weather derivative have event risk related to the weather as well as the potential for model risk and liquidity risk. The investor or external manager will use sophisticated weather forecasting and trading technology to both predict weather patterns and execute trades in the futures markets. Since most weather-related strategies offered to investors are directional in nature, significant losses can occur if the investor or the manager is incorrect. The ability to execute stop losses and manage downside risk is one way to mitigate this strategies drawdown risk.

Trends

The frequency of a wide range of natural disasters is on the rise. In the United States, in 2019, there were significantly more hurricanes than the historical annual average.[10] The same is true for wildfires and many other types of natural disasters. The summer of 2020 saw some of the worst wildfires in the history of the United States, most notable in California. At the same time, the ability to forecast weather-related trends is also improving due to new technology and innovation. The combination of increased demand for reinsurance and hedging tools from insurance providers, increased event risk and an abundance of investor capital looking for higher yields all favor the expansion of capital market and derivative products such as catastrophic bonds and weather futures and options.

Social, Legal and Ethical Considerations

Some investors consider insurance-linked securities such as catastrophic loss bonds to be part of an impact or socially responsible investing asset class. Pandemic bonds are a source of capital to help manage the impact of disease; hurricane triggers provide capital to repair and rebuild homes and businesses. The World Bank and the World Health Organization have even developed something called the Pandemic Emergency Financing Facility. This facility offers more than $500 million of coverage that provides resources to low-income countries that have limited healthcare systems and where the conditions for disease developing into a pandemic are in place. Bonds issued to support this facility were oversubscribed and well received by investors, who see the instrument as one that provides a social good as well as a financial reward.[11]

Academic Research

Academic articles about insurance-linked securities and weather-linked derivatives have become more prominent since the mid-1990s due to increased concerns about climate change and weather trends throughout the world and the increased frequency of financial crises impacting a variety of securities. Many of these academic articles relating to insurance-linked products examine the risk profile, the hedging viability and the returns of utilizing these products.

Marc Gürtler, Martin Hibbeln and Christine Winkelvos examined the impact of the financial crisis and natural catastrophes on catastrophic loss bond prices. They looked at

---

10. "Facts + Statistics: Hurricanes," Insurance Information Institute, accessed Mar. 2020, https://www.iii.org/fact-statistic/facts-statistics-hurricanes.
11. "World Bank Launches First Ever Pandemic Bonds to Support $500 Million Emergency Financing Facility," Press Release, June 2017, http://www.worldbank.org/en/news/press-release/2017/06/28/world-bank-launches-first-ever-pandemic-bonds-to-support-500-million-pandemic-emergency-financing-facility.

how bond-specific and macroeconomic factors influence catastrophic loss bond prices and premiums. The researchers used secondary market data from 2002 to 2012 to examine how the 2008–09 financial crisis and Hurricane Katrina influenced prices. The authors found a very high correlation between bond premiums and corporate spreads during the financial crisis. This shows that a financial crisis can significantly impact catastrophic bond premiums, even in the absence of any increase in catastrophic events or risk. This means that catastrophic bonds premiums are dependent on developments in capital markets and not just the covered events. This positive dependence significantly strengthened after the bankruptcy of the Lehman Brothers. This implies that these bonds are not truly "zero beta" securities, but that they also behave in ways similar to traditional bonds of the same rating. This finding reduces the diversification benefits associated with catastrophic loss bonds during periods of market dislocation. The findings related to natural disasters also showed that the bond market and investors will price event risk differently than the models used by issuer or rating agencies. They found that risk premiums increased significantly after Hurricane Katrina. They also found a positive correlation with other hurricanes included in the sample period.[12]

Daniel Weagly has examined how stress in the financial sector impacts weather derivatives and hedging. Weagly focused on the monthly temperature futures market, which mostly consists of energy and utility companies shorting contracts to offload mild temperature risk and banks and investors buying contracts to speculate or satisfy demand for hedging from energy consumers. Prices for hedging and speculation on the weather should not be related to the financial markets for a number of reasons. One is that contract payoffs are based on local temperatures, which is external to stress in the financial market. Another is that the products require margin and trade on the CME, which is AA-rated. There is no settlement or counterparty risk. There should be little to no correlation between futures prices and financial market stress. The variables selected for financial market stress included in this study include changes in TED spreads (the three-month Eurodollar deposit rates and the three-month Treasury bill rate) and volatility measures like the VIX index and financial crisis measures, for example, the changes in asset prices during the collapse of Lehman Brothers (starting in September 2008 and ending in April 2009). Weagly found that during the 2008 financial crisis, prices of temperature futures one month from maturity decreased by 2.9% and open interest decreased by over 40% and that prices are negatively correlated with the TED spread and the VIX. This means futures prices fell when TED spreads or the VIX rose. Rising TED spreads and VIX levels mean more risk in the markets. The paper also noted that this positively correlated with the capital of participating financial institutions. These findings indicate that the weather futures market may not be as strong a hedging tool or portfolio diversifier as one might expect based on theoretical assumptions. In theory,

---

12. Marc Gürtler, Martin Hibbeln and Christine Winkelvos, "The Impact of the Financial Crisis and Natural Catastrophes on CAT Bonds," *Journal of Risk and Insurance*, July 2014, https://papers.ssrn.com/sol3/papers.cfm?abstract_id=2140653.

there should be no reason for the financial markets and weather to be related to one another.[13]

Researchers Bridget Browne, Aaron Bruhn and Alex Huynh evaluated risk and returns related to mortality bonds in their paper entitled "Catastrophic Mortality Bonds: Analyzing Basis Risk and Hedging Effectiveness." The review discussed how mortality bonds can be used as a hedging vehicle by life insurance companies. It is one of the few articles that addresses hedging effectiveness of mortality bonds. The researchers note that the hedging of life insurance policies written by insurance companies is subject to basis risk based on the use of general population mortality triggers in the construction of catastrophic loss mortality bonds. The paper compares specific portfolio mortality risk and the hedging effectiveness of various instruments. The paper concludes that the hedge effectiveness of mortality bonds may be too low to be acceptable to some insurers and suggests ways to improve the hedging effectiveness for others.[14]

Summary

The insurance-linked market is a market that facilitates risk transfer and hedging of a wide range of business activities. The market is likely to expand given the increase in volatility in the world related to weather and natural disasters and the need for investors to find new and innovative ways to earn attractive yields in today's low rate environment.

Useful Websites and Additional Reading

"The Attractiveness of Insurance-Linked Securities for Investors," https://www.elementumadvisors.com/news/the-attractiveness-of-insurance-linked-securities-for-investors/.

"The Case for Longevity Bonds," https://crr.bc.edu/wp-content/uploads/2010/06/IB_10-10–508.pdf.

"Catastrophe Bonds: An Investment Analysis of Their Performance and Diversification Benefits," https://www.swerma.se/assets/Catstrophe-bonds-Viktor-Karlsson-Emelie-Karneba%CC%88ck.pdf.

"Catastrophe (CAT) Bonds: Risk Offsets with Diversification and High Returns," https://www.econbiz.de/Record/catastrophe-cat-bonds-risk-offsets-with-diversification-and-high-returns-kish-richard/10011566971.

---

13. Daniel Weagly, "Financial Sector Stress and Risk Sharing: Evidence from the Weather Derivatives Market," *Review of Financial Studies*, Aug. 2018, https://academic.oup.com/rfs/article-abstract/32/6/2456/5087740.
14. Bridget Browne, Aaron Bruhn and Alex Hunyh, "Catastrophic Mortality Bonds: Analyzing Basis Risk and Hedge Effectiveness," *Australian Journal of Actuarial Practice*, Mar. 2014, https://ssrn.com/abstract=2688882.

"Convergence of Insurance and Financial Markets: Hybrid and Securitized Risk-Transfer Solutions," https://www.jstor.org/stable/40247567?seq=1#metadata_info_tab_contents.

"The Impact of Natural Disasters on Stock Markets: Evidence from Japan and the US," https://ideas.repec.org/a/pal/compes/v55y2013i4p672-686.html.

"Insurance-Linked Securities Primer," https://www.naic.org/capital_markets_archive/primer 180705.pdf.

"Weather Derivatives Valuation and Market Price of Weather Risk," https://onlinelibrary.wiley.com/doi/abs/10.1002/fut.20122?casa_token=EcjrKEinxFIAAA AA:kb6gFiXNZ2Ed4yQicTU-rfRKQl736kRQHClfFHcjVWWn2-NSJDh1SklDe_ijKxLiTWVV_fpskU9vydc.

"Weather Forecasting for Weather Derivatives," https://www.tandfonline.com/doi/abs/10.1198/016214504000001051?casa_token=md8NLB3bQsgAA AAA:qPvZ5kmJH906krrF_z42WIlj56F-qpGSFoJBb6W1gfsXyrd1mz8CC_vZ5XvosM1nRpzaDBSYJxMFGA.

"What Are Insurance Linked Securities (ILS), and Why Should They Be Considered?" https://www.casact.org/community/affiliates/CANE/0912/Cat-Bond.pdf.

Chapter Seven

TAX LIENS, TAX CREDITS, AIRCRAFT LEASES, STORAGE UNITS AND TRADE CLAIMS

Introduction

This chapter is intended to cover a wide range of investment opportunities where investors can earn premium yields as a result of tax credits, global trade flows, changing demographics and mobility trends, regulatory preferences and protections. Investment opportunities discussed in this chapter include aircraft leases, shipping containers and self-storage units, tax credits, tax liens and trade claims. Each of these investments generates current income and cash flow, and some of them also have the opportunity for capital appreciation. Aircraft leasing provides capital to commercial and private users of aircraft. Tax lien financing provides cash to municipalities for essential services. Investing in trade claims provides cash flow to counterparts in corporate bankruptcies. Tax credit investing provides incentives for firms to invest in important industries or for social good. Shipping container leasing provides capacity for global commerce. Storage unit rentals provide for personal mobility and flexibility for individuals and small businesses. All of these investments have a degree of complexity and are subject to rigorous documentation and unique contract terms.

Industry Associations

The National Aircraft Financing Association is a professional organization that promotes the exchange of ideas and best practices in the aviation finance industry. It provides educational, networking and other resources that help its members. Information about aircraft finance programs, conferences and educational material is available at the association website: https://www.nafa.aero/cpages/home.

The mission of the National Tax Lien Association is to promote legislative and regulatory agenda that support the tax lien industry. It also promotes best practices and ethical conduct and provides education for its members. Information about tax lien investment programs, conferences and educational material is available at the association website: https://www.ntla.org.

The Self-Storage Association is a dedicated trade group that promotes the success of investors in self-storage units. It is an industry group that advocates on behalf of its investor members to increase awareness about the storage unit industry. Information about the self-storage industry, events and educational programs is available at the association website: https://www.selfstorage.org/.

The Trade Claims Association is a membership group of participants in the trade claim industry. The group was formed in 2002 to promote standardization in the trade claim industry. Information about the group can be found on its member website: https://www.argopartners.net/who-we-are/tcba.

The Container Dealers Association was formed in 2011 to promote ethics and behavior among shipping container dealers and to deliver information and education to container buyers. Information about the container industry is available at the association website: http://www.containerdealers-association.org/about.htm.

Investment Opportunities and Unique Risks

Aircraft Lending and Leases

The commercial aircraft industry needs financing for the purchase of its aircraft. Aircraft are extremely expensive and require enormous financial outlays. Most airlines and commercial users will use leases to finance their fleet. Banks and other financial sponsors provide a wide range of financing tools, including loans, leases and structured products, to meet the needs of the airline industry.

IBISWorld research estimates in Figure 7.1 show revenues from the global aircraft leasing market of $11.1 billion in 2019. The industry has a profit margin of 27%. Revenues have grown 2.3% annually from 2014 to 2019 and are expected to grow at a rate of 2.7% annually from 2019 to 2024. Some key market trends affecting future growth include smaller operators failing to secure contracts and exiting the industry, expected contraction in airline customers and corporations cutting travel-related expenses.[1]

Most aircraft leases revenues for 2019, shown in Figure 7.2, are operating leases, which account for 71.7% of the industry, followed by loans at 17.7% and capital leases at 10.6%.[2]

Investors can participate in this industry by buying loans, providing equity to support structured products or by investing in debt issued by financial sponsors to support aircraft leases. The market for aircraft leases is quite complex. It requires large investments and complex assumptions related to the useful life, operating costs and other risk factors associated with an aircraft. The majority of capital providers are banks, large institutions and special purpose aircraft leasing companies.

Many high-yield portfolio managers, private equity funds and other alternative investment managers have entered the market to meet the industry's need for capital and financing solutions. These new sources of funds have generated increased competition for banks and traditional lessors, compressing yields and creating innovative structure solutions and securitization. Increased competition can also serve to elevate risk and

---

1. Devin McGinley, "Commercial Aircraft Leasing," IBISWorld, Dec. 2019, https://www.ibisworld.com/united-states/market-research-reports/commercial-aircraft-leasing-industry/.
2. Ibid.

Total Revenue in 2019	Annual Growth 2014–2019	Annual Growth 2019–2024	Profit Margin in 2019	Wages as a share of Revenue in 2019	Number of Businesses 2014–2019
$11.1 bn	2.3%	2.7%	27.0%	5.1%	0.4%

Figure 7.1. IBIS World statistics related to the aircraft leasing industry at the end of 2019.

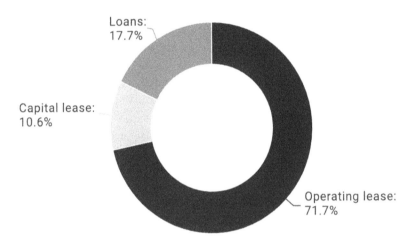

Industry Products & Services Segmentation

Loans: 17.7%

Capital lease: 10.6%

Operating lease: 71.7%

Figure 7.2. IBISWorld breakdown of aircraft leasing industry segments for 2019.

reduce lending standards. Some lenders have lowered loan to value ratios and reduced covenants to win business.

Risk factors for those who provide financing or invest in loans or debt issued by aircraft finance companies include fleet composition and the age of the fleet, counterparty credit quality, interest rate and illiquidity. These factors all play a role in the pricing of any lease or loan. One unique risk to aircraft leasing or loans is estimating the residual value of any aircraft. The rate of depreciation has a direct impact on the collateral supporting the loan or lease. Aircraft that decline in value faster than a loan is repaid exposes the lender or lessor to additional credit risk. Accurate assessment of terminal values of aircraft requires extensive due diligence and an extensive technical knowledge of specific aircraft.

Tax Liens

Homeowners do not always pay their property tax on time. When this occurs, the local municipality that is owed the tax may place a lien on the property until the tax is paid. This lien allows the municipality to foreclose and take possession of the property. The municipality sells the property to cover the tax liability. The process to issue a delinquency notice, place a lien and wait for repayment takes time and exposes the local government to cash flow problems while they are waiting for the taxes to be paid. Tax lien certificates can be sold by a local government to third-party investors as a means to address cash flow concerns. The investor is funding the tax liability for the government with the property assigned as collateral. If the tax is not paid after a set period of time, the municipality can foreclose on the property to pay back the investor. The investors can and usually do get paid on the tax lien certificate prior to any foreclosure. If there is a foreclosure, the investor will tax possession of the property and can realize a windfall if the sale proceeds exceed the value of the taxes owed. Unlike a loan default, the investor does not need to return the excess of the sale proceeds to the homeowner. According to the National Tax Lien Association, approximately 98% of homeowners will pay the taxes owed prior to a foreclosure. Only about .5% of tax lien certificates end up in foreclosure.[3] Interest rates on delinquent tax liens can be significant, as high as 2% per month in some states. However, investors will often accept a much lower rate of return given that the tax lien certificate is managed by the municipality and significantly over-collateralized by the property against which the taxes are owed. The return on tax lien investing is very predictable and not correlated with the markets. Typical returns are in the high single digits.

Investors in tax liens also will want to pay future taxes levied against the property. These taxes must be paid and kept current to avoid their sale to another investor and the creation of additional liens on the property. Investors also should be careful to avoid properties with existing mortgages, since the banks are likely to buy the tax lien themselves in order to protect their investment and avoid the property if sold via a foreclosure.

The primary risk in tax lien investing is that the taxes will not be paid and the foreclosure value of the home is less than the tax liability the investor paid to the local government to buy the lien via an auction. While the investors will have a first lien on the property, it does not ensure the property value will be enough to cover the taxes plus a reasonable rate of return. If there is a foreclosure, and the property sells for less than the taxes originally owed, plus interest, the investor will suffer a loss or have a lower rate of return than initially expected. This means that investors should perform due diligence on the underlying property to ensure it can cover the amount of the tax plus interest. Tax liens also have some operational risk. The local tax collector will be responsible for most communication with the homeowner, including any collections and interest payments. The tax lien certificate owner only communicates with the tax collector. The investor may however be responsible for giving notice to the homeowner that the lien is in place and participating in the foreclosure process or paperwork. If the property goes all the way to foreclosure and sale, the investor may need to pay for improvements and repairs to make the property attractive for a sale. A homeowner who is delinquent in paying taxes is also not likely to be current in other areas such as home repairs and maintenance.

3. Kayleigh Kulp, "Nine Things to Know About Tax Lien Investing," June 2018, https://money.usnews.com/investing/real-estate-investments/slideshows/9-things-to-know-about-tax-lien-investing?slide=2.

Site visits are a good idea to ensure that any property is in fact saleable in a worst-case scenario.

Given the higher level of due diligence on this type of investment and the operational risk associated with owning tax liens, most investors are better off using a commingled vehicle or professional tax lien advisor to facilitate purchases, sales, foreclosures and valuation. Investors need to be wary of not paying too much or receiving too little given the risk involved.

Also, remember, it is not the headline interest rate that the local government might charge a delinquent taxpayer that matters, but rather the rate that is paid on the tax lien certificate to an investor. If the local government could charge the homeowner 18% interest, investors will often bid down the rate during or pay a premium over the amount owed at an auction so that the return to the investor is bid down to only 5%–10%. At some point the risk premium is not enough given the illiquidity and potential risk of loss.

Tax lien investing opportunities generally occur when individuals fail to pay their property taxes. A number of factors such as the loss of a job, death in the family or other adverse events will impact the level of tax delinquency. In theory, delinquency would occur more often during periods of economic downturns. If so, then opportunities to invest in tax liens should rise when the economy and the stock market are doing poorly and unemployment is high. They should also decline when the economy is doing very well and unemployment is low. As such, investments in tax liens should exhibit a low correlation to stock indices.

Tax lien investors can also use this sort of investment as an alternative and cheaper way to acquire real property. Depending on the state, delinquent taxes can result in property foreclosure at the end of some statutory period, for example, after two years. Investors may find themselves with the property title and the right to sell if the taxpayer does not pay their tax bill within a specified period. Normally, someone will buy the property and pay the back taxes before this occurs. A bank holding a defaulted mortgage on a property that has delinquent property taxes will normally pay the taxes to avoid a tax lien being bought from an investor. This protects the bank and allows them to keep all of the proceeds of any foreclosure to settle the mortgage loan.

In the United States, approximately $20 billion to $25 billion of property tax credits go unpaid each year. Of this number, local governments sell between $5 billion and $6 billion to private investors. Florida is the top market for unpaid property taxes, followed by New Jersey, Illinois, South Carolina, Colorado and Arizona.[4] Most cities report their own amount of tax liens sold to investors, such as New York City, which sells about 5,000 liens on properties each year.[5]

---

4. Francys Vallecillo, "U.S. Tax Lien Industry Worth Billions," *World Property Journal*, Mar. 2014, https://www.worldpropertyjournal.com/north-america-residential-news/us-national-tax-lien-association-ntla-tax-lien-auctions-unpaid-property-taxes-brad-westover-tax-foreclosures-tax-lien-sales-8142.php.
5. Justin Bland, "City's Annual Lien Sales Trigger Payments from Owners, Often Exceeding Original Amount Owed," New York City Independent Budget Office, June 2014, https://ibo.nyc.ny.us/iboreports/2014taxlien.html.

Trade Claims

Trade claims are assertions of rights to payment by one counterparty to another. Commercial contracts and activities arise everyday where one company owes another for a product or a service. A trade claim is an unsecured obligation of a firm to pay its vendors or service providers. When a company goes into bankruptcy, the ability to pay any claim is impaired. Other secured claims and those higher in the capital structure will get paid first in any plan of reorganization. The trade claims will generally get paid last. The uncertainty around the amount and timing of any payment on a trade claim associated with a bankruptcy has given rise to an active secondary market where the claims can be sold or traded, usually at a steep discount. Owning a trade claim against a firm who has filed for bankruptcy may also give the owner some rights to participate or vote on a reorganization or convert a claim into equity under favorable terms. Sellers of existing claims against a company in bankruptcy may be motivated to get cash and not wish to or have the capacity to wait until a reorganization plan or liquidation is completed. A particular class of claim against a firm in bankruptcy may only receive a fraction of the value owed under a contract or other form of financial obligation. A bankruptcy judge or trustee will establish a waterfall or sequence of payments that will be distributed payments to all claimants and creditors as assets of the bankrupt company are sold. Investors who purchase claims may do so to profit from any difference between the discounted price paid and the amount actually paid out under the reorganization or liquidation or to increase their influence in a bankruptcy proceeding.

Trades claims can be purchased from vendors and counterparties to a firm in bankruptcy for a deep discount to the projected value. A claim estimated payment can range from just a few cents on the dollar to as high as 95 cents. A buyer would discount the estimated payout another 20%–30%.[6] The discount represents the illiquidity of the claim and the fact that the seller may need the funds sooner than the court-appointed payout date.

One risk of investing in trade claims is of course that the claim will be deemed invalid. This is referred to as notional value risk. It occurs if a purchased claim or transfer of the claim to the buyer has some legal defect that impairs the gross amount that is due under the claim. Another is recovery risk. Recovery risk for any valid claim is the risk that the amount of the payment on the claim will be different than that originally assumed by the investor or that it will take longer to collect. This can occur if the value of assets sold that are allocable to a class of claims is less than the amount originally anticipated or assumed by the investor. There can also be some counterparty risk between the investors and the person from whom they bought the trade claim. Normally, the seller has to make certain warranties about the claim and the status with the bankrupt company. In some cases, a buyer will have an indemnity or seek recourse against the seller if the claim is invalidated or has a defect. Trade claims are also illiquid since the investor holding the

---

6. William Beranek and Stephen Jones, "The Emerging Market for Trade Claims of Bankrupt Firms," *Financial Management*, vol. 23, 1994, https://www.jstor.org/stable/3665741?seq=1#metadata_info_tab_contents.

claim must wait for the payout from the court or sell in the secondary market at a significant discount.

Due diligence on any claim being considered is needed to mitigate risk. Due diligence requires legal review of documentation, an understanding of the company's bankruptcy filing status and evolution and analysis of similar claims and circumstances that may prove useful when estimating the time to collect on a claim. Each claim and case is unique, so the resources to perform due diligence and evaluate will be very specific, require a high level of expertise and be rather time-consuming.

The trade claim market itself and trading of claims between parties is not regulated by any governmental organization. It is self-regulated. The Trade Claim Buyers Association is an industry organization that promotes industry standards and best practices and seeks standardization within the industry.

Opportunities for investing in trades claims are countercyclical. This means that there are more opportunities when the economy is doing poorly and less when the economy is doing well. This means that the returns from investing in trade claims will have a very low correlation to the equity market.

Investment firms active in this space include Sierra Funds, Contrarian Capital Management, Whitebox Advisors and Jefferies Leveraged Credit Products.

Tax Credits

Tax credits are incentives given to business by the Internal Revenue or other government agencies designed to influence behavior. Incentives are designed to promote positive behavior like investing in alternative energy whereas fines and penalties can be used to dissuade firms from exceeding limits on unwanted behaviors such as pollution.

Investors may want to invest in a property or projects that benefits from tax incentive. In this case, the investor is getting a return from the project itself as well as a return from special tax treatment or credits. The government will provide tax relief to projects or firms that use solar and wind power or assess fines or penalties against those that pollute the air or water. At any given time, there may be a differential between the capacity of a firm to engage in a positive behavior and the capacity to avoid a negative behavior. Firms may be allowed to sell their unused capacity to produce solar power or, oddly enough, sell their unused capacity to pollute the environment. Tax credits exist related to low-income housing, rehabilitation of historic sites, sustainable energy and pollution, to name a few. Companies that wish to make larger investments in desirable projects that exceed their eligible tax credit can simply buy them from a firm who is underinvesting and has excess credits. A firm that needs rehabilitation credits may be able to buy them from someone who has not used their full allotment.

Since these credits for socially desirable projects or outcomes have value, investors can sometimes buy them and hold them for resale in the secondary marketplace, separate and distinct from any production process, project or real estate. A firm that is over its permitted level of carbon emissions can buy unused capacity from another firm who does not produce any carbon emissions. The government is satisfied that the aggregate level of emissions is limited, but supports the trading of credits and a means to achieve its long-term goal of lowering pollution with a limited number of fines and penalties. As such, there is an active secondary market where firms can sell tax or other credits and unused capacity to those who can use them.

By its very nature, tax credit investing has significant legal and regulatory risk. Many credits have sunset provisions or expire. Other times, the annual amounts available to claim as credits are changing or subject to new compliance or eligibility requirements to use the credits. Investors need to ensure the returns to any project can be evaluated both on a pretax and after-tax basis, including incentives. Investments that rely solely on their tax relief or credits may be riskier than those that do not. Investing in the secondary market for tax credits comes with liquidity risk and substantial compliance risk. It can also involve complex calculations and assumptions about supply and demand and capacity for covered activities.

Self-Storage Units

A self-storage unit is an investment in a real asset that can generate both appreciation and rents. Demand for units comes from individuals seeking temporary storage of their positions during specific life events. A move, marriage, divorce, downsizing or a variety of other life events can motivate someone to rent a storage unit. According to Green Street Advisors, the demand for self-storage units has increased, with an estimated 8% of the US population using self-storage units, up from just 3% in 2008.[7] One of the attractive characteristics of storage unit rentals, at least from the perspective of the investor, is the ability to change rates over short periods of time. This means that the investment can earn higher returns as demand increases and lower rates to manage occupancy rates and total revenue when demand slumps. Demand and occupancy rates related to self-storage units have been rising since 1987. Occupancy rates in 1987 were just 78.4% compared to 92.8% at the end of 2017.[8] Increased demand and semi-fixed supply gives unit owners pricing power and the opportunity to profit from higher rents when short-term contracts expire with tenants or for pricing new tenants.

A risk in the self-storage industry is that investors and operators will over-expand and create more supply than is required to keep rents stable and increasing. Natural disasters and storms can be harmful to storage owners, necessitating repairs or rebuilds and loss of capacity and occupancy. Another risk is simply that pricing is too high. In the current low-yield environment, many of the pricing for units and the share price of publicly traded REITs are too high to generate attractive returns. REITs tend to behave more like stocks during periods of market self-offs despite their fixed income or rental

---

7. "Specialized REITs ETFs Find Support from Rising Demand for Self Storage," ETF Trends, Dec. 2018, https://finance.yahoo.com/news/specialized-reits-etfs-support-rising-202958963.html.

8. "2018 Self Storage Almanac," MiniCo, 2018, https://www.ministoragemessenger.com/product/2018-self-storage-almanac/.

characteristics leading to additional market risk concerns. Private investments and direct investments that do not trade in the public markets would likely do better during periods of declining publicly traded stock prices.

The life events that support demand for self-storage rentals, at least theoretically, do not appear to be correlated to the economy. Life, death, marriage and divorce should be independent of changes in GDP or markets. Investments in self-storage units should also provide some downside protection during a recession. In addition, rising unemployment and falling home prices during a recession could provide support for rental unit investments as it might force more downsizing and a need for storage units for personal property until the economy recovers and their personal situation improves.

Public companies that operate storage units include Public Storage, CubeSmart, Life Storage and Extra Space Storage. These are all REITS that have exposure to storage units on a regional or national level.

According to IBISWorld data for 2019, shown in Figure 7.3, the industry had a total revenue of $38.6 billion and a profit margin of 40.1% in 2019. Growth is expected to slow between 2020 and 2025.[9]

The breakdown of storage unit revenue, in Figure 7.4, shows that the majority of revenue is from smaller units designed for residential use, with the most popular being the 10 foot by 10 foot self-storage unit.[10]

Shipping Containers

Shipping containers are another real asset that can be owned, rented or leased to companies who wish to ship goods from one location to another by water. Shipping companies tend to invest their capital in vessels and more often will lease shipping containers rather than own them outright. This allows investors in shipping containers or firms that produce and lease them to capture leasing fees and rents. Shipping line profits are a function of the charter rates they can charge to companies who wish to ship goods, the cost of the shipping line operation, including fuel and insurance, and the cost of shipping containers to carry the goods around the world. An increase in global trade has caused demand for shipping container production, sale and leasing to expand over since 2010. According to the Textainer 2018 annual report, shipping container trade continued has consistently grown at a faster rate than global GDP. The report also noted that leasing companies purchased over 60% of the new container production and that lease terms tended to average between three and eight years.[11] The estimated size of the global transportation

9. Qing Zheng, "Storage and Warehouse Leasing in the U.S.," IBISWorld, Dec. 2019, https://my.ibisworld.com/us/en/iexpert-risk/53113/iexpert-risk#snapshot.
10. Zheng, "Storage and Warehouse Leasing in the U.S."
11. Hyman Shwiel et al., *Textainer Group Holdings Limited Annual Report 2016*, Textainer Group, 2019, http://investor.textainer.com/annual-reports.

Total Revenue in 2019	Annual Growth 2014–2019	Annual Growth 2019–2024	Profit Margin in 2019	Wages as a share of Revenue in 2019	Number of Businesses 2014–2019
$38.6 bn	2.6%	0.7%	40.1%	12.3%	2.7%

Figure 7.3. IBISWorld statistics related to the self-storage industry at the end of 2019.

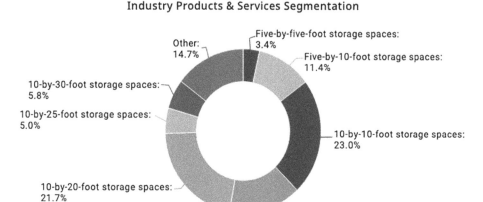

Figure 7.4. IBISWorld breakdown of self-storage industry revenue by segment for 2019.

market at the end of 2019 was approximately $2.7 trillion with sea-based transportation making up over $850 billion.[12]

There are several dominant public companies in the shipping container leasing business that trade on public exchanges. CAI, Textainer, Triton, Invesco Shipping ETF, Maersk are public leasing and shipping companies. There are also ETFs and private funds that offer exposure to the transportation and shipping industry. Fortress Transportation and Infrastructure is a publicly traded closed-end fund investing in a wide range of sea, land and air investments.

Risks in shipping container investments primarily include pricing risk, liquidity risk and utilization rates. During periods of economic slowdown, lease rates and revenue could be significantly impaired. Longer-term leases are one way to mitigate this risk. Containers are not very liquid and have limited uses beyond carrying freight. Demand is also concentrated in a finite number of global shipping lines. Freight and shipping prices also tend to be quite volatile.

The global shipping industry is regulated by a United Nations agency called the International Maritime Organization.

---

12. "Portfolio Overview," Fortress Transportation and Infrastructure, accessed Apr. 2020, https://www.ftandi.com/investment-portfolio.

Benchmarks and Indices

The IHS Markit Global Carbon Index tracks the total return from tradable carbon credits using futures market prices. Components include futures contracts on European Union Allowances, California Carbon Allowances and the Regional Greenhouse Gas Initiative. Information about the index and historical data can be found at the index provider's website: https://indices.ihsmarkit.com/Carbonindex

The Ascend Aircraft Leasing Index is a proprietary index maintained by Ascend Advisory that allows investors to compare investments in different assets using their Sharpe ratio. Their research shows that a passive investment in commercial aircraft offers an attractive risk-adjusted return compared to traditional and alternative asset classes. According to their research, the unleveraged return from aircraft leasing was 6.2% with a volatility of 5.7% over the 21-year period from 1991 to 2012. This compares favorably to returns offered by the S&P 500 of 6.9%. However, the volatility is significantly lower, resulting in a much higher Sharpe ratio. The research report and information about the index can be found at http://aviatia.ro/wp-content/uploads/docs/Ascend_Aircraft_Investment_Index_Aircraft_Leasing.pdf.

Drewry Supply Chain Advisors maintains several indices important to the container and shipping industry. The World Container Index is a composite of container freight rates on eight major routes to and from the United States, Europe and Asia. Another index, the Global Port Throughput index, is a monthly report on a series of volume indices based on monthly throughput data for a sample of over 220 ports worldwide. Information about Drewry Supple Chain advisor indices can be found at https://www.drewry.co.uk/supply-chain-advisors/supply-chain-expertise/world-container-index-assessed-by-drewry.

Firms, Funds and Platforms

AerCap Holdings is a Dublin-based global aircraft leasing company that serves around 200 airlines in approximately 80 countries. In late 2013, AerCap acquired International Lease Corp. for over $5 billion, thus bringing its total owned aircraft above 1,000. For more information, visit the company's website at https://www.aercap.com.

Air Lease Corp is a Los Angeles–based aircraft leasing company that was founded in 2010. The company manages approximately 375 aircraft with leases to over 100 customers in over 59 countries. For more information, visit the company's website at https://airleasecorp.com.

Shipping Container Leasing is a Bermuda-based container leasing company to ship, rail and truck transportation companies. As of early 2020, it held a fleet of over 6 million 20-foot equivalents of containers. Triton operates 20 offices in 16 countries and is a major lessor to all top five global container shipping companies. For more information, visit the company's website at https://www.tritoninternational.com.

Textainer Group is a Bermuda-based container lessor that was founded in 1979. As of early 2020, it owned more than 3 million 20-foot equivalents of containers that are leased to about 250 customers. Textainer Group is also a reseller of used containers and,

Table 7.1. The return, risk and correlation of an aircraft leasing, tax lien, shipping container and storage unit composite to the S&P 500 between January 2016 and December 2019.

	Taxes and Leasing	S&P 500
Correlation	0.64	NA
Standard Deviation	26.67%	11.56%
Average Annual Return	14.33%	14.33%
Simplified Sharpe	0.54	1.24

from 2014 to 2019, resold approximately 140,000 containers each year. For more information, visit the company's website at https://www.textainer.com.

Public Storage is a California-based owner and operator of self-storage facilities. It owns nearly 2,500 facilities in the United States that are used by more than 1 million customers. The company is structured as a real estate investment trust. For more information, visit the company's website at https://www.publicstorage.com.

Extra Space Storage is a Utah-based real estate investment trust that owns and operates self-storage units. The company operates in more than 1,800 locations in 40 states, making it the second largest owner of self-storage units in the United States. For more information, visit the company's website at https://www.extraspace.com.

Kite Tax Lien Capital offers investments in tax lien certificates secured by real property. They deploy proprietary research and strategies to maximize opportunities in the tax lien and related real estate markets. The company's mission is to provide investors with superior returns, access to a unique asset class and diversification. For more information visit the company website at http://ktlc.us/index.html.

Lumentum is a platform for investors in tax liens. It provides investors with the tools and information they need to evaluate and invest in tax liens. The company also operates a secondary market for trading tax liens. For more information, visit the company website at https://www.lumentumllc.com.

Composite

The return from a composite of aircraft leasing, tax lien, shipping container and public storage unit vehicles between January 2016 and December 2019, shown in Table 7.1, is similar to the S&P 500. It also had more than double the volatility and a lower Sharpe ratio. The composite has a relatively low correlation of 0.64.

A $1,000 investment in an aircraft leasing, tax lien, shipping container and public storage unit composite in January 2016, shown in Figure 7.5, would have grown to $1,708 by December 2019, the same as an investment in the S&P 500.

Academic Research

Research by Russell Thompson analyzed the effectiveness of R&D tax credit and its ability to induce investments. While most published analyses are based on firm-level

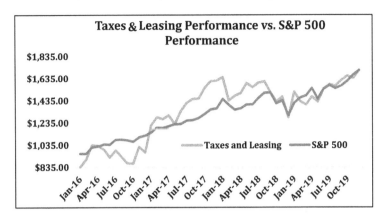

Figure 7.5. The growth of $1,000 invested in aircraft finance, container and storage unit vehicles for the period from January 2016 to December 2019.

data, this analysis fails to reach a consensus across multiple studies. Instead, Thompson proposes a cross-country analysis as an alternative, which exploits the variation between different countries' policies. To accomplish this, the paper uses cross-country industry-level data from the Organization for Economic Cooperation and Development (OECD) to identify the elasticity of R&D investment with respect to tax price. The data covered 29 industries in 26 OECD countries from the years 1987–2006. The research found that there is a tax price elasticity of R&D investment of −0.50. This falls within the range of previously published studies. This result means that reducing the tax price of R&D by 10% induces an additional 5% R&D investment. Another conclusion the paper made is that a country with a corporate income tax rate of 35% that is considering introducing an R&D tax credit would create short-run R&D investment increases of 60 cents for every dollar of current tax revenue forgone. Long run, the analysis shows an elasticity of 4, which is regarded as high but in line with other studies. The overall conclusion is that there will likely be some crowding out of tax revenue forgone in the short run, but that tax incentives induce more R&D than their cost to governments in the long run.[13]

Another study by Alessandro Gavazza studied the way asset liquidity affects lease contracts, using aircraft leases as the focus of the study. The leasing market for capital-intensive industries is very large, with 80% of US capital-intensive companies using leasing as a source of funding. In the aircraft market, more than 50% of aircraft are financed through leases. There is an important distinction between the two types of leases: capital and operating leases. In a capital lease, the lessee acquires ownership of the asset at the end of the lease's term. In an operating lease, the ownership reverts to the lessor. The difference between these two types of contracts affects which companies offer one contract versus the other. Operating lessors are typically companies with deep

13. Russell Thompson, "The Effectiveness of R&D Tax Credits: Cross-Industry Evidence," University of Melbourne, June 2013, https://papers.ssrn.com/sol3/papers.cfm?abstract_id=2275094.

knowledge of the market for the assets they lease, whereas capital lessors are usually banks or financial institutions that provide lending to firms. The paper discussed two main factors which affect the liquidity of an aircraft: production of new units and the retirement of old units. The paper gives the example of the Boeing 727, which was very popular and liquid in the 1970s when production was high, but now is illiquid as it has been phased out of production. Gavazza also evaluated the focal point of an aircraft lease contract, which is the salvage or liquidation value of the asset. For this analysis, only passenger planes were included in the data set. The paper conducted an empirical analysis to see how lease contracts vary systematically across the airplane leasing market wherein they analyzed the characteristics of airplanes of differing liquidities. They analyzed two data sets, one that contains active aircraft from 1963 to 2003, and the other containing details of who operated the aircraft at that point in time. They analyzed the liquidity of an aircraft by using the bid–ask spread as a proxy for market demand and charted it against the stock of an aircraft of the same type. Gavazza found that airplanes with a high aircraft per type ratios experience higher turnover, higher capacity utilization, lower dispersion of utilization levels, higher mean price and lower dispersion of transaction prices, which are properties of liquid assets.[14]

An article by Caroline Enright discusses the privatization of delinquent property tax liens and tax sale surplus in Massachusetts. Massachusetts, as well as 28 other states, allow municipalities to sell delinquent property tax liens to private investors. While this has allowed for municipalities to recover delinquent debt, Enright argues that it is devastating for the most economically vulnerable members of society, and that legislation action is required to fix this problem. Enright argues that the privatization of tax liens is unethical. Private entities often drive up costs and charge high interest rates, which allows investors to hold financially distressed taxpayers' homes hostage to create a windfall. One example is of Bennie Coleman, a retired Marine sergeant suffering from dementia, who missed a $134 property tax bill. When Coleman's son heard that the municipality was going to foreclose his father's house, he found out the municipality sold off the tax lien to a private investor. Coleman's son couldn't afford to pay the taxes and all the interest and fines that had accrued on the tax certificate, so Bennie Coleman ended up losing his $197,000 home. There are dozens of other cases that Enright sources with similarly low dollar amount tax liens which ended up with investors taking people's homes. She goes on to make the argument that this practice is unconscionable. Selling tax liens allows for predatory agents to affect the most vulnerable members of society, that is, the sick, the poor and the elderly. Minority groups are often severely affected by this practice as well, as gentrification has caused property taxes to skyrocket in urban centers, and allows for private investors to snatch up homes for pennies on the dollar. Enright advocated for

---

14. Alessandro Gavazza, "Asset Liquidity and Financial Contracts: Evidence from Aircraft Leases," London School of Economics, Oct. 2008, https://papers.ssrn.com/sol3/papers.cfm?abstract_id=931456.

lawmakers to change this practice based on the predatory nature of the private tax lien industry.[15]

Summary

Aircraft leasing, tax liens and trade claims are examples of seemingly complex investments that command a premium. They offer yields that are attractive relative to their interest rate and credit risks, primarily due to their lack of liquidity. Shipping containers and storage units offer returns and yields that have both appreciated and rental income. Shipping containers and storage units are hybrid investments that offer an opportunity for both appreciation and income. The returns from a composite set of investments related to aircraft leasing, tax liens and shipping and storage units were similar to the S&P 500 between January 2016 and December 2019, with more volatility.

Useful Websites and Additional Reading

"12 Tips for First-Time Investors in Self-Storage Real Estate," https://www.sparefoot. com/self-storage/news/44-advice-for-self-storage-investors/.

"Aviation Industry Leaders Report 2019," https://assets.kpmg/content/dam/kpmg/ie/ pdf/2019/01/ie-aviation-industry-leaders-report-2019.pdf.

"EY's Aviation Finance: An Interesting Prospect for Long-Term Investors" https://www. ey.com/Publication/vwLUAssets/ey-aviation-finance-as-a-long-term-investment/ $File/ey-aviation-finance-as-a-long-term-investment.pdf.

"Efficiency and Tax Incentives: The Case for Refundable Tax Credits," https://heinonline. org/HOL/LandingPage?handle=hein.journals/stflr59&div=10&id=&page=.

"How Have Public Aircraft Leasing Companies Performed?" https://assets.kpmg/ content/dam/kpmg/ie/pdf/2020/03/ie-aviation-finance-leasing-series-how-have-public-aircraft-leasing-companies-performed.pdf.

"The Interaction of Financing and Investment Decisions When the Firm Has Unused Tax Credits," https://www.jstor.org/stable/2327994.

"Leveraged Aircraft Leases: The Lender's Perspective," https://www.jstor.org/stable/ 40687017?seq=1.

"Nine Things You Need to Know About Tax Lien Investing," https://money.usnews.com/ investing/real-estate-investments/slideshows/9-things-to-know-about-tax-lien-investing.

"Self-Storage Is an Investment Alternative," https://money.usnews.com/money/ blogs/the-smarter-mutual-fund-investor/articles/2018-01-11/self-storage-is-an-investment-alternative.

"What Is Self-Storage?" https://www.sparefoot.com/self-storage/blog/78-what-is-self-storage-2/.

---

15. Caroline Enright, "Privatization of Delinquent Property Tax Liens and Tax Sale Surplus in Massachusetts," *Boston College Law Review*, Feb. 2020, https://lawdigitalcommons.bc.edu/bclr/vol61/iss2/6/.

Chapter Eight

ESPORTS, GAMING, FRANCHISES AND ENTERTAINMENT

Introduction

The eSports, gaming, gambling, sports franchises and entertainment industries are being transformed by rapidly changing technology and innovation. In this chapter, we will explore some of the reasons this is the case. We will also examine some of the public and private opportunities available to investors who want exposure to these types of exotic alternative investments.

People have been playing sports, investing in their own skills, attending tournaments and events, gambling on outcomes at casinos and investing in brands associated with athletes and entertainers for many years. However, the notion of investing in eSports is something relatively new. It is something that has evolved from the gaming industry and is able to leverage trends in technology and our preoccupation with the sports and entertainment world.

Traditional sports franchises and venues have been big business for a long time. Football, baseball and basketball teams, even those without rings or championships, are all valued in the billions of dollars today. George Steinbrenner bought the New York Yankees in 1973 for a mere $8.8 million. According to Forbes, the Yankees are the highest valued baseball sports franchise today at almost $5 billion. The Yankees rank number four among all professional sports teams, trailing only the FC Barcelona soccer club, the Golden State Warriors and the Los Angeles Lakers basketball franchise. [1]

Many sports teams, arenas and venues are privately owned by the team founders, families and sometimes fans. A handful of teams from various sports are available to the public and can be traded on an exchange. However, sometimes, public ownership of a team is more about bragging rights than profits. The Green Bay Packers of the National Football League are the only publicly owned franchise in the NFL. Their shares have limited financial value, do not trade on any exchange and the owners are not entitled to share in the team's profits. They can, however, attend the annual meeting and get special updates and information about their team. There has also been significant growth in public companies in the sports and entertainment industry that own assets related to horse racing, auto racing, ski resorts and professional wrestling.

---

1. "MLB Team Valuations," *Forbes*, Apr. 2019, https://www.forbes.com/teams/new-york-yankees/#196cc6604e6e.

Electronic gaming products are being created and developed by companies for individual and professional consumers alike. Some games tend to be designed for multiplayer and team competitions, whereas others are more individual. Companies like Sony, SEGA, Electronic Arts, Microsoft, Activision Blizzard and many others have been making gaming platforms like PlayStation and Xbox as well as participating in the designing of games for decades. Smartphone and tablet games are a more recent development. The broad-based gaming industry sales across all sorts of platforms and products were estimated to be worth $120.1 billion in 2019, according to market researcher SuperData's 2019 year-end report. One game in particular, Fortnite, alone accounted for $1.8 billion of that amount in the same year.[2]

eSports is an extension of the sports and gaming industry. It comes about from an association of professional gamers playing on teams and in tournaments rather than just individual players playing electronic games for their own personal enjoyment or in individual competitions. *Fortnite, Mortal Kombat* and *League of Legends* are games that can be played in teams and tournaments or as individuals. Professionals can make huge sums of money by joining teams, getting sponsors and winning tournaments just like traditional athletes. Individuals can also get paid from playing video games if they can attract viewers and followers in much the same way as other social media influencers. eSports is driving much of the products being designed and developed by companies for both individual enjoyment and professional consumers.

One interesting and fast-growing development in the sports, entertainment and gaming business is the development of online platforms for legalized sports betting outside of casinos. Platforms allow people to bet on outcomes or compete for points related to specific players, sports and teams. Sports gambling was legalized in Pennsylvania in 2017. New Jersey legalized sports gambling in June 2018. So far, approximately 20 states have legalized sports gambling. New York and several other states are watching closely and many more are expected to legalize gambling. Companies such as FanDuel, DraftKings, Willian Hill and many casinos and gaming companies now offer platforms where individuals, professionals or even some boutique portfolio managers can place bets on a wide range of sports and celebrity outcomes.

Another interesting development is the ability to buy exposure to a professional athlete or personality by investing in them directly in exchange for a percentage of their future financial success. Several well-known and up-and-coming athletes and entertainers have sold their personal equity as investments to those who want to own a percentage of their high-profile future earnings from their contracts, endorsements, films and concerts. One company trying to make this happen is Fantex Inc. The company has offered public and private investments backed by stakes in a professional athlete's future contract revenue, select endorsements, appearance fees and much more. The portfolio spans the sports of baseball, football and basketball.[3] Another company called the Hollywood

---

2. "2019 Year in Review—Digital Games and Interactive Media," SuperData Research, 2019, https://www.superdataresearch.com/reports/2019-year-in-review.
3. Homepage, Fantex Inc., accessed Mar. 2020, https://fantex.com/.

Stock Exchange (known as HSX.com) offers shares that are linked to the performance of everything from specific films and television shows to movie stars and comedians.[4]

Television networks also derive a great deal of their revenue from promoting and airing sporting events that will generate advertising revenue. Viacom, Disney, CBS, AMC and other networks are heavily invested in long-term deals with professional sports teams.

In most cases, people participating in any sport, including eSports tournaments, or sponsoring a team or gambling on sporting events do so as a hobby and in the interest of making money on the side. The platforms that have arisen to support gaming and gambling for consumers and individuals have also given rise to several new and exciting investment opportunities.

Market Size and Activity Measures

Information and data on the specific size and scope of the eSports market and many of its activity variables about viewership, profits and revenue are still emerging. The industry is relatively new and sources to measure its size and scope will certainly develop over time.

One data source is Roundhill Investments. Roundhill Investors is an investment advisor, data provider and fund manager active in the eSports industry. The fact sheet for the Roundhill BITKRAFT Sport Index is one useful source of information about the size and scope of the esports industry. According to the index fact sheet, the global industry exceeded $150 billion in revenue in 2019 and is growing at almost 10% per year, with 2.5 billion people playing video games worldwide, and with almost 500 million people watching video games annually.[5]

The video gaming industry is a broad industry group that includes the development and sale of video games and platforms. Industry players range from very small gaming companies to large multi-dimensional players like Microsoft, Sony, GameStop, Activision and Nintendo.

Video game industry revenue and performance measures for the United States from IBISWorld for 2019 are shown in Figure 8.1. Annual revenue was $63.4 billion, with a profit margin of 17.6%. Video game revenues had grown at a 14.4% annual rate from 2014 to 2019 and are projected to continue to grow at almost 6% per year through 2024.[6]

The majority of the revenues from this industry come from online games and software sales. Figure 8.2 from IBISWorld for 2019 shows that online games and software made up 63.8% of revenue in 2019 followed by physical games and consoles at 17% and 13.1%, respectively.[7]

4. Hollywood Stock Exchange Homepage, accessed Mar. 2020, https://www.hsx.com.
5. "Roundhill Bitkraft eSports Index," Roundhill Investments, Mar. 2020, https://www.roundhillinvestments.com/assets/pdfs/Roundhill_Fact_Sheet.pdf.
6. Nick Masters, "Video Games in the U.S.", IBISWorld, Dec. 2019, https://my.ibisworld.com/us/en/iexpert-risk/nn003/iexpert-risk.
7. Ibid.

Total Revenue in 2019	Annual Growth 2014–2019	Annual Growth 2019–2024	Profit Margin in 2019	Wages as a share of Revenue in 2019	Number of Businesses 2014–2019
$63.4 bn	14.4%	5.5%	17.6%	47.4%	12.8%

Figure 8.1. IBISWorld data for the US video game industry for 2019.

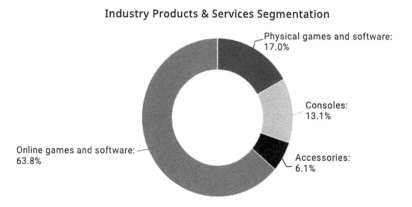

Figure 8.2. IBISWorld breakdown of video game revenue in the United States for 2019.

Traditional sports franchises benefit from increased consumer demand to attend and view games. Franchises are limited by the respective leagues to protect regional franchises against direct competition. Unsuccessful franchises will be taken over and actively managed by the respective league and may be relocated or closed if they do not become successful.

Research from IBISWorld in Figure 8.3 shows that revenue from the traditional sports franchise industry in the United States was $37.7 billion in 2019. Revenue had grown at an annual rate of 5.4% from 2014 to 2019 and is expected to grow at a rate of 1.2% annually from 2019 to 2024. The business had a profit margin of almost 10%. Key drivers for continued revenue growth include changes in disposable income, media rights contracts negotiations and changes in athletes' collective bargaining negotiations.[8]

Most of the revenue stream shown in Figure 8.4 comes from broadcasting and media rights, which represents 37.9% of reported revenue. Other categories include ticket sales at 32.3%, advertising at 15.4%, concessions at 3.5%, merchandise at 1% and other sources at 9.9%.[9]

---

8. Ryan Roth, "Sports Franchises in the US," IBISWorld, Nov. 2019, https://www.ibisworld.com/united-states/market-research-reports/sports-franchises-industry/.
9. Ibid.

Total Revenue in 2019	Annual Growth 2014–2019	Annual Growth 2019–2024	Profit Margin in 2019	Wages as a share of Revenue in 2019	Number of Businesses 2014–2019
$37.7 bn	5.4%	1.2%	9.5%	63.7%	4.0%

Figure 8.3. IBISWorld statistics related to the traditional sports franchise industry in December 2019.

Industry Products & Services Segmentation

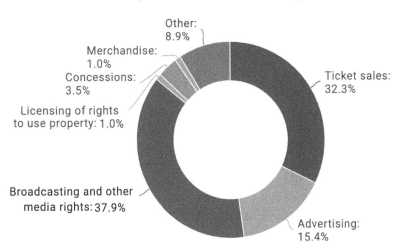

Other: 8.9%
Merchandise: 1.0%
Concessions: 3.5%
Licensing of rights to use property: 1.0%
Broadcasting and other media rights: 37.9%
Ticket sales: 32.3%
Advertising: 15.4%

Figure 8.4. The IBISWorld breakdown of traditional sports franchise revenue by segment for 2019.

According to the UK Gambling Commission, from 2008 to 2009, 68% of the population engaged in some form of gambling. In 2016, the UK Gambling Commission stated that online gambling has overtaken traditional gambling. Between April 2015 and March 2016, online gambling operators reported a gross gambling yield of $5.62 billion, which is about 33% of the total market yield.[10]

The US commercial casino industry reported record revenues of $41.68 billion in 2018, which marked a 3.5% increase over 2017. As many as 12 of the 24 states with commercial casinos reported record annual gaming revenue in 2018. The United States has 465 commercial casinos. Increased revenues were brought on by the Supreme Court

10. Daniel Perez Liston and Juan P. Gutierrez Pineda, "Financial Performance of Internet Gambling Stocks: Empirical Evidence from the UK," *Review of Integrative Business and Economics Research*, 2020, https://sibresearch.org/uploads/3/4/0/9/34097180/riber_9-3_01_b19-021_1-19.pdf.

overturning the Professional and Amateur Sports Protection Act, which was a 1992 federal law that restricted lawful sports betting to Nevada.[11]

Opportunities and Strategies

Playing a sport and making individual bets is not a financially sound strategy for most people. That being said, playing a sport or betting on one high-profile individual can certainly be profitable. Being a celebrity or entertainer, becoming a professional golfer, a successful comedian or singer, a basketball player or a football player or joining an eSports team can be quite lucrative. However, the likelihood of this happening has a very low probability. Nonetheless, for those with the requisite skill level, the payoff can be significant. This is also true in eSports today. For example, in September 2018, a 19-year-old named Austin Etue won $250,000 playing Fortnite in a tournament sponsored by the game's developer, Epic Games.[12]

Betting on specific sporting events or players is also another way to make money and get exposure. This process also considers very-low-probability events, yet every day there are those who do win big in Vegas or win the lottery! The bottom line is that the average individual playing a sport or betting on celebrities is living out a personal dream or participating in a hobby. It is not a sound form of investing.

Investors, on the other hand, are individuals or organizations seeking to leverage long-term opportunities from the sports, gaming, gambling and entertainment industry, not those playing or making individual bets.

Investors can invest in many publicly traded companies in the sports and entertainment business that own teams, arenas or cable companies and streaming services. Some may not provide pure exposure to specific sports, gaming or entertainment assets, but rather offer diversified cable, telecom, entertainment or hospitality exposures along with a sports team or brand. Several professional sports teams are owned by media organizations or holding companies who themselves are owned privately or listed publicly. The Yankees are owned privately by the Steinbrenner family, the Toronto Blue Jays, Raptors and Maple Leaves are all owned by a public company named Rogers Communications. The New York Knicks and Rangers are both owned by a public company called the Madison Square Garden Co., named after the "world's most famous arena" in New York City where they both play. Manchester United, a soccer club from the United Kingdom, is listed on the New York Stock Exchange under the symbol MANU. Investors who want diversification or liquidity are best suited for these investments and their related ETFs. Investors can also get more narrow exposure to sub-segments of the sports industry by

11. William C. Miller et al., "State of the States 2019," American Gaming Association, June 2019, https://www.americangaming.org/wp-content/uploads/2019/06/AGA-2019-State-of-the-States_FINAL.pdf.
12. Tom Huddleston Jr., "How This 19-Year-Old Amateur Gamer Won $250,000 Playing Fortnite," *CNBC*, Nov. 2018, https://www.cnbc.com/2018/11/20/how-teenage-gamer-austin-morgausse-etue-won-250k-playing-fortnite.html.

investing in names like the Churchill Downs Co., Vail Resorts, International Speedway Corp. and World Wrestling Entertainment Inc.

Investors are also able to get exposure to the gaming industry by researching and investing in any number of publicly traded sports teams or gaming companies like GameStop, Sony or Activision. These firms are well positioned to profit from the increased visibility that eSports and gaming bring to the products, games and platforms that they sell to consumers. These firms profit from software, games and platforms used to play the games they watch the professionals play. Fans who attend tournaments or view them online and want to compete against their friends online can provide con- sumers for these brands and their products. Some of these companies, such as Sony, are integrated across hardware, software, content and services, while others are more narrow, pure plays into specific segments of the market. Publicly traded stocks, mutual funds and ETFs are available for investors who wish to take this approach.

Investors can of course profit from investing in companies that make a profit from gambling or related services and businesses. This can be done by investing in traditional casinos, related service companies or online gambling platforms. Traditional casinos include names such as MGM Grand, WinStar, Las Vegas Sands and many more. They offer on-site gaming and also profit from a wide array of hospitality services. Casinos make a profit by acting as a principal on bets and established odds designed to favor the casino over time and from the fees for services they provide to their guests. Expenses include personal equipment leases and purchases, rent and other operating costs. Casinos are also highly regulated businesses. Some investors may prefer indirect ways to get expo- sure to casinos and hotels. Companies like Scientific Games and International Game Technology supply items like tables, equipment and technology to casinos and hotels. Another way to get exposure to casinos and hotels is to invest in real estate investment trusts that own the land that casinos and hotels use to operate their business. This strategy is very accessible and can be implanted using publicly traded stocks, mutual funds and ETFs as well.

Some investors choose to invest in this space by privately sponsoring new or up-and- coming athletes, entertainers, teams, players or leagues. Venture capital opportunities to invest in a traditional or new eSports team or even a new baseball, basketball or football league such as the XFL are available from time to time. Venture capital will provide funds to buy existing teams or to launch teams or new leagues related to both traditional and eSports industries. Access to opportunities may be limited to high-net-worth individuals and deals may be hard to come by for many interested investors.

The intersection of all forms of eSports, gaming, and the legalization of the online gambling industry has opened up opportunities and strategies that some investors and financial advisors may find quite interesting. Investing in online gambling or fantasy gaming platforms is yet another option. This would include investing in companies like Fan Duel and Draft Kings. Some of these companies have positioned themselves as gaming companies and not necessarily gambling. They offer cash prizes to players who accumulate points and earn their revenue from player entrance fees for games and tournaments plus advertising. This business is an extension of the fantasy sports league concept, as players can compete beyond family, coworkers or friends. They can compete against an expanded universe of all the players on the platform. The online platform gaming business model is a hybrid that straddles the gambling and gaming worlds. In some states, the platform is considered gambling and must be explicitly approved and regulated, while in others, the platform is viewed purely as a technology and gaming site and not betting at all. The revenue is based on advertising, subscriptions and fees and creating related businesses or services to support customers, such as data services, analytics and live betting hubs and destinations. Besides paying out prizes, company expenses are heavily weighted toward technology and client acquisitions. Investors may need to take venture or private equity stakes to get exposure to these companies when they first launch. Some are now available to the public via business development corporations or direct exchange listings. There are also opportunities to invest in companies that provide online casino games like Blackjack and Texas Hold'em. This opportunity tends to be in mostly online and mobile applications.

Today there are some private hedge funds that are leveraging such new technologies and betting platforms by creating algorithms that actually place bets and use probability and player research to bet on sporting events and player performance. Strategies can be predictive. In this strategy, algorithms are used to predict the odds or a win or loss and a traditional bet is placed on one or more betting platforms. Strategies can also seek to arbitrage or exploit mispriced bets occurring on a platform at a specific point in time. Data and analytics play a critical role in algorithmic or computer-based sports gambling. Information advantages related to player or team statistics, weather and injuries can provide investors with enhanced outcomes and profits.

There are also opportunities to invest in athletes or celebrities by using platforms like FANEX and HSX.com.

Finally, investing in the ticket brokerage industry is yet another way to participate in the growth of many kinds of sports and entertainment events. Individuals can buy tickets on the primary market when sold to the public by Ticketmaster or Live Nation, then hold them and resell the tickets at a higher price. There are many platforms that exist today that allow for the legal resale of tickets on a secondary market such as StubHub or Vivid Seats. One strategy is to invest in these primary market distributors directly by buying shares in Live Nation or other similar publicly listed companies.

Who Invests?

Institutions will invest some of their traditional equity allocation to publicly listed sports, gaming and entertainment companies as part of their normal asset allocation process to stocks and stock indices. Institutional investors will own stakes in public companies like Sony or Nintendo and may have exposure to casinos and many types of media and telecommunications companies. They will over- or underweight the sector based on their research and relative risk and return perspectives. However, most institutions are not necessarily ready to jump into specific eSports, gaming and entertainment strategies or early-stage opportunities as a direct investment or even as part of their alternative's allocation.

High-net-worth individuals and family offices are some of the biggest investors in traditional sports teams, as well as eSports franchises and gaming, whether in the form of private equity stakes or public equity stakes. Many athletes, entertainers and traditional franchise owners are prominent investors in eSports as well. Mark Cuban, who comes from the sports, technology and entertainment industry, is one example of a major investor in eSports. Cuban owns both the Dallas Mavericks and a number of eSports investments. According to a 2018 article by Tom Huddleston Jr., other notable investors in this space include high-profile former athletes like Michael Jordan, Stephen Curry, Steve Young and Alex Rodriquez and entertainers such as Drake, Ashton Kutcher and Jennifer Lopez. Michael Jordan owns a stake in the Miami Marlins along with Derek Jeter. Michael Jordan is also part of an investor group that acquired a stake in aXiomatic, which owns an eSports company called Team Liquid. The entertainer Drake owns a company that invests in an eSports organization called 100 Thieves, which invests in teams that compete in games such as *League of Legends* and *Call of Duty*.[13]

Retail investors interested in this space can get exposure to the sports and gaming industry by buying shares in companies like MSG, Activision Blizzard or ETFs such as GAMR. ETFs offer investors more diversified exposure to the sector than individual companies.

Benchmarks and Indices

The Forbes Sports Money Index is a comprehensive source of information about money and sports. It provides detailed data on over 400 athletes, teams and brands as well as sports agencies. The information covered includes revenues, expenses, valuations, contracts and a wide range of financial measures about athletes and teams. For more information, visit https://www.forbes.com/sports-money-index/#3e21fdae1d35.

The Roundhill BITKRAFT eSports Index is an index designed to track the performance of the market related to eSports. The index consists of an equal-weighted portfolio of listed companies that participate in the gaming industry. This index includes video game publishers, streaming network operators, video game tournament and league operators and owners, competitive team owners and hardware companies. More information about the index can be found at https://www.roundhillinvestments.com/assets/pdfs/Roundhill_Fact_Sheet.pdf.

The Roundhill BITKRAFT eSports Index shown in Figure 8.5 outperformed the S&P 500 during the first half of 2019 and underperformed during the second half of 2019, ending the year up almost 30%.

Firms, Funds and Platforms

The eSports, gaming, sports franchise and Internet-based firms span the globe. Some firms develop and publish games and content, others produce and manufacture

---

13. Tom Huddleston Jr., "From Michael Jordan to Drake: The Athletes and Celebs Who Invested Millions in eSports in 2018," Dec. 2018, https://www.cnbc.com/2018/12/19/from-michael-jordan-to-drake-athletes-celebrities-invested-millions-esports.html.

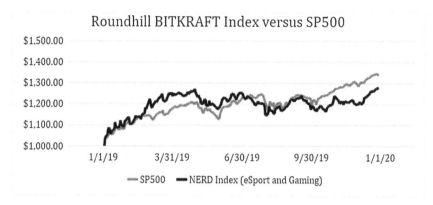

Figure 8.5. The growth of $1,000 invested in the Roundhill BITKRAFT eSports Index of eSports and gaming versus the S&P 500.

hardware and software, some operate platforms or own teams and revenues. There are many public, private and commingled funds that offer exposure to various segments of this industry. Some firms and investment vehicles are narrow and participate in only one or two industry segments, whereas others are broad and participate at many levels.

Tencent specializes in various Internet-related services and products, entertainment, artificial intelligence and technology. It is a Chinese company that was founded in 1998. Tencent operates the largest online gaming platform in China. The company trades under the symbol TCEHY. Information about the company can be found at https://www.tencent.com/en-us/about.html.

Activision Blizzard is engaged in the development and publication of interactive entertainment products and games. According to the company's website, it operates five divisions that develop and distribute different games and product offerings. Activision develops entertainment for gaming consoles, mobile and tablets including well-known titles such as *Skylanders* and *Call of Duty*. Blizzard Entertainment develops and distributes games like *World of Warcraft*. King Digital Entertainment offers titles such as *Candy Crush*. Major League gaming operates products and services designed for fan experiences. Activision Blizzard Studios makes original film and television from the library of games and other content owned by the company. The company trades under the symbol ATVI. Information about the company can be found at https://www.activisionblizzard.com/about-us.

Electronic Arts engages in the provision of digital interactive entertainment and develops and delivers games, content and online services for Internet-connected consoles, mobile devices and personal computers. The company trades under EA. Information about the company can be found at https://www.ea.com.

Sony and Nintendo are firms that participate in the development, design, manufacture and sale of electronic equipment, instruments, devices, game consoles and software for consumers, professionals and industrial markets.

NetEase engages in the provision of Internet technology services. It operates through the following business segments: online games, e-commerce, advertising services, email and others. TakeTwo engages in the development, publishing and marketing of interactive software games. Huya is a leading gaming and video streaming company in the Chinese market. Glu Mobile is a developer and publisher of mobile games for smartphone and tablet devices.

Gamestop sells new and pre-owned video game hardware, video game software, pre-owned and value video games and video game accessories, including controllers, gaming headsets, virtual reality products, memory cards and other add-ons for use with video game hardware and software. The company trades under the symbol GME. Information about the company can be found at https://gamestop.gcs-web.com.

Nvidia designs, develops and markets three-dimensional graphics processors and related software. The company offers products that provide interactive graphics to the mainstream personal computer market that are essential to gaming and other applications. Information about the company can be found at https://www.nvidia.com/en-us/.

Vectors Video Gaming and eSports ETF is a broad-based investment vehicle that tracks the price and performance yield of companies involved in video game development, eSports and related hardware and software. Vectors Gaming ETF is another ETF that seeks to track the overall performance of companies involved in casinos and casino hotels, sports, betting, lottery services, gaming services, gaming technology and gaming equipment. An eSports and Digital Entertainment ETF is designed to track the performance of the eSports market. This includes but is not limited to video game publishers, streaming network operators, video game tournament and league operators and owners, competitive team owners and hardware developers. Defiance Next Gen Video Gaming ETF seeks to track the performance of the BlueStar Next Gen Video Gaming Index. ETFMG Video Game Tech ETF tracks an equity index of global firms that support, create or use video games.

Roundhill BITKRAFT is an active eSports investment fund that seeks to invest in early- and growth-stage companies. Vision Venture Partners LLC operates as a private equity and venture capital firm. It focuses on investments in eSports, digital entertainment and the lifestyle and food and beverage industries. Information about the company can be found at https://www.roundhillinvestments.com.

Sports teams' investments include investments in the Manchester United British soccer club, Liberty Media and the Liberty Braves which own stakes in the Atlanta Braves, Madison Square Garden which owns the New York Knicks and New York Rangers and Rogers Communication which owns the Toronto Maple Leaves, Raptors and Blue Jays.

Sports venue investments include Churchill Downs, which owns and operates horse racing tracks, as well as International Speedway, which owns and operates auto racetracks, and Vail Resorts, which owns and operates ski resorts. Finally, World Wrestling Entertainment is a company that owns and operates a number of successful wrestling brands and profits from both live and broadcast revenue, merchandise and film opportunities.

Table 8.1. The performance, risk and correlation of a composite of eSports and gaming investment vehicles versus the S&P 500 between January 2016 and December 2019.

	Gaming	S&P 500
Correlation	0.66	NA
Standard Deviation	18.87%	11.56%
Average Annual Return	24.36%	14.33%
Simplified Sharpe	1.29	1.24

Table 8.2. The performance, risk and correlation of a composite of traditional sports franchises investment vehicles versus the S&P 500 between January 2016 and December 2019.

	Sports	S&P 500
Correlation	0.72	NA
Standard Deviation	12.55%	11.56%
Average Annual Return	21.39%	14.33%
Simplified Sharpe	1.70	1.24

Table 8.3. The performance, risk and correlation of a composite of a combined eSports, gaming and traditional sports franchise investment vehicle composite versus the S&P 500 between January 2016 and December 2019.

	Sports and Gaming	S&P 500
Correlation	0.75	NA
Standard Deviation	14.83%	11.56%
Average Annual Return	23.34%	14.33%
Simplified Sharpe	1.57	1.24

Composites

A composite of eSports and gaming investments shown in Table 8.1 had a correlation of 0.66 to the S&P 500. The composite had better performance than the S&P 500 between January 2016 and December 2019 with a return of 24.36% versus 14.33%. It had higher volatility and a similar Sharpe ratio of 1.29 versus 1.24.

A composite of traditional sports franchises, venues and arenas, shown in Table 8.2, shows a correlation of 0.72 to the S&P 500 between January 2016 and December 2019. The composite outperformed the S&P 500 with a return of 21.39% versus 14.33%, with similar volatility and a much higher Sharpe ratio of 1.70.

On a combined basis, a composite of eSports, gaming and traditional sports franchise investments, shown in Table 8.3, produced higher returns, with only slightly higher volatility than the S&P 500. It had a higher Sharpe ratio of 1.57 compared to 1.24 for the S&P 500 between January 2016 and December 2019.

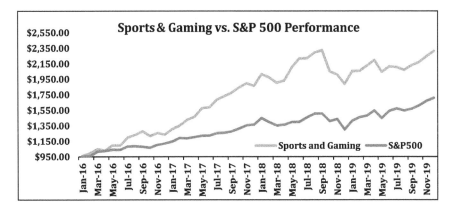

Figure 8.6 The growth of $1,000 invested in a composite of eSports, gaming and traditional sports franchises vehicles versus $1,000 invested in the S&P 500 from January 2016 to December 2019.

A $1,000 investment in an eSports, gaming and traditional sports franchise composite in January 2016, shown in Figure 8.6, would have grown to almost $2,400 by December 2019 compared to $1,708 for the S&P 500.

Unique Risks

Value is created by sports franchises by attracting players and fans alike. Winning championships, creating a brand and getting the best players are some of the primary ways the value of a particular franchise is increased. The risks tied to investing in any sports team or franchise include what happens if the teams or players fail to perform, if fans stay away and advertising dollars dry up or if fan preferences change and fans switch to another sport altogether. Negotiating with unions and collective bargaining arrangements have a material impact on traditional sports franchises and their profits; investors and franchise owners must watch them carefully. eSports investors must also consider the timing of game releases, trends in gamer demand, the risk of over-investing in short-lived fads and any shifts in player or consumer preferences. They must also consider the continual pressure of competing offerings, as well as the increased technology costs to deliver the product to consumers and the need for ongoing innovation to maintain and grow market share.

Some aspects of the gaming industry are also subject to regulatory risk. The Entertainment Software Ratings Board was established in 1994 to assign ratings to video games. Ratings range from "M for mature" to "E for everyone." Some games can be sold unrated. Ratings are voluntary, meaning retail stores and online sellers are not required to restrict product distribution to those who fall outside the rating category. In fact, in 2011 the US Supreme Court ruled that restricting sales based on content was a violation of individuals' right to choose.

Piracy and the sale of competing knock-off games is another risk to software investments related to video games. Some countries are notorious for the piracy of all sorts of media products, including music and games. Lower-cost bootleg and counterfeit games limit profits and market share and restrict pricing power for legitimate products. This can eat into revenue growth.

Moreover, investments in ticket brokers and resellers like Vivid Seats are also subject to fraud risk. The resellers must guarantee that the tickets bought and sold on their platforms are legitimate. This means that any fraud becomes a drag on profits. It can also lead to a loss of consumer confidence. There is also a proliferation of competing platforms and intense price competition.

Investing in casinos requires an investor to research the specific segments of the market that a company has exposure to and can profit from in the future. Many times, the company's assets will be regional, located in places like Las Vegas or Hong Kong, and will be subject to a great deal of regulation. Casinos also need to address threats from online and mobile applications.

High valuation, limited profits, a lack of history and unclear demand for the demand of IPOs are all risks that could impact valuations and lead to losses from eSports investments. Valuations of eSports teams or franchises, as with many new technologies and opportunities, may be very expensive due to hype, limited market size and investor enthusiasm and a limited track record. According to some industry observers, the multiples for eSports teams are trading more akin to tech companies than sports franchises or entertainment companies. Many lack current profits as well and have unclear paths to profits.[14]

Online gaming platforms like Fan Duel and Draft Kings and other electronic gambling companies are also still early-stage businesses. They need a lot of cash for investment in technology and customer acquisition and many are not yet profitable. Both Fan Duel and Draft Kings are losing money and face stiff competition and many regulatory challenges.

Investing in an individual athlete's contract and future endorsement earnings via equity stakes may seem enticing. It may well have terrific payoffs if the player meets or exceeds expectations. However, what happens if a player's performance on or off the field is suboptimal or worse or if an entertainer falls out of favor? Future earnings could plummet with no way to recover, making any investment worthless.

Hedge funds investing in the outcomes of sporting events or gambling are brand new and have limited track records. It also may be difficult to backtest or validate results in many cases. Another challenge is considering the size of the bets being placed and scaling the initial returns. It may not be possible to replicate the results earned when betting small sums with large sums. Individual casinos or online platforms may not be willing to accept or handle high dollar value or high-volume computer-generated trades without their systems blocking trades or crashing.

---

14. Josh Chapman, "How to Invest in Video Gaming," Gaming Street, Oct. 2019, https://www.gamingstreet.com/how-to-invest-in-video-gaming.

Social, Legal and Ethical Considerations

There are certainly a number of arguments that can be made against investing in some of the sports, gaming, gambling and entertainment strategies discussed in this chapter. Let's briefly highlight a few of those arguments.

One risk is simply that, to many people, gambling is not considered a socially responsible activity and therefore should not be considered a socially responsible investment. Many investors will include casinos and gambling as investments to be avoided, despite positive returns or a bright outlook.

eSports and gaming may also suffer from the risk of simply not being taken seriously as a sport or, even worse, being considered a health threat and an activity subject to abuse or addiction. In 2018, the Japanese eSports association petitioned the International Olympic Committee to include eSports in the Tokyo 2020 Olympics. It was rejected without much debate or discussion. The committee did take the time to comment that the World Health Organization does not even recognize eSports as a sport since it does nothing to promote individual health and well-being. In fact, there was concern expressed by the World Health Organization that excessive participation in eSports and gaming can lead to mental health issues. According to the 11th International Classification of Diseases ICD 11 released in 2018, "gaming disorder" was classified as a form of mental illness.[15]

Data protection and privacy issues are two other concerns related to eSports and gaming. Participating in online gaming often requires user registration and the use of emails and personal data in order to participate. Security over personal data in a new and emerging industry can certainly be a concern for many participants. This may become an issue for investors if there is a breach by a product manufacturer that leads to damage to a brand and a loss of participants or sales.

Buying tickets to events like a concert that are, for example, originally sold for $50, and then reselling them on Stub Hub for $500 is not without issue. Companies that take such actions to profit are viewed as acting in a way that restricts event attendance to only the wealthiest in society, those who can afford to pay an exorbitant price for a popular event like a World Series, NCAA final or popular Broadway show. Some question whether this is a fair way to make a profit. After all, "scalping" tickets was illegal in many states until fairly recently. Why is a secondary market in ticket resale any different? Many performers have gone to great lengths to ensure their fans are getting their tickets at reasonable prices. They are increasingly seeking out ways to limit ticket resale, such as requiring buyers to be registered or to prove they are only buying for personal use.

Another consideration here is the morality of owning and trading people's wages and futures earnings like stocks. Taking stakes in people and trading their personal equity as stocks may not be considered investing per se; it may be viewed as more of a social contract than an investment and should therefore be avoided.

---

15. "Gaming Disorder," WHO, Sept. 2018, https://www.who.int/features/qa/gaming-disorder/en/.

Trends

According to a recent Deloitte research report, eSports currently represent less than 5% of the video gaming market in the United States. Those who label themselves as gamers and who actively play video games tend to watch eSports more than other consumers. Among those identified as gamers, 40% watch eSports events at least once a week and those who do watch tend to do so for more than four hours per week. While a small percentage of the gaming market today, eSports is destined to grow as millennials and others become larger parts of the economy.[16]

The increased popularity of eSports and gaming is something that could have both positive and negative effects on the traditional telecom and media industry. Gaming consoles can now be used for a wide range of streaming media services. This may be a threat to telecom and cable companies. On the other hand, the increased popularity of mobile gaming presents an opportunity.

New technologies that enable live casino gambling on the Internet and virtual reality gambling will increase the attractiveness of online casino games for many potential consumers. Access to more data and analytics will also be an enabler for online gambling and competition in the future. Deals between gaming and gambling platforms and sports franchises like the NBA and NFL are on the rise. Platforms will be able to give players real-time updates on games and access to injury reports and trend information relevant to placing bets before entering the competition.

Traditional casinos that cannot adapt may find their business model under siege from the multitude of online and virtual options available to consumers in the future.

The use of cryptocurrencies is also becoming an important feature for many of the online eSports platforms and brick-and-mortar style casinos. In fact, several casinos and platforms already accept Bitcoin. More may follow in the future as platforms compete for global consumers. The use of cryptocurrencies provides consumers with the ability to remain anonymous and protect their personal data when using gaming sites.

Academic Research

Researchers Donghun Lee and Linda Schoenstedt sought to explain how eSports consumption patterns compared to traditional sports consumption. To do this, the research team used a sample of 515 college students and athletic event attendees as their sample size. This paper utilized 14 eSports consumption motives in their analysis, which included social interaction, fantasy, identification with sport, diversion, competition, entertainment, sports knowledge application, arousal, design/graphics, pass time, control, skill-building for playing actual sports, permanence and peer pressure. In order to compare these consumption motives to traditional sports, seven items measuring involvements in traditional

---

16. Kevin Westcott et al., "Digital Media Trends 2019," Deloitte, June 2019, https://www2.deloitte.com/us/en/insights/industry/technology/digital-media-trends-consumption-habits-survey/trends-in-gaming-esports.html.

sports were added: game participation, televised sports viewing, purchase of team merchandise, use of the Internet specific to a sport, using print media about a sport, listening to the radio specific to a sport and game attendance. To analyze this data, the researchers used descriptive statistics, correlation analysis and multiple regression analysis. They found that the correlation between eSports consumption and involvement in the seven traditional sports behavior indicated both similarities and differences that exist between the very different forms of sport consumptive behaviors. The similarities they found included that televised sports viewing and Internet-usage-specific with traditional sports are more related to eSports. Notable differences in consumption behaviors existed between eSports and three other traditional sports consumption behaviors: game participation, radio listenership and team merchandise purchase. Additionally, there was no significant overlap between eSports and traditional sports in-game attendance and using print media about sports. Based on these findings, this paper recommended that it is essential for marketers to develop effective marketing strategies for eSports to reach specific target audiences. Marketers and investors might fulfill their goals of higher purchases and larger market shares by developing tailored messages that drive consumption behaviors of target audiences to specific games.[17]

Tobias M. Scholz and Volker Stein discuss the business model network of eSports and performed a case study on the internationally acclaimed game Overwatch. According to the authors, the absence of a standardized governance structure in eSports causes the industry to be generally self-organizing and mostly business-driven. The authors state that the eSports industry does not follow traditional business rules because of its young audience, global approach and digitized environment. The business model network focuses on value integration, with an emphasis on cooperation rather than competition and threats. Despite the threats of new entrants, buyer power, supplier power, risk of substitution and competitive rivalry, there is a need for cooperation to develop synergies. The authors find that eSports operate markedly differently than traditional businesses. Every stakeholder is inclined to share resources and potentially some sources of profit with other stakeholders to create a sustainable and thriving business model network. The authors present a brief case study for the popular Overwatch League, which is an eSports league based on the popular video game Overwatch.[18]

Joseph Macey and Juho Hamari investigated the relationship between eSports and gambling. Gambling in eSports refers to activities such as betting on eSports matches, playing fantasy eSports, paying to access randomly generated in-game items, using in-game items or currencies as wagers in third-party gambling sites and social network gambling games. Specifically, the study investigated the relationship between a range of gambling activities, the consumption of video games as a whole and the eSports industry. The researchers constructed a Partial Least Squares model to investigate data, as this

17. Donghun Lee and Linda J. Schoenstedt, "Comparison of eSports and Traditional Sports Consumption Motives," *Journal of Research*, 2011, https://www.academia.edu/3305551/Comparison_of_eSports_and_Traditional_Sports_Consumption_Motives.
18. Tobias M. Scholz and Volker Stein, "The Business Model Network of eSports: The Case of Overwatch," University of Siegen, 2019, http://www.digra.org/wp-content/uploads/digital-library/DiGRA_2019_paper_18.pdf.

method is best used for predictive studies. They gathered this data via an international online survey, which included a sample of 869 video gamer players across social media channels and online discussion forums dedicated to video gaming and eSports. In 2017, industry analysts estimated the number of mainstream eSports gambling participants to exceed 2.25 million. Additionally, it is estimated that over 3 million people actively participate in the informal markets surrounding in-game items, such as skin lotteries. Skin lotteries are virtual goods from a game, primarily weapons and clothing, which don't have any effect on gameplay but which do change the appearance of the game. Gamers deposit skins to a third-party lottery site where increases in deposits translate to a greater chance of success. The study found that increased consumption of video games has a positive association with game addiction score. However, game addiction has a negative correlation with both video game-related gambling and the PGSI (Problem Gambling Severity Index). This means that there is an unidentified aspect of video gameplay which serves to reduce the appeal of gambling for heavy gamers. Lastly, and most surprisingly, video game addiction was found to be negatively associated with offline gambling, online gambling and problem gambling. This means that contemporary video games are not associated with increased potential for problematic gambling.[19]

An interesting study by Daniel Liston and Juan Pineda examined the financial performance of an online gambling portfolio in the United Kingdom. The goal of the paper is to examine the financial performance of an online gambling portfolio and compare it to the market portfolio. The paper also studied the performance of online gambling stocks during a period of significant financial instability, in this case, the Great Recession. The study found that a portfolio of online gambling stocks underperformed market benchmarks. It also found that traditional brick-and-mortar gambling stocks outperformed market benchmarks. On a combined basis, they found that the industry showed no significant differences using traditional performance measures. However, they observed different results when performance measures were designed for periods of negative average returns, such as during times of financial instability. When estimating modified Sharpe ratios, the rankings of the portfolios changed significantly, with the online gambling portfolio performing much worse. Furthermore, Treynor ratios and Jensen's alpha also show that the online gambling portfolio underperforms the market portfolio.[20]

Finally, in another study, Daniel Rascher discussed an alternative valuation technique for sports franchises. Some franchises may have a small amount of, or even zero, net income. However, many owners do receive utility value for owning the sports franchise. The researchers proposed a hybrid income and market approach method that adjusts for the weaknesses in the comparable model. They gave an example of two NBA franchises. The first one generates $100 million in revenues, has zero income and is

19. Joseph Macey and Juho Hamari, "Investigating Relationships between Video Gaming, Spectating eSports, and Gambling," *Computers in Human Behavior*, Jan. 2018, https://www.researchgate.net/publication/321192069_Investigating_Relationships_Between_Video_Gaming_Spectating_Esports_and_Gambling.

20. Liston and Pineda, "Financial Performance of Internet Gambling Stocks."

valued at $320 million, which would imply a price to revenue ratio of 3.2. The second franchise generates $260 million in revenue and $50 million in profit. The application of a 3.2x price to revenue ratio from the former franchise to the latter would imply a valuation of $832 million, which would only account for revenue differences, but not income differences. The paper stated that a zero-income franchise only has utility value, because it consistently produces zero profit, and that an alternative valuation technique is required to account for this difference. They proposed a hybrid income and market approach method that adjusts for the weaknesses in the comparable model that would take the $320 million as the zero-profit value of owning a franchise. This deduction is due to the utility value of owning it and adding to it the capitalization of earnings value of the $50 million in income. At a discount rate of 9% and annual growth rate in earnings of 3%, this implies an "income-driven" value of $833 million which would be added to the utility value of $320 million to get $1.15 billion in value. This methodology would help compare a team like the Los Angeles Lakers, a team that reportedly has high profits, to a team like the New Orleans Pelicans, which reportedly has low or zero profits. This approach would allow for a meaningful way to compare the valuations of sports franchises.[21]

Summary

It is no secret that people love sports, games and gambling. New technologies, regulations and social media are all acting in concert to facilitate new forms of investing in this space. Many of the available eSports opportunities are new, so direct investors need to be careful. However, there are also safer, more liquid and diversified ways to benefit from the popular rise of eSports and gaming, such as investing in more established firms that own a combination of exposures to this sector. eSports, personal equity stakes and hedge fund gambling algorithms have the most risk and the highest potential. However, investing in Sony or MSG can still capture some but not all of the upside, with much less risk.

Useful Websites and Additional Reading

"Beyond Solitary Play in Computer Games: The Social Practices of eSports," https://journals.sagepub.com/doi/abs/10.1177/1469540514553711.

"The Celebrity Stock Market," https://ssrn.com/abstract=3361319.

"Deloitte's Digital Media Trends Survey," https://www2.deloitte.com/us/en/insights/industry/technology/digital-media-trends-consumption-habits-survey.html.

"Growth Effects of Sports Franchises, Stadiums, and Arenas: 15 Years Later," https://papers.ssrn.com/sol3/papers.cfm?abstract_id=3191302.

"Harvard Law School Forum on Celebrity Stock Markets," https://corpgov.law.harvard.edu/2019/06/25/celebrity-stock-market/.

---

21. Daniel A. Rascher, "Valuing Highly Profitable Sports Franchises," University of San Francisco, July 2019, https://papers.ssrn.com/sol3/papers.cfm?abstract_id=3421632.

"The Rise of eSports Investments," https://www2.deloitte.com/content/dam/Deloitte/us/Documents/finance/drfa-rise-of-esports-investments.pdf.

"Roll the Bones: The History of Gambling," https://digitalscholarship.unlv.edu/lib_articles/458/.

"Sports Betting Hedge Funds," https://www.sportsbettingdime.com/guides/finance/hedge-funds-betting-on-sports/.

"What Is eSports and Why Do People Watch It?" https://www.emerald.com/insight/content/doi/10.1108/IntR-04-2016-0085./full/html.

Chapter Nine

FARMLAND, TIMBER, WATER RIGHTS AND AIR RIGHTS

Introduction

Real assets can be a useful part of an inventor's portfolio. They can provide a combination of current income and appreciation as well as some inflation hedge and downside protection. All real asset investments provide some degree of diversification due to their low correlations to traditional stocks and bonds. Farmland, timber, air and water rights are examples of real assets that have very attractive diversification benefits and meaningful downside protection. Each represents an investment whose value is based on several underlying factors, including the usage cash for the asset itself. Land has value due to its limited supply and related to its specific usage cases. Sometimes land generates rent and at other times appreciation. Often it generates both. The level of appreciation and rent may be a function of the usage case for the land. Land that is used for commercial or residential property development will have different characteristics than land that is used for growing different commodities. Air rights have value based on their relationship to commercial and residential real estate prices and their scarcity value. Water rights have value based on the demand for clean water, rising commodities prices and their potential scarcity value.

A Few Definitions and Key Terms

Permanent crops are trees and plants that produce fruit annually and only get planted once. Apples grown on apple trees are an example of a permanent crop.

Row crops are single-season commodities such as soybeans that get planted and harvested annually.

Cash rent is computed per acre based on a farm's tillable acres and is normally paid in full before any crops are planted. Sometimes a portion of the rent may be collected in the spring and the balance after the harvest. The farmer assumes all the risks associated with planting, growing and harvesting the crop.

A crop share arrangement is one where the landowner is paid rent based on a percentage of the crop's revenue. In this case, the landlord and the farmer both assume risk.

A flex lease is a hybrid arrangement that combines a cash-based lease with a revenue-sharing arrangement if commodity prices reach certain levels. Farmers like both crop share and flex lease because some risk is being shared with the landowner.

Air rights are a developmental right to develop a specific amount of unused air space above real property. A property has air rights if it is vacant or if the building and improvements on the property are less than the permitted state and local laws and regulations.

Air space parcels are certain volumes of air space that are owned and can be sold, leased or rented.

Expansion space means all air space located directly above an Air Space Parcel extending upwards without limitation.

Air rights lease agreements give one party the rights to use a specific air space parcel for development in exchange for rents or fees.

Water rights are the rights that real property owners have to access water under or adjacent to their land. Land in certain states can lease or sell rights to the water under their property to third parties for commercial usage.

Riparian rights give landowners with a property adjacent to a river or stream the right to use the water for only those purposes authorized by local regulations. Some regulations may prohibit an owner from pumping the water or using it for commercial enterprise without approval. These rights generally may not be able to be sold separately from the land.

Prior appropriation rights allow a landowner to establish access rights and withdraw water on essentially a first come, first serve basis. Water rights in states with a prior appropriation system can be sold separately from the land, subject to local or federal regulations.

Timber refers to a wide range of trees and wood products that can be sold or processed into commercial or consumer goods such as planks, boards and paper.

Farmland Investing

In the United States, there is a limited supply of land available for any commercial use. Demand for land for specific crops or for their by-products is on the rise in many cases. Supply of land is limited and, in some cases, shrinking. Productivity gains of the past 25 years related to genetics and crop science are not repeatable at the same rate and some have been found to have negative consequences that damage land use. Environmental pressure to restrict land use or raise the cost of development is also on the rise in many states. Soil quality, water supply and commodity prices all converge to uniquely influence land valuations, rents and the returns on farmland investing.

Also, contrary to what some might think, farmland in the United States is still very much a family-run business. Individual owners tend to be the operators or landlords more often than large corporations. Smaller tracts of land run by individual farmers are the norm, not the exception.

Corporate ownership and professional investing in farmland are increasing as education and knowledge about the potential benefits are more widely dispersed. In addition, we have seen a surge in entrepreneurs and financial innovators seeking to launch funds and products that allow for commingled or individual exposure to real estate used for a wide range of purposes including farming. Many of these individuals and funds are applying sophisticated science and financial techniques to improve land productivity, yields and liquidity of real estate and farmland investing. Despite the progress and recent innovations, the institutionalization of farming as an asset class is still in its early stages.

Farmland investors can benefit from global increased demand for food, the expanding middle classes in China, India and Africa, and the resulting changes in diets, demand for alternative fuels produced from crops as well as demand for land for wind turbines. Limited land supply only increases opportunity further.

There are numerous players in the farm investing space. The industry includes farmers, real estate brokers, property owners, consumers, futures markets and many more. Real estate brokers specializing in farmland facilitate the purchase, sale and transfer of farming properties between market participants. The farmers are the operators of the land and often take all the risk associated with any land usage case. A farmer or farming coop or conglomerate that does not own the property will enter into rental agreements with the property owners and thus incurs a liability due immediately or in the future. The amount owed under any land lease must ultimately be funded by the return on the sale of the crop each year. The farmer often bears 100% of the risk of loss associated with a failed crop or a downturn in prices. Farmers can ensure certain risks or hedge them using commodities futures. In many cases, the property owner bears little to no direct risk exposure to the underlying crop or commodity.

Hedging vehicles for individual crops can be traded on the Chicago Mercantile Exchange (CME). Farmers are investors in the commodity they grow. They can reduce price risk by selling futures contracts that expire at or near the anticipated date the crops being grown or harvested will be sold in the cash market.

During the 2002 and 2008 financial crises, returns from investing in farmland and timber were actually positive, while the S&P 500 was down significantly.

Market Characteristics

The value of farmland real estate in the United States was $2.68 trillion dollars in 2018, which has been steadily rising since 2004, when the value was $1.21 trillion.[1] The number of farms in the United States for 2018 was just above 2 million. Total land in farms was estimated to be 900 million acres, and the average farm size is 443 acres.[2]

The US Department of Agriculture provides regular research and statistics about farmland in the United States in varying uses. They recently reported that farmland and structures account for about four-fifths of the total value of US farm assets, that farmland values have leveled off since 2014 after a long period of appreciation following the

1. M. Shahbandeh, "Total Value of Farm Real Estate in the United States from 2004 to 2018," Statista, July 2019, https://www.statista.com/statistics/196392/total-value-of-farmland-and-buildings-in-the-us-since-2004/.
2. "Farms and Land in Farms 2018 Summary," USDA, Apr. 2019, https://www.nass.usda.gov/Publications/Todays_Reports/reports/fnlo0419.pdf.

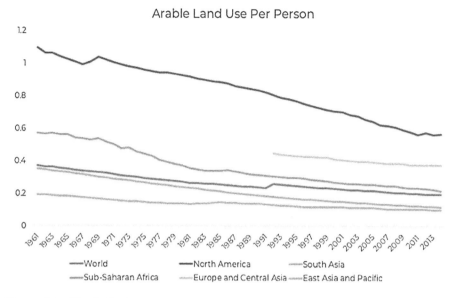

Figure 9.1. The decline in acres per person over time for different geographies.
Source: AcreTrader.com, Food and Agricultural Organization of the United Nations and NCREIF

farm crisis of the 1980s and that growth in farm real estate values has been relatively flat since 2014.[3]

One of the advantages of farmland investing, at least in theory, is that it will appreciate over time due to its scarcity value. Unlike stocks and bonds which depend upon the performance of a business, the value of farmland depends primarily on the usage case for the land. The amount of arable land for use in farming at any point of time is fairly stable. As global demand for food increases, so too does the demand for land available to grow that food. Figure 9.1 shows the declining amount of arable land per person that has occurred concurrently with the rising population over the past 50 years. It is logical to assume that if this trend continues, the value of farmland will also continue to grow.

According to the NCREIF Farmland Index data analyzed by AcreTrader and shown in Figure 9.2, the average annual return of farmland from 1991 to 2018 has been 11.5%. Farmland volatility was only 6.7% compared to approximately 17% for the S&P 500.[4]

In addition to low correlation and higher returns than investing in stocks, analyses of farmland and the S&P 500 return data, shown in Figure 9.3, from periods of financial crisis in 2002 and 2008 show that farmland investing provided investors with significant downside protection in both the 2000–02 and 2007–09 financial crises.

3. Scott Callahan, "Farmland Value," USDA, Aug. 2019, https://www.ers.usda.gov/topics/farm-economy/land-use-land-value-tenure/farmland-value/.
4. AcreTrader.com, https://www.acretrader.com/learn/farm-land-good-investment-opportunity.

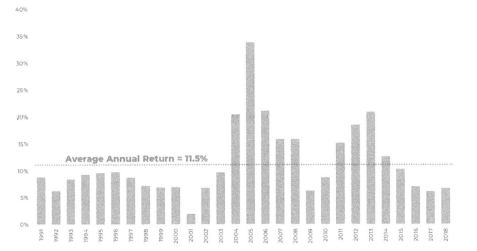

Figure 9.2. The annual return to farmland investing from 1991 to 2018.
Source: AcreTrader.com, Food and Agricultural Organization of the United Nations and NCREIF

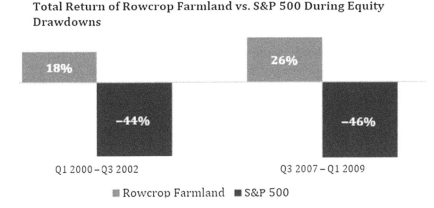

Figure 9.3. The performance of farmland investments compared to the S&P 500 during periods of financial crisis.
Source: NCREIF Row Crop Index, S&P 500 Index

Opportunities and Strategies

There are many ways to profit from investing in farmland. One strategy is to invest in row crops. This involves buying and leasing farmland used to grow crops such as soybeans, corn or feed crops. Row crops that focus on feed for dietary staples are benefiting from mega-trends in China and emerging markets. For example, an increase in demand for meat from China means that they will need more soybeans to feed hogs. This has caused a long-term increase in demand that supports farmers and rents. Another way to invest is to invest in permanent crops. Investors in land used for row crops essentially own the dirt into which crops are planted. The farmer bears the operational risk and the risk of disease or crop failure. Permanent crops may not be supported by the same mega-trends as row crops and can be more volatile. Land used for permanent crops tends to grow products such as apples or oranges that are in lower demand in emerging markets and places like China. Investors in permanent land used for permanent crops also own the trees and plants bearing the fruit in many cases and this more operational risk. The demand for permanent crops is generally more regional and subject to consumer preferences since the products are more discretionary.

Investing in farmland is also a way to profit from the scarcity of clean water outside the United States. Farmers will export water-intensive crops like almonds, wheat or corn to markets where clean water for commercial agriculture is in short supply. A country with a growing population and limited water resources will import crops that are water-intensive as a way to maximize their domestic water resources.

Unique Risks of Farmland Investments

Agricultural industry factors impact the value of farmland based on the use of the specific tract or parcel of land. Land used for commodities that are in high demand can obtain higher rents than others. A collapse in agricultural prices for a specific crop might also impact the tenant's ability to pay rent (impacting their creditworthiness) or lower rents under flexible lease arrangements.

Default risk on farm leases can often, but not always, be a factor. This risk, if present, can be mitigated by upfront payment or the collection of all or some of the amounts due under the lease.

Reduced water resources to support crops will of course lead to losses. The same is true for disease and pestilence. Anything that destroys permanent crops or impairs the ability of row crop farmers to pay rents will negatively impact farmland valuations and returns.

Environmental liability for damages to water supplies, protected animal or plant species, air quality or other protected categories may be present or arise in some cases. This can be mitigated by use of professional environmental studies in advance of any purchase and adequate knowledge of local rules and regulations.

A lack of diversity in crop types or a concentration in one specific crop within a portfolio can lead to price volatility or over-exposure to a particular agricultural market. This may also impact future lease payments and rents that are available. Falling rents would lead to lower returns.

Commodity prices are subject to many factors such as weather, government policies, shifts in supply and demand curves, population growth and changes in standards of living or cheaper substitutes. The price of agricultural products can also be affected by factors such as pestilence and disease that might cause crop failures or reduced harvests.

Geographical diversity is also important. Concentration in one specific locale may lead to exposure to local economic cycles. Geographic concentration makes a portfolio more exposed to local events such as hurricanes or floods. Farmland investments

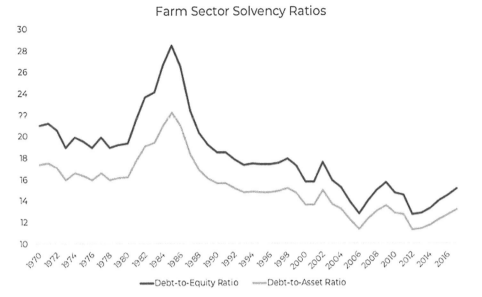

Figure 9.4. The improvement in solvency ratio and a decline in leverage from 1970 to 2016. *Source:* AcreTrader.com, FDA and NCREIF

tend to be illiquid. Illiquidity may limit an investment portfolio's ability to raise cash to meet redemptions or exchange investments to take advantage of different economic opportunities.

State and local real property taxes are a factor that impact investment returns. Taxes that are not deductible on federal tax returns or increases and decreases in tax assessments will have an adverse impact on performance and really cannot be hedged. In addition to changes in rates or deductibility, landowners are also subject to higher taxes as a result of an increase in the assessed valuation of a property. Higher assessed values lead to higher tax payments and liabilities.

The use of leverage in a farmland property is shown in Figure 9.4. The use of financial leverage by farmers will also increase risk. In the 1980s, many farms were over-leveraged, leading to insolvency when rents or prices fell. Since then, leverage has been declining, and in many high-quality farmland investment portfolios, debt is avoided altogether.

Air Rights

Air rights are a developmental right to develop a specific amount of unused air space above real property. A property has air rights if it is vacant or if the building and improvements on the property are less than those permitted by state and local laws and regulations. Air space parcels are certain volumes of air space that are owned and can be sold, leased or rented. Expansion space means all air space located directly above an air space parcel extending upwards without limitation. The lease agreements for air rights give one party the rights to use a specific air space parcel for development in exchange for rents or fees.

Many major cities around the world have regulations allowing for the purchase and sale of air rights. Companies who wish to develop high-rise office buildings and residential space can purchase air rights to allow construction in space that is above local restrictions. One common way for developers to expand above local limitations for height or floors is to invest in air rights by buying them from another property or properties that are adjacent to the property that is being developed and is subject to the same zoning code. In effect, one person's unused air space can be sold to another person who wishes to exceed local limitations. This is interesting because the transfer of these air rights grants developers the permission to build taller and bigger buildings than the city zoning code allows. A buyer of air rights can generate future rent, income and cash flows from a resale or development of the air rights. A seller can profit by increasing cash flow that will never be released, such as selling the space above a church or museum. The value of air rights is also heavily dependent on supply and demand imbalance in a particular city. When a city's population density rises, space becomes very limited, causing both land and air rights to rise in value. According to a University of Michigan study, approximately 84% of the US population currently lives in urban areas. That number is expected to rise to 90% by 2050. This trend of continued urbanization supports new development and the need for developers to maximize both land and air space.[5] Investors who buy and hold air rights can benefit from leasing or outright sale as the value of the space increases over time. The rights are priced, sold and eased in based on dollars per square foot. Manhattan air rights averaged more than $300 per square foot citywide in 2017.[6]

The size of the development rights market in terms of transactions is not particularly large. NYU's Furman Center for Real Estate and Urban Policy conducted a study that identified 421 development rights transactions in New York City between 2003 and 2011. There are three ways property owners can transfer development rights. The first and most common method is through a process called a "zoning lot merger." This type of transaction permits a building owner to transfer development rights to adjacent properties on the agreement to group their properties together and have them treated as one lot for zoning purposes. This allows underbuilt properties to transfer unused development rights to other properties. "Landmark transfers" allow the owners of landmarks to transfer unused development rights to adjacent parcels on the same block, across the street or next to any lot on another corner that touches the same intersection. Upon agreement, the building owner enters into a binding agreement to maintain the landmark. These types of transactions are highly sought after but extremely rare. "Special purpose district transfers" are used to tailor zoning to specific neighborhoods. In these cases, the city creates several special purpose districts that each have their own unique land use rules. For instance, in some of these districts, tailored zoning resolution allows air

5. "U.S. Cities 2019 Factsheet," Aug. 2019, http://css.umich.edu/factsheets/us-cities-factsheet.
6. Lois Weiss, "Offices Buying More Air Rights than Residential Condos," Mar. 2018, https://nypost.com/2018/03/20/offices-buying-more-air-rights-than-residential-condos/.

right transfers from grantor zones to any property in a designated receiving zone, voiding the strict adjacency requirements present in a zoning lot merger. In the theater district of midtown Manhattan, select Broadway theaters have been able to transfer unused air rights to any other lot in the theater district. Embedded in these deals is an agreement stating that the granting site will remain a theater to support city preservation efforts.[7]

A recent groundbreaking deal took place in March of 2018 when JP Morgan Chase bought 680,000 square feet of air rights from Grand Central Terminal for $240 million, the price per square foot being approximately $353.[8]

Today, New York City currently has 1.6 billion square feet in unused air rights. Manhattan is the most popular borough for air rights transactions and there remain only 33 million square feet of unused air rights at present. Go to the PropertyShark.com website for a full map of unused air rights in New York City: https://www.propertyshark.com/Real-Estate-Reports/2019/04/29/1-6-billion-square-feet-of-unused-air-rights-in-nyc/.

Water Rights

Water Rights are investments that give investors access to water from sources such as lakes, groundwater and rivers. Once you have the right to use the water, you can charge companies and governments for access to the water covered in your investment contract. The water rights market is increasingly attractive for private investments but is often difficult to navigate due to its fragmented geographic and ownership characteristics. Unlike other commodities, water markets are highly regionalized due to infrastructure or regulatory burdens that restrict water transfers between regions. Water resources in the United States are primarily regulated at the state level of government. In some states, water rights are considered a property right that may be transferred separately from land ownership, allowing water markets to emerge. Each state has developed unique systems for administering water rights, resulting in a variety of asset classes traded with varying levels of regulatory complexity. Investors can buy shares of public companies that develop water, water utilities and environmental services companies that clean, purify and distribute it.

Underground water rights come in different forms. Absolute ownership is an unrestricted right to any use you want from underneath your own land, even if the underground aquifer you are draining extends under many other parcels of land. Water rights may not always be absolute and can have limitations related to waste or overconsumption or prejudicial or negative motives.

Many of the world's banks and investment firms have been buying up water rights in recent years. Wealthy tycoons such as T. Boone Pickens, former president George H. W.

7.   Vicki Been and Josiah Madar, "Buying Sky: The Market for Transferable Development Rights in New York City," NYU Furman Center, Oct. 2013, https://furmancenter.org/research/publication/buying-sky-the-market-for-transferable-development-rights-in-new-york-city.
8.   Charles V. Bagli, "With $240 Million Deal, Floodgates Open for Air Rights in Midtown East," *New York Times*, Mar. 2018, https://www.nytimes.com/2018/03/02/nyregion/jp-morgan-chase-midtown-east-air-rights.html.

Bush and his family, Hong Kong's Li Kashing, the Philippines' Manuel V. Pangilinan and other billionaires are buying thousands of acres of land with aquifers, lakes, water rights, water utilities and shares in water engineering and technology companies all over the world.[9]

Strategies for investing in water not only include direct investments in water rights, but also investments in water filtrations, distribution, recycling, purification and bottling. Opportunities exist to invest in infrastructure to convert untreated water into drinkable water both in the United States and in many countries around the world. The lack of available water also makes investments in bottled water and other beverages more attractive. Water-related investment funds include public companies, water-focused mutual funds, ETFs and hedge funds. Today there are ample opportunities to obtain exposure via public and private funds and vehicles investing in water assets and resources.

Timber

Timber is an investment that is more institutional than many other exotic alternative investment categories. Investing in timber covers a wide variety of geographies and products. Different regions and different types of trees and wood products all have different weather, scarcity value and supply and demand characteristics. Timber prices tend to be more volatile than land values themselves. Investors in timber are investing in trees and wood products and often lease the land from the landowner. Growth rates and forecasts of weather can be complex in ways similar to agricultural products. Valuation of timber licenses or production and distribution is a function of discounting the cash flows from operations and futures sales. In this regard, it is subject to interest rate risk. Timber tends to hold its value during recessions or slumps in other markets because it has intrinsic value. It is also often a good hedge against inflation.

Timber can be owned by buying land and planting trees and then selling the trees or the by-products directly. There are also many public companies and mutual funds and real estate investment trusts that own land and trees for resale. Some of the larger public vehicles are offered by real estate investment trusts operated by public companies. ETFs and timber investment management corporations are also available for investing in timber and wood.

Revenue from the timber industry, shown in Figure 9.5, was $1.6 billion in 2019. The revenue has grown 5.1% annually from 2014 to 2019 and is expected to grow at a rate of 1% annually from 2019 to 2024. The industry is expected to grow 1% per year over the next five years. Rising wages and a decrease in the number of businesses are also putting pressure on profit margins. The industry profit margin was 7.2% in 2019.[10]

---

9. Jo-Shing Yang, "The New 'Water Barons': Wall Street Mega-Banks Are Buying Up the World's Water," Global Research, Oct. 2019, https://www.globalresearch.ca/the-new-water-barons-wall-street-mega-banks-are-buying-up-the-worlds-water/5383274.

10. Thomas Henry, "Timber Services in the US," IBISWorld, Mar. 2020, https://my.ibisworld.com/us/en/industry/11311/industry-at-a-glance.

Total Revenue in 2019	Annual Growth 2014–2019	Annual Growth 2019–2024	Profit Margin in 2019	Wages as a share of Revenue in 2019	Number of Businesses 2014–2019
$1.6 bn	5.1%	1.0%	7.2%	17.8%	-1.6%

Figure 9.5. IBISWorld statistics related to the timber industry for 2019.

Industry Products & Services Segmentation

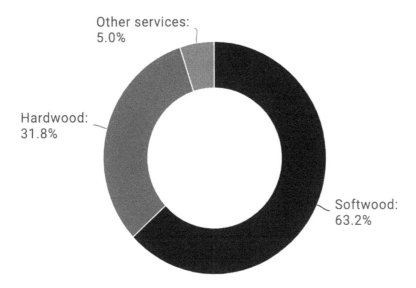

Other services: 5.0%

Hardwood: 31.8%

Softwood: 63.2%

Figure 9.6. IBISWorld segmentation of the timber industry for 2019.

The largest revenue segment, shown in Figure 9.6, is softwood at 63.2%, followed by hardwood at 31.8% and with all other sources accounting for just 5%.[11]

Who Invests in Farmland, Air, Water and Timber?

According to a survey by U.S. Trust of its high-net-worth- and ultra-high-net-worth individual clients in 2016, the use of real assets in portfolios, including farmland and timber properties, is both significant and increasing. Nearly half of the wealthy surveyed owned tangible assets, up from 41% in an earlier survey in 2016. Investors were attracted to the asset due to its low volatility. The ability of these sorts of investments to provide downside

---

11. *2016 U.S. Trust Insights on Wealth and Worth—Annual Survey of High-Net-Worth and Ultra-High-Net-Worth Americans*, 2016, https://www.privatebank.bankofamerica.com/publish/content/application/pdf/GWMOL/USTp_ARXDJKR8_2017-05.pdf.

protections and their relatively low correlation to traditional stocks and bonds are some of the reasons for the increased use in asset allocation. Other reasons include this asset class' ability to deliver attractive risk-adjusted returns with both income and long-term growth.[12]

Institutional investors also invest in farmland and timber as part of an alternative investment allocation. They are attracted to the asset class' strong risk-adjusted return and hybrid characteristics of providing both growth, income and a hedge against inflation.

How to Invest?

Like many other alternative investments, you can choose to invest directly in land or negotiate air and water rights for specific domains, invest in companies that operate farms, grow and process timber, own and manage water or purchase and sell air rights or in funds that invest directly or own companies that have exposures. Direct investments can be obtained by using platforms as well. This provides investors with direct exposure to individual assets. The investors can build their own portfolio as they wish. Many investors choose to invest in public companies, mutual funds, ETFs or private funds to gain exposure. This allows investors to obtain additional diversification and allows for reliance upon expert managers to run the portfolio and manage exposures.

Benchmarks and Indices

The NCREIF Farmland Index is a time series composite measure of the return from a large pool of individual farmland properties owned by private market participants for investment purposes. The index can be filtered by both permanent cropland and annual cropland. The index can be found at https://www.ncreif.org/data-products/farmland/.

S&P Global Timber and Forestry Index (SPGTTF) is an index that comprises the 25 largest publicly traded companies engaged in the ownership, management or the upstream supply chain of forests and timberlands. The index launched in August 2007. For more information, visit the company's website at https://us.spindices.com/indices/equity/sp-global-timber-and-forestry-index.

There are several water-related indices and benchmarks available. Indices and benchmarks in this sector include the Credit Suisse Water Index, HSBC Water, Waste and Pollution Control Index, Merrill Lynch China Water Index, S&P Global Water Index, First Trust ISE Water Index Fund (FIW) and the International Securities Exchange's ISE-B&S Water Index. The ISE Clean Water Index can be found at https://indexes.nasdaqomx.com/Index/History/HHO.

---

12. *2016 U.S. Trust Insights on Wealth and Worth.*

Firms, Funds and Platforms for Farmland, Timber, Air and Water Investments

Farmland Partners Inc. (FPI) is a publicly traded real estate company that owns and seeks to acquire high-quality farmland addressing the demand for food, feed, fiber and fuel. As of March 2019, FPI owned over 162,000 acres throughout 17 states which are farmed by over 125 tenants growing over 30 crops. As of October 2019, the company had a market cap of $349 million. For more information, visit the company's website at http://www.farmlandlp.com.

The iShares Global Timber and Forestry ETF is a publicly traded ETF managed by iShares that seeks to track the investment results of an index composed of equities in or related to the timber and forestry industry. The ETF was founded in 2008 and is traded on the NASDAQ. The fund's benchmark is the S&P Global Timber and Forestry Index. As of October 30, 2019, the ETF had 25 holdings including Svenska Cellulosa, Weyerhaeuser REIT, West Fraser Timber and Suzano SA and $250 million in assets under management. For more information, visit the company's website at https://www.ishares.com/us/products/239752/ishares-global-timber-forestry-etf.

Invesco MSCI Global Timber ETF is managed by Invesco and seeks to mimic the MSCI ACWI IMI Timber Select Capped Index by allocating at least 90% of its capital to securities held by it. The fund tracks the performance of securities engaged in the ownership or management of forests, timberlands and production of products using timber as raw materials. The ETF was founded in November 2007, and as of October 2019 had holdings including UPM-Kymmene Oyj, Weyerhaeuser Corp., Mondi PLC, Avery Dennison Corp. and Westrock Co. and assets under management of $139 million. For more information, visit the company's website at https://www.invesco.com/portal/site/us/investors/etfs/product-detail?productId=CUT&ticker=CUT&title=invesco-msci-global-timber-etf.

The Organics ETF is managed by Janus Henderson and seeks to track the Solactive Organic Index and provide investors with exposure to companies globally that service, produce, distribute, market or sell organic food, beverage, cosmetics, supplements or packaging. The fund was founded in June 2016 and as of October 2019 had $7.35 million of AUM with holdings including Hansen Holding' Sprout's Farmers Market Inc., Hain Celestial Group Inc. and Ariake Japan Co. Ltd. For more information, visit the company's website at https://www.janushenderson.com/en-us/advisor/.

Invesco Water Resources ETF seeks to replicate the results of the NASDAQ OMX US Water Index SM. The fund will generally invest at least 90% of its total assets in common stocks, American depositary receipts (ADRs) and global depositary receipts (GDRs) of companies in the water industry that comprise the Underlying Index. As of October 2019, the ETF has around $1 billion AUM. For more information, visit Invesco's website at https://www.invesco.com/portal/site/us/investors/etfs/product-detail?productId=PHO.

The Invesco S&P Global Water Index ETF seeks to replicate the results of the S&P Global Water Index. The fund will generally invest at least 90% of its total assets in equities that comprise the index as well as ADRs and GDRs that support the index's holdings. As of October 2019, the ETF had around $700 million AUM. For more information, visit Invesco's website at https://www.invesco.com/portal/site/us/financial-professional/etfs/product-detail?productId=CGW&ticker=CGW&title=invesco-s-p-global-water-index-etf.

First Trust Water ETF seeks to generate investment results that generally match the ISE Clean Edge Water Index. The fund will typically invest at least 90% of its net assets in common stocks and depository receipts that comprise the index. As of October 2019, the ETF had around $500 million AUM. For more information, visit First Trust's website at https://www.ftportfolios.com/retail/etf/etfsummary.aspx?Ticker=FIW.

Weyerhaeuser is a public company traded on the New York Stock Exchange. It is one of the world's largest private owners of timberlands. Weyerhaeuser began operations in 1900 and owns/controls about 12 million acres of timberlands in the United States and Canada. In 2018, the company generated $7.5 billion of revenue, and as of October 2019 had a market cap of $21.3 billion. For more information, visit the company's website at https://www.weyerhaeuser.com.

Rayonier is a real estate investment trust that is traded on the NYSE. The company holds timberland real estate across the United States and New Zealand. As of October 2019, Rayonier controlled 2.6 million acres of timberlands and has customers in 38 countries with a market cap of $3.9 billion. For more information, visit the company's website at www.rayonier.com.

Potlatch Deltic is a real estate investment trust traded on NASDAQ. The company owns 1.9 million acres of timberlands throughout the six states and has a strong focus on environmental conservation and sustainability. The company also operates saw mills, plywood mills and a rural timberland sales program. As of October 2019, the company had a market cap of $2.85 billion. For more information, visit the company's website at https://www.potlatchdeltic.com.

American Water Works Co. Inc. is a public utility company based in Camden, New Jersey. It was founded in 1886 and operates in both the United States and Canada. AWK provides regulated and market-based drinking water, wastewater services and other related services to an estimated 14 million people. As of October 2019, AWK had a market cap of $21 billion. For more information, visit the company's website at https://amwater.com/corp/.

American States Water Co. is an American water and electricity utility company based in San Dimas, California, and is the parent company of the Golden State Water Co. and American States Utility Services Inc. AWR primarily manages water and wastewater on military bases throughout the country under long-term private contracts with the US government. As of October 2019, AWR held a market cap of around $3.5 billion. For more information, visit the company's website at http://www.aswater.com.

Agua America is a water and wastewater utility company that provides drinking water and wastewater services to about 3 million people in Pennsylvania, Ohio, North Carolina, Illinois, Texas, New Jersey, Indiana and Virginia. As of October 2019, WTR had a market cap of around $10 billion. For more information, visit the company's website at https://www.aquaamerica.com.

Calvert Global Water Fund seeks to generally mimic the performance of the Calvert Global Water Research Index. The fund typically allocated at least 80% of its assets to both domestic and international equities whose primary services involve water-related services or technologies. Additionally, the fund only invests in companies that perform their services sustainably and in a manner that promotes efficiency and access. CFWAX, as of October 2019, held net assets totaling around $400 million. For more information, visit the fund's website at https://www.calvert.com/Calvert-Global-Water-Fund-CFWAX.php.

Allianz RCM Global Water Fund allocates at least 80% of its net assets in equities of companies that are tracked by at least one of the S&P Global Water Index, the NASDAQ OMX US Water, Global Water Indices or S-Network Global Water Index. All primary operations held by the company are water-related. As of October 2019, the fund held around $625 million of net assets. For more information, visit the fund's website at https://us.allianzgi.com/en-us/products-solutions/mutual-funds/allianzgi-global-water-fund-a-awtax.

Ceres Partners is a private equity fund focused on food and agriculture. The manager has two funds: Ceres Farms LLC, which invests in US farmland, and Ceres Food and Agriculture Opportunity Fund, which invests growth equity in food and agriculture businesses. Ceres Farms LLC is a commingled fund that launched in 2007 to acquire and manage agricultural land. As of March 31, 2019, the fund had total assets of $787 million. For more information, visit the manager's website at https://www.cerespartners.com.

Homestead Capital is a private investment firm focused on acquiring farmland assets throughout the US Homestead Capital USA Farmland Fund II closed in 2016 with a committed capital of $400 million. The fund acquires farm investments in the Mountain West, Pacific, Midwest and Delta regions and constructs a diversified portfolio of assets. Homestead has raised a total of $923 million across three funds. For more information, visit the manager's website at http://www.homesteadcapital.com.

Stafford Capital Partners is a private investment fund that provides investment and advisory services in agriculture and food, infrastructure and timberland. Stafford was founded in 2002 and most recently raised Stafford International Timberland VIII to an amount of $612.5 million. Stafford has over $5.3 billion under management, according to its website. For more information, visit the manager's website: https://www.staffordcp.com.

BTG Pactual Timberland Investment Group is a private investment fund that is now one of the largest timberland managers globally. According to its website, it has nearly $3.5 billion in assets and commitments with over 2.2 million acres currently under management. For more information, visit the manager's website: https://timberlandinvestmentgroup.com.

Water Asset Management LLC is a hedge fund manager based in New York that employs a long and short equity strategy to make investments in the global water and water infrastructure industries. WAM manages TRF Master Fund, which was created in March 2012 and as of October 2019 had $341 million AUM, according to Preqin data. For more information, visit the fund's website at http://waterinv.com.

Table 9.1. The performance, risk and correlation of a composite of farmland, timber and water investment vehicles versus the S&P 500 between January 2016 and December 2019.

	Timber, Farmland, Air Rights	S&P 500
Correlation	0.86	NA
Standard Deviation	12.67%	11.56%
Average Annual Return	13.54%	14.33%
Simplified Sharpe	1.07	1.24

XPV Water Partners is a Canada-based private equity fund that invests growth capital in emerging water companies that focus on any business that improves the management of water. Since its inception in 2005, XPV has raised $400 million, according to Preqin data. For more information, visit the fund's website at https://www.xpvwaterpartners.com.

There are also a few exchanges and websites that offer water rights for purchase and sale, such as waterrightexchange.com, watercolorado.com and waterbank.com.

Composite

A composite of farmland, timber and water investments, shown in Table 9.1, had returns and volatility similar to that of the S&P 500 between January 2016 and December 2019. The correlation was 0.86 and the Sharpe ratio was slightly lower at 1.07 versus 1.24.

A $1,000 investment in a farmland, timber, air and water rights composite in January 2016, shown in Figure 9.7, would have grown to almost $1,662 by December 2019 compared to $1,708 for the S&P 500. Most of the underperformance during the period came during 2019.

Social, Legal and Ethical Considerations

Arguments against private use of seemingly natural or public resources have existed in the United States and other countries for many years. Investing in natural resources that are of a limited supply is not without controversy. Many environmentalists take issue with the accumulation of land and water resources by financially oriented investors who are focused on profits alone. Some view these resources as public goods that should be highly regulated, available to all and not hoarded for profit. Some people are critical of large-scale commercial land projects that use a disproportionate amount of water at the expense of locals who need water for daily living.

Trends and Outlook

Natural resources like land, water and airspace will likely experience increased demand as the global and emerging market population demand for materials, space and food increases faster than increases in the relatively fixed supply of these resources or gains related to productivity. This will tend to support prices for a variety of land, water and airspace usages including farming, water consumption and urban development.

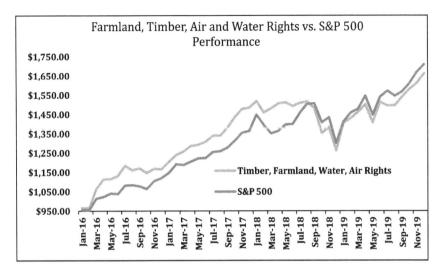

Figure 9.7. The growth of $1,000 invested in farmland, water and timber investments versus the $1,000 invested in the S&P 500 from January 2016 to December 2019.

Farmland values have benefited for a long-term fall in interest rates since the 1990s. Increases in land acquisition costs and values naturally lead to higher rents. These trends tend to benefit owners of land and investors at the expense of farmers. According to a report from the USDA, in 2018, US farmland values rose significantly from 2000 to 2015. Average per-acre farm real estate values doubled from $1,483 per acre in 2000 to $3,060 per acre in 2015. The report found that cropland appreciated faster than pastureland. The study went on to say that rising land prices were putting pressure on returns and that future returns would be heavily impacted by changes in interest rate. Rising rates could lead to a significant drop in values.

In addition, trade wars between the United States and China could negatively impact demand for many crops that are currently supported by exports to China. Lower demand and rising rates could squeeze the profitability of some farmland investments over time.[13]

According to a report from the United Nations Environment Program, half the world will face water stress by 2030 as demand outpaces supply in most parts of the world. The report states that agricultural demand accounts for some 70% of all global freshwater demand. As the global population increases, it is likely that agriculture will continue to exert growing pressure on a limited universe of clean water resources.[14]

---

13. Christopher Burns et al., "Farmland Values, Land Ownership and Returns to Farmland, 2000–2016," USDA, Feb. 2018, https://www.ers.usda.gov/webdocs/publications/87524/err245_summary.pdf?v=0.
14. Shereen Zorba, "Half the World to Face Severe Water Stress by 2030 Unless Water Use is 'Decoupled'," UN Environment Program, Mar. 2016, https://www.unenvironment.org/news-and-stories/press-release/half-world-face-severe-water-stress-2030-unless-water-use-decoupled.

Better management of water resources and waste in many urban centers is seen as one way to perhaps make better use of available supply and meet increases in demand. Improvements in farmland productivity and water usage initiatives can also help manage water resources.

Demand for timber to be used in construction is seeing an increase in many markets in the United States. Improvements in safety and new technology are positioning commercial and industrial sites built with wood as a green alternative that is more sustainable than steel and concrete structures. Some industry groups, architects and designers view wood as a natural and self-sustaining resource that can be managed effectively to meet demand without adding cost or compromising safety.[15]

Trends in air rights are closely tied to trends in urbanization and real estate development. Air rights will generally increase in value in cities where urban expansion is taking place.

Manager Perspectives and Insights

Carter Malloy, CEO, AcreTrader

Carter grew up in a farming family and has a lifelong passion for investing and agriculture. Prior to AcreTrader, he was part of an equity investment firm for five years. Before joining AcreTrader in 2013, Carter was a managing director with Stephens Inc., a large private investment bank where he was an equity research analyst focused on the internet, data and analytics and real estate processing sectors. Prior to Stephens, he owned small businesses focused on Internet marketing and sustainable fuel technologies. He graduated from the University of Arkansas with a Bachelor's degree in Physics and has previously held Series 7, 63, 86 and 87 licenses with the Financial Industry Regulatory Authority (FINRA).

Why do you believe farmland is an attractive investment?
Land is one of the oldest investment classes in existence, producing enormous wealth over generations. We think US farmland represents an attractive, long-term investment while providing significant relative capital preservation during times of economic turmoil. At a risk of oversimplifying the economics, there is a limited and shrinking amount of supply (we lose three acres of farmland per minute in the United States (source: American Farmland Trust)) and consistently increasing demand via a growing global population. This has led to stable increases in farmland values of roughly 6% annually for the past approximately 50 years [source: USDA]. In addition to asset appreciation, the landowner typically receives cash rent from the farmer that can be 3%–5% of yield annually. Assuming reinvestment of returns, farmland has produced over 11% annual unlevered returns to its investors since 1990 [source: NCREIF].

---

15. Think Wood, https://www.thinkwood.com/about.

With a growing global population and shrinking US farmland acreage, the laws of supply and demand are clearly in favor of farmland investing. As a result, the aforementioned farmland returns have consistently beat other asset classes over time. Perhaps more impressive is the consistency of farmland returns over time. While the value of gold or stock markets can go down over 30% or 40% in a single year, farmland returns have been positive every year since 1990 (the first year of the NCREIF index).

What are the risks associated with farmland investing?

As with any form of investing, there are asset-specific as well as macro risks associated with farmland investing. While the price impact of these risks has been muted on an aggregate basis historically, each is worth substantial investor diligence.

Asset-specific risks are risks that are typically unique to agriculture and/or real estate. Agricultural risks include the quality of soil, long-term access to water and the quality/size of the local tenant pool. In particular, having sustainable access to water is critical; without water, dry land farming such as wheat can be substantially less lucrative than irrigated crops. The local tenant pool is also a unique risk to farmland. Assuring that your current tenant is well qualified and is adhering to best practices is important, but it is equally important to make sure there are alternative leases in the area should things not work out with your current tenant.

Some of the big picture risks of farmland investing include overpaying for land and potential long-term commodity price pressures. With regard to overpaying, the simple real estate adage of "you make your money when you buy" applies well to farmland. Making sure that the farm-specific factors are all attractive is important, but it is also vital to apply proper valuation to each farmland investment.

In addition to purchase price, commodity prices are an important long-term macro risk. In general, a growing global population has led to commodity price inflation over time, in turn leading to increased farm income and increased farmland prices. However, trade wars and their associated tariffs are a specific risk that impact US commodity export volumes and thus commodity prices received by US farmers. While these may be short-term in nature, reduced commodity prices can lead to income volatility for the farmer and potential pressures for the landowner as well.

Please note that the above risks are only a limited sample, as each farm and each local area presents idiosyncrasies perhaps not spelled out here. This is why it is important to work with a well-qualified local representative or investment portal like AcreTrader when evaluating farmland investments.

Where does or should farmland fit into portfolio construction and asset allocation?

We see varying levels of asset allocation to farmland, with some farmers having upwards of 100% of their investments being in land and some online investors looking to make farmland 10% or 20% of their overall portfolio. We don't provide investment advice, but there are some great resources online, including research done by various institutional investors such the Teachers Insurance and Annuity Association of America, showing these types of allocation levels as a target.

What is perhaps most interesting is that the vast majority of investors have no farmland investments at all and that is why we created AcreTrader. Given the attractive historical risk-adjusted returns of farmland in the context of little correlation to other asset classes, we think it makes sense as a consideration for any well-diversified modern investment portfolio.

Barbara Keady, Director of Marketing, Ceres Partners

Barbara Keady is the director of Marketing at Ceres Partners, based in South Bend, Indiana. Ceres Partners is a specialist investment manager focused exclusively on food and agriculture. Ceres Partners manages two investment vehicles with distinct strategies and investment objectives. Ceres Farms LLC invests in US farmland and the Ceres Food and Agriculture Opportunity Fund invests in growth equity in emerging operating businesses in food and agriculture. Barbara is responsible for new business development and guiding the firm's overall marketing efforts. She received a B.S. from the McIntire School of Commerce at the University of Virginia and an MBA in Finance from Columbia University. Barbara started her career at Bankers Trust Co. in their fixed income sales department, covering pensions, corporations and money funds in the Mid-Atlantic region. She then worked as an associate in the Private Wealth Management group at Morgan Stanley in New York, selling the firm's asset management services to high-net-worth individuals, endowments and foundations. She serves as a director of Sprott Focus Trust (FUND) Board and holds the 7, 63 and 24 securities licenses.

What sort of properties or geographies does the fund buy or focus on?
Ceres is a row-crop-focused, US farmland fund with a focus on the corn belt and lake states. We look to be a value buyer, leasing our properties to sophisticated tenant partners who view us as a capital partner. We believe row crop farmland provides better risk/return metrics over the long term. We own the land, but are passive, not active operators. In addition to commodity crops, we allocate to specialty crops which historically provide a higher return for the fund. We focus on the US Midwest because this is the low-cost region of the low-cost country with plentiful water resources. We focus on the United States because we are confident in the rule of law here and lack of political volatility relative to other growing regions in the world.

What is the expected return relative to traditional investments?
There are three components of return: rental income, passive appreciation of the farmland and any value add that is made installing irrigation, clearing timber and so on. Looking at the return of farmland versus other asset classes over a 20-year period, you will note that on a risk-adjusted basis, farmland has equity-like returns with bond-like volatility.

What are some of the biggest risks?
There are several risks in farmland investment. A strong dollar, overall excess supply due to perfect weather conditions globally and of course a trade war. Permanent crops have individual idiosyncratic risk, that is, are almonds more in vogue than walnuts or pistachios? Weather, access to water and the rule of law are important considerations when determining your geographic investment. As a row crop manager, we spend a

tremendous amount of time sourcing our tenant farmers. We need to have confidence in their ability to be good stewards of the land as this is a long-term investment for our LPs.

Advances in technology can also provide both risk and reward. Will the impossible burger make a dent in overall beef consumption? How have milk substitutes such as almond, soy, coconut affected dairy production?

Where does this investment fit in terms of asset allocation for investors and what sort of investors are investing today?

There really is no "typical" bucket within which farmland is placed. Given its attributes of income generation, historically low volatility, inflation protection and diversification, I have seen it placed in the following allocations: Real Assets, Real Estate, Inflation Protection, Bond Substitute and Natural Resources.

There is very little institutional ownership of US farmland, estimated at less than 3%. Most farms are owned by passive landlords (i.e., trusts and estates). Farm turnover per year is also extremely low at approximately 1%. We are seeing an increase in interest across all verticals with respect to farmland investment. Pensions, endowments and family offices recognize the benefits of direct farmland investments mentioned above. As more research is done on the space, I expect more managers will look to raise funds across the agriculture complex globally.

Academic Perspectives and Research

Academic articles relating to farmland and water rights as an investable asset began to take prominence in 2007. During this time, commodities were experiencing a price boom, which subsequently meant that farmlands attached to commodities were booming as well. Institutional investors became interested and started investing in the sector. Even after the 2008 recession, while there was a short dip in farmland prices, the uncertainty in overall investment opportunities caused investors to seek out alternative, more secure places to store their money and farmland was an attractive solution to this problem. Investors found farmland an attractive investment because of the continued capital gains appreciation in the land itself, as well as the productive uses of growing crops. Recent academic articles provide an overview of how the farmland industry has evolved, investment vehicles that can be used to participate in the industry and how the system can be changed for the better.

One prominent article by Madeleine Fairbairn examines investment vehicles for farmland and the potential risks it poses to agricultural operators. One investment vehicle used to gain exposure to farmland is a FIMO or a Farmland Investment Management Organization. FIMOs typically require a minimum investment of $50 million, which make them accessible only to institutions and extremely wealthy individuals. Traditionally, FIMOs tended to take a long-term view of farmland assets where land was held for many years or sometimes decades, as a source of rental income and a store of value. More recently, two new types of FIMOs have emerged that have their roots in the financial and agricultural operator sectors, respectively. The first structure is a farmland private equity fund, which is usually structured with a standard 2/20 fee structure. While the farmland private equity fund may have higher fees, they typically have a much lower barrier to entry, with a minimum of $200,000 investment. With the private equity structure, they must return funds to investors after an agreed-upon period, typically anywhere from five to ten years. Managers of the fund return capital by either taking the entire fund public, selling the properties or rolling the properties over to a new fund. The second structure originates from agricultural operators that are looking to capitalize on the high rates of appreciation of their land. The operators do this by spinning off their farmland portfolio into a separate asset management business. By doing this, it allows the farmland operators to acquire much more land from the new funds and participate in the price appreciation of the assets. Fairbairn concludes the article with the dangers that the securitization of finance plays in the farmland sector. Many farms in the United States are small businesses and the financialization tends to prefer consolidation into larger plots of land. In parts of the country where legal title is murky, but where families have held the property for at times generations, a financial institution with an ironclad property title will come at the expense of the residents. Additionally, short-term, speculative investments pursued by private equity funds could lead to careless treatment of the soil and water resources on the property and surrounding areas.[16]

Another article by Bill Howard from the Callan Investments Institute provides an overview of investing in farmland. The purpose of the paper is to examine key characteristics of investing in farmland and risks posed to outside investors. The paper stated that investors sensitive to inflation or those that would like to shift assets away from fixed income to boost returns without increasing overall volatility would be good candidates for investing in farmland. The biggest risk of investing in farmland is supply and demand. Overharvesting in seasons can lead to excess supply, which would decrease the price of the crop and the underlying land. Economic slowdowns, trade barriers and changes in farming subsidies could lead to drastic changes in demand, which could also decrease the price of farmland. Other large risk factors include weather and disease, which would severely impact the quality of the farmland and decrease the asset's value.[17]

Another article by Mike Young from the Federal Reserve Bank of Kansas City examines how water management in the United States can be improved to increase its value. Young provides an overview of Australia's successful water reform back in the 1990s and how the United States could use their success as a model. Young also provides an overview of the US water market. Finally, Young speculates on what the United States could change to improve its water market.

Australia implemented national agreements and laws that resulted in massive benefits for rural communities, the economy and the environment. Additionally, the value of water rights in the Southern Connected River Murray System, which is Australia's most

---

16. Madeleine Fairbairn, "Like Gold with Yield," *Journal of Peasant Studies*, Jan. 2014, https://www.tandfonline.com/doi/full/10.1080/03066150.2013.873977.

17. Bill Howard, "Farmland Investing: An Overview," Callan Investments Institute, Dec. 2005, https://www.pionline.com/assets/archive/docs/Callan%20Farmland%20Investing%20Paper.pdf.

important and largest water source, increased by well over 15% per year for a decade. The author suggests that this directly contrasts how water rights are viewed in the United States where water reform is seen as a zero-sum game or a fight for the biggest share of the pie. Next, Young outlines how water trading and the water market work. There are two types of trading in the water market: allocation trading and entitlement trading. Allocation trading occurs with a specific volume of water that may be taken from a system within a nominated period of time. Entitlement trading is a perpetual entitlement to a share of all allocations made. Lastly, Young states that while the Australian water reform can serve as a base model, there are complications with their system and context-specific issues that the United States will need to adapt to. Despite this caveat, Young provides four central concepts that would improve the water trading system and market in the United States. These central concepts are unbundling, improving and validating existing water rights, establishing robust water resource plans, transitioning toward decision-making structures characterized by trust, efficiency and rigorous enforcement and assigning water entitlements to the environment. From these broad concepts, Young lays out 10 concrete opportunities for the United States to improve its water system.[18]

Summary

Global trends related to population growth and urbanization tend to support the conclusion that demand is increasing faster than the supply for farmland, timber, water and air rights. This may lead to a higher return on investment in these assets in the future. Global trade wars, changes in interest rates and improvements in technology are certainly risks that could lead to lower prices and returns. However, the correlation of these investments to traditional stocks and bonds should provide investors with an opportunity to lower portfolio risk and improve Sharpe ratios, if not absolute returns.

Useful Websites and Additional Reading

"Air Rights," https://www.planning.org/pas/reports/report186.htm.
"Buy Me a River: Purchasing Water Rights to Restore River Flows in the Western USA," https://onlinelibrary.wiley.com/doi/full/10.1111/1752-1688.12808?casa_token=CW9o-mruSjIAAAAA%3AQ8eT6-77arcFCpQ9N9KdJseH4IFjHs3kOs VUA2pAtpn09ZJsiLiUGlo7r13RPR84eaKpQwgskSlMxdo.
"Diversify Your Portfolio by Investing in Timber," https://money.usnews.com/investing/real-estate-investments/articles/2018-09-07/diversify-your-portfolio-by-investing-in-timber.
"The Economics of the Tropical Timber Trade," https://www.taylorfrancis.com/books/9780429352249.

---

18. Mike Young, "Water Allocation in the West: Challenges and Opportunities," Federal Reserve Bank of Kansas City, 2016, https://aquadoc.typepad.com/files/si16young.pdf.

"From Financialization to Operations of Capital: Historicizing and Disentangling the Finance–Farmland Nexus," https://www.sciencedirect.com/science/article/pii/S001671851630046X?casa_token=TwaK9X-hSk0AAAAA:Fl-slVVSR4ssD2IR47h2z72QIzMwDQRCsBXs14vls1kjDbw4bMgTO2cwzLF_wzwPSVuqDn3r_Os.

"The Great Air Race," https://www.nytimes.com/2013/02/24/realestate/the-great-race-for-manhattan-air-rights.html.

"Investing in Agribusiness Stocks and Farmland: A Boom or Bust Analysis," https://digitalcommons.usu.edu/etd/7162/.

"'Like Gold with Yield': Evolving Intersections between Farmland and Finance," https://www.tandfonline.com/doi/full/10.1080/03066150.2013.873977.

"Markets in Tradable Water Rights: Potential for Efficiency Gains in Developing Country Water Resource Allocation," https://www.sciencedirect.com/science/article/abs/pii/0305750X94000751.

"Sustainable Farmland Investment Strategies," https://cbey.yale.edu/sites/default/files/2019-09/Sustainable%20Farmland%20Investment%20Strategies_Nov%202016.pdf.

Chapter Ten

CANNABIS AND ALTERNATIVE MEDICINES

Introduction

Today there are quite a few new and emerging drugs and therapies used for medical, commercial or recreational applications, including medical and recreational cannabis, homeopathic products and genome therapies. The focus of this chapter is on the investment potential offered by cannabis-related products and applications.

Cannabis

Cannabis has had a long history of use in the United States, albeit mostly an illegal one. That is until recently. Nowadays, depending on the applicable laws and regulations, plant extracts can be used for recreational, medicinal or cosmetic applications. It is a popular drug that has gained a lot of attention given its dual recreational and medicinal applications. The potential impact of legalized cannabis on tobacco, alcoholic beverages and the medical, pharmaceutical and cosmetics communities is significant. It has the potential to be a potential substitute for tobacco and/or alcoholic beverages for some portion of the populace, as well as being a replacement for existing medicines and a new treatment for many types of illnesses or pain management. It is also a source of new products and applications for the healthcare and cosmetics industries.

Many, if not most, people associate cannabis with recreational usage in the form of marijuana. In this way, it may be a substitute or alternative to alcohol and tobacco. However, today we increasingly see more opportunities for the plant to be used for both its far-reaching medical benefits and in cosmetic products such as make-up, facial creams or oils. Cannabis plant extracts are used in the treatment of a wide range of diseases beyond just pain management. Today it is being used to treat symptoms associated with cancer, chronic pain, depression, arthritis, diabetes, glaucoma, migraines, epilepsy and Alzheimer's, among other illnesses. The current growth in the legal cannabis industry is being driven by a shift in in demand of black-market recreational users moving over to the legal market, by the increasing number of medical professionals recommending cannabis for its medicinal and therapeutic benefits and by a rising demand from the cosmetics industry.

The marijuana industry lacks uniform federal regulations. This is despite the fact that according to some surveys, more than 62% of Americans are in favor of federally legalized marijuana.[1] Canada was the first G7 country to legalize marijuana at the national level. It will likely serve as a template for federal legalization and regulation in the United States as well.

In 1996, California passed Proposition 215, also known as the Compassionate Use Act. California was the first state in the United States to legalize medical marijuana as part of the treatment of certain serious diseases, including cancer and AIDS. In 2012, Colorado and Washington became the first two states to legalize the recreational use of marijuana. Today, there are 33 states that have legalized cannabis in some form or another. As many as 10 of those states have fully legalized marijuana for recreational use.[2] Florida has legalized medicinal marijuana but does not permit recreational use of the drug. Florida has granted 22 licenses for the cultivation of marijuana and is in the process of establishing a scalable program that awards new licenses as the patient database of eligible users increases over time.[3] The supply of marijuana licenses has not kept pace with the demand, creating huge premiums for those wishing to buy or sell a license on the secondary market. A license to cultivate and sell marijuana in Florida recently sold for $40 million. New York has decriminalized marijuana and legalized limited medical usage, but not legalized it. Even so, a license to grow marijuana recently sold in New York for $26 million.[4] Elsewhere in the United States, there is growing acceptance of marijuana in the medical field; for example, in 2018, the largest healthcare provider in Utah gave its physicians permission to recommend medical marijuana to patients where appropriate. Eventually, supply will most likely catch up to demand. For example, Colorado has issued approximately 1,400 licenses for cultivators for a population of just 5.5 million people.

A Few Definitions, Key Terms and Phrases

Cannabis is a plant with two important species. These two variants are known as either marijuana or hemp plants. Marijuana and hemp are variants of one plant species consisting of hundreds of chemical compounds such as cannabinoids, flavonoids, terpenes, proteins and amino acids. These chemical compounds can interact to create a unique experience or effect. The cannabis plants produce both cannabinoids and cannabidiols.

1. Hannah Hartig and A. W. Geiger, "About Six-in-Ten Americans Support Marijuana Legislation," Fact Tank, Oct. 2018, https://www.pewresearch.org/fact-tank/2018/10/08/americans-support-marijuana-legalization/.
2. Hannah Hartig and A. W. Geiger, "State Medical Marijuana Laws," *National Conference of State Legislatures*, Sept. 2019, http://www.ncsl.org/research/health/state-medical-marijuana-laws.aspx.
3. Dara Kam, "Florida Gov. Ron DeSantis Approves 8 New Medical Marijuana Licenses," *Orlando Weekly*, Apr. 2019, https://www.orlandoweekly.com/Blogs/archives/2019/04/19/gov-ron-desantis-approves-8-new-medical-marijuana-licenses.
4. Kris Krane, "Cannabis Cultivation Will Be a Race to the Bottom," *Forbes*, Apr. 2018, www.forbes.com/sites/kriskrane/2018/04/25/cannabis-cultivation-will-be-a-race-to-the-bottom/#4a63a29a4184.

The most well-known cannabinoid is Tetrahydrocannabinol (THC). It is the chemical that comes from the marijuana plant that is responsible for most of cannabis's psychological effects and thus its recreational usage.

Cannabidiols or CBD are the chemical ingredients derived from the hemp plant that is used mostly in cosmetic or pharmaceutical applications.

Hemp is the name given to the strain of cannabis plant with a low THC component and a high CBD component

Medical marijuana is a form of a CBD produced for medical use and only obtainable by prescription It is used to treat a variety of medical conditions such as pain, anxiety, nausea and glaucoma.

Edible cannabis products refer to those that are orally consumed and often include brownies, gummy bears and other foods or beverages.

A grower is someone who plants and cultivates either traditional cannabis or hemp plants. A dispensary is a store that can legally sell cannabis products, for either medical or recreational use.

A useful glossary of common terms and concepts related to cannabis and the cannabis-infused food products industry can be found using the following National Environmental Health Association link: https://www.neha.org/eh-topics/food-safety-0/cannabis-resources.

Market Participants and Industry Players

The cannabis industry is made up of growers, dispensers, consumers, regulators, researchers and many others. The industry is quite fragmented and has not consolidated in the United States, primarily due to the legal and regulatory risks associated with the industry.

Growers are mainly small-scale individual proprietors, as opposed to the larger-scale farmers found in other agricultural sectors in the United States. Individual proprietors can grow marijuana indoors for recreational use and resale. Growers allocate capital to invest in seeds, soil and lights and to spend money on electricity. It takes approximately 90 days for one growth cycle to occur. The grower's primary costs after real estate and seeds are lighting equipment, air conditioning and electricity.

A dispensary is a store located within a state that has approved marijuana for either recreational or medical sale and consumption. A typical dispensary in California could be set up with an annual operating cost of $500,000 for rent, staffing, business equipment and professional services, with an application fee of $1,000 and a license costing about $120,000.[5] According to COVA, a marijuana industry consultant, the average profit margin for recreational and medical cannabis dispensaries is typically between 15% and 20% after taxes. A dispensary that buys or grows marijuana at a cost of $1,200 per ounce and sells marijuana for $1,500 per ounce makes a 20% profit margin on sales. The store

---

5. Gary Cohen, "How Much Does It Cost to Open a Cannabis Dispensary?" Cova, May 2017, https://www.covasoftware.com/blog/the-true-cost-of-opening-a-cannabis-dispensary.

breaks even if it sells approximately 4–5 ounces per day. Stores that sell 10 ounces per day or more on a 365-day operational basis would generate over $1 million in annual profits. Private and public companies have been established that own one or more dispensaries in states that have legalized distribution.[6]

Large beverage companies, pharmaceutical companies and cosmetics companies have been investing opportunistically in research and development and buying stakes in smaller firms that are creating new products. Cannabis growth as a recreational drug directly competes with the alcohol and tobacco industries. It can replicate the effect of alcohol, with zero calories. This means that large food beverage and tobacco companies will either lose market share or, more likely, will add cannabis-related investments and products to their business model as a hedge against potential business disruption.

Many cannabis applications to the wellness and beauty sectors are also emerging. CBD, a hemp plant by-product, is making an impact as an additive to everyday foods such as granola and has been included as a wellness supplement in vitamins. According to the National Conference of State Legislatures, 41 states have set up cultivation and production programs to regulate the production of hemp for commercial and industrial usage.[7]

If the regulatory issues associated with cannabis become more certain or get resolved favorably, the industry is likely to consolidate and investment would likely accelerate. This means the industry players would shift from small-time owners and organizations to becoming controlled by large agricultural firms on the production side, large retailers on the distribution side (such as pharmacies) and global food, beverage and healthcare firms on the product development side. There is even some anecdotal evidence that Cannabis is helping solve pet anxiety problems, although it is not yet widely prescribed by veterinarians.[8]

Industry Associations and Best Practices

The Cannabis Trade Federation (CTF) was recently formed by 14 founding board members from the industry. According to the organization's website, CTF is a national coalition of cannabis-related businesses that represent all aspects of the industry, including cultivators, dispensaries, wholesalers, distributors and ancillary businesses. CTF's board is focused on creating a professional, credible and unified organization for the industry. For more information, visit the association's website at https://www.cannabistradefederation.com.

---

6. Ibid.
7. "State Industrial Hemp Statutes," National Conference of State Legislature, Aug. 2019, http://www.ncsl.org/research/agriculture-and-rural-development/state-industrial-hemp-statutes.aspx.
8. Kathleen Gray, "Pot for Pets: Here's How Vets and Others Say It Can Help," *Detroit Free Press*, Mar. 2019, https://www.freep.com/story/news/marijuana/2019/03/13/medical-marijuana-pets/3134109002/.

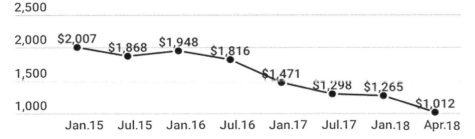

Figure 10.1. The market rate per pound of marijuana in Colorado from 2015 to 2018. *Source:* Colorado Department of Revenue

Estimates of Market Size

Global illegal market revenue from marijuana sales is estimated to be about $50 billion per year.[9] In 2015, retail sales of marijuana products reached $4.8 billion in revenue.[10] Jefferies estimates the legal marijuana industry will grow to $50 billion by 2029. These projections only capture the major markets where cannabis is currently fully legalized. Estimated employment in the cannabis industry exceeds 100,000 jobs in the United States already, many of them in high-tech agricultural jobs, as well as in the manufacturing, distribution and retail sectors.[11]

Migration of marijuana-based products from black markets to legitimate markets will generally have the effect of lowering prices. In Colorado, the price of a pound of marijuana flower has been steadily decreasing for some time. Figure 10.1 shows that a pound of marijuana has fallen from a high of approximately $2,007 in January 2015 to a recent low of approximately $1,000 in April 2018. This decline can be explained by an increase in legitimate suppliers and cultivators that started to appear in 2018. In this case, the supply is growing faster than demand. Despite the fall in price, Colorado has sold almost 500 tons of legal marijuana and topped $1 billion in revenue in 2018.[12]

9. Will Yakowicz, "Illegal Pot Sales Topped $46.4 Billion in 2016, and That's Good News for Marijuana Entrepreneurs," *Inc.*, Jan. 2017, https://www.inc.com/will-yakowicz/marijuana-sales-2016-50-billion.html.

10. Debra Borchardt, "Marijuana Industry Projected to Create More Jobs than Manufacturing by 2020," *Forbes*, Feb. 2017, www.forbes.com/sites/debraborchardt/2017/02/22/marijuana-industry-projected-to-create-more-jobs-than-manufacturing-by-2020/#4889b5643fa9.

11. Emily McCormick, "Jefferies Initiates Cannabis Coverage," *Yahoo Finance*, Feb. 2019, https://finance.yahoo.com/news/cannabis-coverage-industry-could-reach-130-billion-183926744.html.

12. Ryan Borzykowski, "Colorado Grows Annual Cannabis Sales to $ 1 Billion as Other States Struggle," *CNBC*, July 2019, https://www.cnbc.com/2019/07/10/colorado-cannabis-sales-hit-1-billion-as-other-states-rush-to-market.html.

Total Revenue in 2019	Annual Growth 2014–2019	Annual Growth 2019–2024	Profit Margin in 2019	Wages as a share of Revenue in 2019	Number of Businesses 2014–2019
$8.1 bn	25.7%	12.7%	11.6%	26.1%	21.3%

Figure 10.2. IBISWorld revenue and activity measures for the medical and recreational marijuana industry as of November 2019.

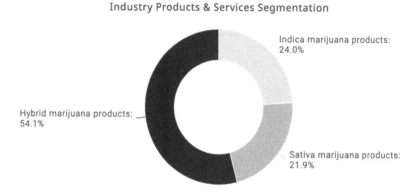

Industry Products & Services Segmentation

Indica marijuana products: 24.0%

Hybrid marijuana products: 54.1%

Sativa marijuana products: 21.9%

Figure 10.3. IBISWorld breakdown of the marijuana industry revenue by segment as of November 2019.

Revenue in the United States for the legal cannabis industry, shown in Figure 10.2, was $8.1 billion in 2019 according to IBISWorld research data. This figure has grown at an annual rate of 25.7% from 2014 to 2019 and is expected to grow at a rate of 12.7% from 2019 to 2024. Support for continued growth comes from a projected increase in discretionary income, more states legalizing recreational cannabis and increased physician visits growing the demand for medical cannabis. The industry profit margin was 11.6% in 2019.[13]

There are three types of revenue streams from products, shown in Figure 10.3. Sativa refers to products producing a high and Indica refers to products that relax the body. Revenues from Sativa products are estimated to be 21.9% and the revenue from Indica is estimated to be 24%, with the majority of revenues coming from at 54.1% of revenue.[14]

---

13. Cecilia Fernandez, "Medical & Recreational Marijuana Growing," IBISWorld, Nov. 2019, https://www.ibisworld.com/united-states/market-research-reports/medical-recreational-marijuana-growing-industry/.

14. Ibid.

Opportunities and Strategies

Opportunities to profit from the use of marijuana comes from any one of a number of strategies. The potential exists to profit from investing in production and licenses for either medicinal or recreational markets, investing in distribution facilities, investing in new beverages or tobacco products or investing in cosmetic products or companies who are likely to use such products to grow their market share or protect themselves against potential loss of market share and, finally, from investing in medicinal and therapeutic applications and opportunities.

There are several stages and investment opportunities that exist in marijuana. Each part of the supply chain has its own economics and risks. Investment can be made in seeds, plants and production or by taking equity stakes in growers. Growers will in turn require the employment of hydroponic farmers, master growers and botanists, and developing distribution relationships and an understanding of the science involved in extraction of chemical compounds for specific markets. Investments can be made purely in distribution companies. An equity stake or loan can be made to an individual dispensary or a chain of stores that sells marijuana and related medicinal or recreational products to individuals.

Investing in marijuana growers or dispensers is a relatively high-risk proposition given the fact that the products are illegal at the federal level and profits can be seized by federal authorities under certain circumstances. Some investors have focused on delivery services that bring marijuana directly to the consumer's door. Other strategies to invest include investing in tools and devices such as pipes and vaporizers. Still other strategies include investing in those contractors, plant trimmers and other support services that focus on marijuana growers. Safer opportunities exist to invest in larger companies in the food and beverage or healthcare and cosmetic industries that are willing to take risk on marijuana investments as a hedge or as a strategic investment to protect existing products or generate growth. Today there are a wide range of individuals and companies specializing in each phase of the product life cycle available for investors to consider.

Some investment strategies are limited to private companies who will benefit from industry growth and consolidation. Investing in a portfolio of private cannabis companies that eventually gets purchased or goes public is similar to many other venture capital or private equity-related approaches. Other strategies include investing in large companies that are adding cannabis products to existing product lines or creating new ones.

Who Invests?

Several well-known and respected individual investors have also begun to diversify into marijuana as a viable form of investment and diversification. One such investor is Leon Cooperman. Cooperman is currently invested in CannTrust, a medical cannabis provider in Canada, and Green Thumb Industries, a Chicago-based national distributor of packaged goods that also operates a chain of retail stores called Rise. Beyond these investments, Cooperman is also invested in iAnthus, which owns and operates a vertical supply chain in the United States.[15]

Today's investors in cannabis also include corporations looking to hedge or expand their businesses, as well as opportunistic individuals. The cannabis industry is still considered a new and somewhat novel industry. People are only recently familiarizing themselves with the industry as regards different aspects of production, supply chain, risks, catalysts and valuations. There are several food and beverage and cosmetic companies that have acquired stakes in marijuana companies as a hedge or in order to gain insights about the use of cannabis in product development or extension. Many of these investments have been small or tenuous given the legal and regulatory issues in the United States. The investment of Constellations Brands in Canopy Growth is an example of one such investment.

So far, pensions, endowments and foundations have been slower to embrace cannabis investments due to reputational concerns and legal risks. As some of these regulatory and legal issues get resolved in favor of the industry, and if cannabis can be legalized at the federal level in the United States, there will be significantly more institutional investors, companies and investment firms drawn to this market.

How to Invest?

Direct investment in a license or production capability or in a grower is one way to get exposure. Another is to invest in distribution by buying a dispensary. Marijuana production and cultivation requires obtaining a license, finding a buyer for production, sourcing seeds or clones, testing soil for contaminants, installing water systems, purchasing pesticides and fertilizer, planting, harvesting and testing. Investment can be in medical, recreational or commercial marijuana cultivation. This sort of direct investment is beyond the scope of most individual investors seeking to diversify their portfolio. Instead, this is a sector that has mostly been funded by high-risk venture capitalists looking to take advantage of the opportunity available during the early phase of marijuana decriminalization and state-by-state legalization.

Another option is to invest in distribution capabilities. In states where cannabis can be sold legally, investors can explore opening a retail store focusing on cannabis oils or edibles or paraphernalia shops offering equipment for recreational users. Many state applications and licensing fees for a new dispensary operator can exceed $10,000. Most states will also have working capital minimums. In Nevada, for example, $250,000 in capital is needed to start a medical marijuana dispensary. In Massachusetts, it is necessary to provide proof of at least $500,000 in liquid capital before applying for a license. In Pennsylvania, $150,000 in capital is needed.

---

15. Thomas Franck, "Billionaire Leon Cooperman Explains How He Ended Up Investing His Personal Money in Pot Stocks," *CNBC*, Oct. 2018, www.cnbc.com/2018/10/17/billionaire-leon-cooperman-on-how-he-ended-up-investing-in-pot-stocks.html.

Public companies invested in the marijuana industry also exist. Several Canadian, American and global firms invest in marijuana as a source of new revenues or as a hedge against disruption of existing product sales.

Public companies and ETFs in the marijuana space have seen quite a bit of volatility and significant price increases on both an absolute and a relative basis. Horizons Marijuana Life Sciences Index ETF, for example, doubled in value from mid-2016 to the end of 2019, exceeding the increase in the S&P 500 from 2,000 to 3,000.

Private funds investing in licenses, production and distribution are also an option. There are a number of private equity and hedge funds that offer exposure to investors. Navy Capital Green Fund, for example, invests in emerging growth opportunities presented by the global legalization of medicinal and adult-use cannabis. The fund was launched in May 2017. It currently has assets under management of approximately $75 million. Another example is Native Roots, the largest dispensary chain in the state of Colorado, which has 21 dispensary locations. It is known for its inexpensive products and skate shop vibes. Native Roots is also trying to develop lotions, edibles, dog treats and coffee, as well as CBD vaporizer products. Native Roots is backed by venture capitalists and private investors.

Benchmarks and Indices

Cannabis Benchmarks is a division of New Leaf Data Services, a leading provider of financial, business and industry data for the North American cannabis markets. The company produces both spot and forward indices on the price per pound of marijuana. For more information, visit the company's website at https://www.cannabisbenchmarks.com.

New Cannabis Ventures is a news and media company that provides information and indices related to cannabis investing. The company maintains several indices and subindices related to marijuana companies. For more information, visit the company's website at https://www.newcannabisventures.com/american-cannabis-operator-index/.

Firms, Funds and Platforms

Privateer Holdings is based out of Seattle. It is a private equity fund that has raised over $100 million dollars since its inception in 2010. Privateer operates based on its philosophy that cannabis is a mainstream product consumed by mainstream people, that the end of cannabis prohibition is inevitable and that brands will determine the future of the cannabis industry. As so, the fund focuses on building a diversified portfolio of cannabis brands. For more information, visit the firm's website at https://www.privateerholdings.com.

Tuatara Capital is headquartered in New York. Tuatara Capital invests across multiple facets of the cannabis industry. The private equity firm was founded in 2014. According to Preqin, the minimum investment for an LP to buy into the fund is $250,000 and Tuatara collects a 2% management fee for all committed capital. The fund's focus includes companies that conduct research and testing for the cannabis industry, cultivate the product, process it and provide technology to the industry. For more information, visit the firm's website at https://tuataracapital.com.

Poseidon Asset Management was founded in 2013 and operates two funds across multiple sub-sectors of the cannabis industry. The company aims to invest in 15 companies privately held Cannabis companies that specialize in cultivation, processing, distribution and retail. For more information, visit the firm's website at https://www.poseidonassetmanagement.com.

Casa Verde was founded and backed by Snoop Dogg in 2015. Casa Verde focuses on investing in businesses that support the cannabis industry rather than producers and suppliers of cannabis. Casa Verde's first fund closed in 2018 with $45 million in committed capital. For more information, visit the firm's website at https://www.casaverdecapital.com/

Phyto Partners is a venture capital firm that focuses its investments on technology and big data companies that support the growth of cannabis producers. According to Preqin, the firm was started in 2015 and has launched two funds since. For more information, visit the firm's website at https://www.phytopartners.com/overview-2/.

Hypur Ventures is a Scottsdale, Arizona–based venture capital fund that invests across the entire cannabis supply chain using its newest $500 million fund called Hypur Ventures II, which launched in March of 2018. The fund seeks to invest $1 million to $25 million in cannabis companies that specialize in the cultivation, distribution, retailing, genetics and technology associated with cannabis. For more information, visit the firm's website at https://hypurventures.com/overview/.

CB1 Capital Management is a hedge fund whose primary strategy is long/short equity. It invests in the supply chain of cannabinoids and companies that create medical cannabis solutions to various health issues. The Wellness Fund was opened in 2017 and, as of September 2019, had committed capital of nearly $14 million, according to Preqin data. For more information, visit the fund's website at https://www.cb1cap.com.

Measure 8 Venture Partners is an asset manager that invests through its Measure 8 Full Spectrum Fund. Based out of Delaware, Measure 8 is, at its core, a long/short equity fund that invests in all facets of the cannabis industry. However, it is also open to making private investments. The fund was opened in August of 2019 and requires a minimum investment from its LPs of $250,000 while taking a 2% management fee and 20% performance fee on profits, according to Preqin. Measure 8 Full Spectrum Fund manages roughly $20 million of public equities. For more information, visit the fund's website at http://www.m8vp.com.

Navy Capital is a hedge fund manager that invests through the Navy Capital Green International. According to Preqin data, Navy Capital managed $150 million as of December 2018. The primary strategy of the fund is long/short equity and focuses on public companies that benefit from the legalization of medicinal cannabis. The minimum investment for LP's is $500,000 and, as of April 2019, the fund had raised just over $5 million. There is a standard 2% management fee on committed capital and 20% performance fee on profits. For more information, visit the fund's website at https://www.navycapital.com.

Alternative Harvest ETF is the first and largest ETF in the cannabis industry with holdings in 40 companies that are both domestically and internationally based. The ETF is managed by ETF Managers Group based in New Jersey. MJ began trading on December 3, 2015, on the NYSEArca. The ETF tracks the Prime Alternative Harvest Index and has large stakes in cannabis cultivators, producers, marketers and distributors such as Tilray, Canopy Growth, GW Pharma and Aphria. The total value of MJ's common stock holdings as of May 31, 2019, was $1.22 billion. For more information, visit https://etfmg.com/funds/mj/#footnote-holdings-1.

Horizons Emerging Marijuana Growers Index ETF is an ETF that provides investors the opportunity to invest in small cannabis companies that have the potential to produce outsized returns. Horizons ETFs are managed by Horizons ETFs Management Inc. in Canada which is owned by Mirae Asset Global Investment based in South Korea. HMJR is designed to mirror the Emerging Marijuana Growers Index run by Solactive. The fund began trading on the Aequitas NEO Exchange in Canada on February 13, 2018, and has holdings in over 60 companies primarily based in North America. As of October 4, 2019, HMJR had net assets of $5,187,297 Canadian dollars. For more information, visit https://www.horizonsetfs.com/etf/HMJR#.

Evolve Marijuana ETF symbol SEED is a Canadian traded ETF that was first listed in February of 2018 and trades on the Toronto Stock Exchange. SEED has holdings primarily in large-cap marijuana companies like Tilray and Aurora Cannabis. It also invests nearly half of its $8 million Canadian dollars, as of September 2019, in ancillaries and emerging cannabis companies. SEED is managed by Evolve Funds Group Inc. and tracks its performance against the North American Marijuana Index. For more information, visit https://evolveetfs.com/product/seed/.

American Growth Fund Series II is the only mutual fund that invests in the cannabis industry and has holdings of the top marijuana producers and ancillaries. Series II is managed by American Growth Fund Inc. It opened in February 2011 as a diversified mutual fund. In July of 2016, Series II was converted into a cannabis industry-focused mutual fund. For more information, visit the firm's website at http://www.agfseries2.com.

Aurora Cannabis is a public company trading on the Toronto Exchange. It has an estimated annual production of 700,000 kilograms of cannabis and is considered to be the largest producer of cannabis in the world. Aurora has infrastructure in place to strongly accelerate its Canadian sales. The company is well positioned to grow as additional derivative products come into the market, and with increased access to the US market. For more information, visit the firm's website at https://www.auroramj.com.

Canopy Growth produces approximately 530,000 kilograms of cannabis annually. Canopy Growth trades on NYSE. Canopy Growth was Canada's first publicly traded medical cannabis company, as well as the first diversified licensed producer under current regulations. In October 2017, the company announced that it had received a $250 million investment from alcohol beverage giant Constellation Brands. Approximately one year later, Constellation upped its stake, adding another $5 billion to its holdings. Constellation now owns approximately 38% of the company. Canopy has helped the Canadian cannabis industry establish significant credibility and now seeks to expand its brand internationally. For more information, visit the firm's website at https://www.canopygrowth.com.

Cronos Group is currently trading on NASDAQ. This company was founded in 2013 and was originally known as PharmaCan. It was one of the earliest licensed producers with a global footprint in cannabis. The company signed an agreement with Ginkgo Bioworks to produce rare cannabinoids at a significantly larger scale than had been done in the past. This agreement will serve to accelerate the company's goal of being a global cannabinoid company, rather than simply a cannabis company. The company's mission is to build an organization that follows best practices from other similar industries, that is, alcohol, fragrances, consumer products, whereby it will prioritize investment in functions such as research, intellectual property protection and strategic planning and support. Marlboro cigarette maker Altria said in December 2018 that it would take a $1.8 billion stake in Canada's Cronos Group. For more information, visit the firm's website at https://thecronosgroup.com.

Tilray provides an example of the impact of the recent frenzy around publicly traded marijuana stocks. The company has a limited float of shares. Shares available to the public have thus far seen tremendous volatility and price movements, rising from $20 to $300 per share in just over three months following its initial public offering. Tilray's massive moves say more about the shortage of attractive investment options for those seeking direct exposure to marijuana production and distribution than the company's business fundamentals. For more information, visit the firm's website at https://www.tilray.com.

What to Look For?

What does the company or investment do? Is it a grower in cultivation, a dispensary in distribution, a technology play, an investment in product research or does it create new products and applications?

Moreover, what are the costs? If the company is a producer, what is the cost to acquire and grow its products and what is the company's operating margin? Cost per gram information is one common metric. On the other hand, if the company is a dispenser, we must consider the margins and payroll costs. If the company is doing research or is science-based investment, how much is being spent and what is the expected return on investment? Does the company own any intellectual property rights?

Other questions to consider include questions such as: where will growth come from? Is the sector over-supplied? Some estimates today say that the state of Washington already has a surplus supply of marijuana for recreational and medical use that exceeds six years of demand. How will this over-supply impact prices?

What is the set of supplier or distributor relationships in place today and are there any long-term or government entity contracts?

How are profits handled? Where is cash deposited? Many banks will not accept cash or make loans to businesses in states with legal marijuana due to the illegal federal status. Credit unions, Bitcoin and other creative ways to store cash and profits need to be understood and evaluated.

Unique Risks

The most unique risks in the cannabis industry are the obvious legal risks associated with the product, as well as the overcapacity of supply and the threat of industrialization and commercialization of all aspects of the supply change by big agricultural, pharmaceutical, food and beverage, tobacco and retail players. Marijuana producers also have all the risk associated with farming crops such as weather, pestilence and other factors that might contribute to a bad harvest.

Social, Legal and Ethical Considerations

The distribution, possession and use of cannabis with over .3% THC is illegal in the United States under federal law. As a Schedule I drug under the Federal Controlled Substances Act of 1970, cannabis is considered to have no accepted medical use and to have the potential for abuse and physical or psychological dependence. Under Federal Law in the United States, the only legal use of cannabis is limited to FDA-approved research programs.

Despite this, individual states have enacted legislation decriminalizing possession and permitting exemptions for various uses, mainly for medical and industrial use but also including recreational use. Banking regulators from 25 states recently sent a letter to Congress to urge the enactment of the SAFE Act in the hope of permitting banks to service cannabis companies that are compliant with state laws, despite violating federal regulations.[16]

Concerns over federal legalization include arguments that legalization may lead to a push to expand the legislation of drugs beyond cannabis. Secondly, there are medical warnings regarding the use of cannabis. For example, former FDA Commissioner Scott Gottlieb and others argue that the use of cannabis impacts the development of the brain and that marijuana use has been linked to schizophrenia.[17]

Public polling data from the Pew Research Center suggest most Americans believe marijuana should be legal. According to a recent survey conducted by the Pew Research Center in October 2017, approximately 61% cent of US respondents believe marijuana should be legal, as opposed to the 37% who believe the substance should remain illegal.[18]

---

16. Tom Angell, "State Financial Regulators Press Congress to Allow Marijuana Banking Access," *Forbes*, Apr. 2019, https://www.forbes.com/sites/tomangell/2019/04/16/state-financial-regulators-press-congress-to-allow-marijuana-banking-access/#594bf78755c9.
17. Scott Gottlieb, "Statement by FDA Commissioner Scott Gottlieb...," FDA, June 2018, https://www.fda.gov/news-events/press-announcements/statement-fda-commissioner-scott-gottlieb-md-importance-conducting-proper-research-prove-safe-and.
   Is There a Link between Marijuana Use and Psychiatric Disorders? (National Institute on Drug Abuse, 2019), https://www.drugabuse.gov/publications/research-reports/marijuana/there-link-between-marijuana-use-psychiatric-disorders.
18. Hartig and Geiger, "About Six-in-Ten Americans Support Marijuana Legislation."

There also appears to be broad bipartisan support for initiatives aiming to expunge the records of individuals who have committed minor offenses at the federal level related to cannabis possession. One of the central points of issue is whether the offense expands beyond minor possession to involve distribution. These concerns are also controversial. Anything that can be framed as increasing the number of active drug dealers could derail cannabis legislation.

Homeopathic Medicines

Homeopathy is a type of alternative medication practice. The homeopathy products market is categorized into neurology, analgesic and antipyretic, immunology, respiratory, dermatology, gastroenterology and many others. There is a growing use of homeopathy for the treatment of various chronic diseases. The dermatology segment has accounted for a significant share of the global market due to rising incidences of skin-related diseases globally. The global homeopathy products market is estimated to reach $16.2 billion by 2024. that would represent a CAGR of 16.8% over the forecast period. According to the OECD, in 2014, the healthcare expenditure in Germany was around $390 billion, whereas in France it was $290 billion and in the United Kingdom it was $270 billion. The Middle East and Africa hold promising opportunities in the future of homeopathy, as homeopathy is the second largest system of medicine in these regions, with a growth rate of 20 to 25% each year. According to the National Institutes of Health, over 6 million people in the United States use homeopathy, mainly for self-care related to specific health conditions. As many as 1 million of these individuals are children.[19] The increase in healthcare expenditure and use of homeopathy products as a substitute for allopathic products is driving this market's growth.[20,21]

Boiron was established in 1932 by brothers Jean and Henri Boiron in Lyon, France. Boiron is the largest producer of homeopathic medicines in the world, employing over 3,700 people in 59 countries. The company is best known for its flu medicine, Oscillococcinum, and pain reliever, Arnicare. In the United States, Boiron is FDA-certified. For more information, visit the firm's website at https://www.boironusahcp.com/about-boiron/.

---

19. Press Releases, Market Reports, Global Market Insights, https://www.gminsights.com/pressrelease.
20. "The Prevalence of Homeopathy in the World," Goldenstein Research, Jan. 2019, https://www.goldsteinresearch.com/pressrelease/global-homeopathy-product-market.
   Joel John, "Global Homeopathy Products Market Will Reach USD 15.98 Billion by 2024," Zion Market Research, Oct. 2018, https://globenewswire.com/news-release/2018/10/29/1638266/0/en/Global-Homeopathy-Products-Market-Will-Reach-USD-15-98-Billion-by-2024-Zion-Market-Research.html.
21. Joel John, "Global Homeopathy Products Market Will Reach USD 15.98 Billion by ...." Zion Market Research, October 2018, https://globenewswire.com/news-release/2018/10/29/1638266/0/en/Global-Homeopathy-Products-Market-Will-Reach-USD-15-98-Billion-by-2024-Zion-Market-Research.html.

Heel Inc. is a pharmaceutical company that specializes in the production of natural-ingredient medicines. Some of Heel's most successful medicines include Zeel, a tablet that is intended to help with arthritis pain, Neurexan, a tablet that helps users with patterns of irregular sleep disturbances, and Traumeel Ointment, a cream to help relieve muscle and joint pain. For more information, visit the firm's website at https://www.heel.com/en/home.html/.

Nelson and Co. Ltd. was founded in 1860 in London, England, as a producer and distributor of homeopathic medicines. Nelsons is known for its Rescue Remedy, a mix of different flower essences developed by Dr. Edward Bach. For more information, visit the firm's website at https://www.nelsons.net/.

Hahnemann Laboratories Inc was founded by Michael Quinn in 1985. Hahnemann Labs is a producer of homeopathic medicines that prides itself on selling the most potent single-ingredient products in the industry. Based in California, Hahnemann Labs produces FDA-approved remedies that can stimulate the body's natural defense against myriad illnesses. For more information, visit the firm's website at https://www.hahnemannlabs.com.

Natural Health Supply is based in New Mexico. Natural Health Supply provides homeopathic remedies and ancillary products to its customers. Uniquely, it offers kits that allow clients to make their own remedies, glassware, clinic supplies and other products related to the production of natural medicine. For more information, visit the firm's website at https://a2zhomeopathy.com/index.html.

Genomic Medicine

Genomic medicine is the field of study that looks into our genes and investigates the complex biological details of an individual as well as the use of these details for effective diagnosis and tailor-made medical treatment. According to Global Market Insights, the genetic testing market could be worth over $22 billion by 2024 and register a CAGR of 10.65% during the time frame between 2019 and 2024.[22]

A report by research firm Battelle Technology Partnership Practice estimates that between 1988 and 2010, federal investment in genomic research generated an economic impact of $796 billion. This fact proves impressive when we consider that the Human Genome Project spending between 1990 and 2003 amounted to just $3.8 billion.[23]

Most genetic tests are not sold as stand-alone products. The services performed by clinical laboratories are regulated under the Clinical Laboratory Improvement Act amended in 1988. This bill was enacted to strengthen federal oversight of clinical laboratories and to ensure accurate and reliable tests after Congress found widespread poor quality of laboratory services. Some major players and investment opportunities in

---

22. Press Releases, Market Reports, Global Market Insights.
23. Jonathan Gitlin, "Calculating the Economic Impact of the Human Genome Project," NHGRI, June 2013, https://www.genome.gov/27544383/calculating-the-economic-impact-of-the-human-genome-project.

Table 10.1. The performance, risk and correlation of a composite of marijuana and alternative investment vehicles versus the S&P 500 between January 2016 and December 2019.

	Alternative Medicine	S&P 500
Correlation	0.57	NA
Standard Deviation	37.09%	11.56%
Average Annual Return	33.28%	14.33%
Simplified Sharpe	0.90	1.24

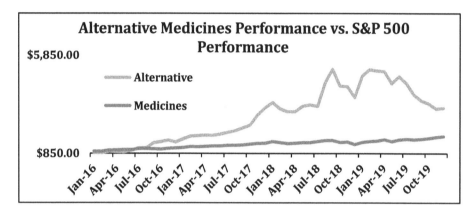

Figure 10.4. The growth of $1,000 invested in cannabis, homeopathic and genome vehicles versus the $1,000 invested in the S&P 500 from January 2016 to December 2019.

this field include Illumina, Exact Sciences, Myriad Genetics, Genomic Health and Ark Genomic Revolution ETF.

Composite

A composite of recreational and medical cannabis, genome and homeopathic medicines, shown in Table 10.1, had significantly higher returns and risk than an investment in the S&P 500 between January 2016 and December 2019. The Sharpe ratio was 0.90 versus 1.24. The correlation was also very low at 0.57.

A $1,000 investment in cannabis and alternative medicine composite in January 2016, shown in Figure 10.4, would have grown to over $3,155 by December 2019 compared to $1,708 for the S&P 500.

Trends and Outlook

The major trend facing the marijuana industry is deregulation. It appears that momentum is gaining and that this trend will continue. The next most important trend is that of falling prices and a potential for over-supply. Another favorable trend is the increasing number of applications for cannabis extracts in the cosmetic, cream and healthcare businesses. Despite significant returns to date, the outlook may be challenging. Large operators from the food, drug and beverage industries as well as big pharmaceutical companies may cannibalize the small operators who grow and distribute cannabis today. Many of these first movers are owned by venture capital firms and are the primary players in the US market today.

Manager Perspectives and Insights

Richard Travia, Founder, Wildcat Advisory Group

Richard Travia founded Wildcat Advisory Group in 2017 and Wildcat Investment Management in 2018. Wildcat Advisory Group is a diversified business and investment consultant that advises small- and medium-size public and private companies, institutional investors such as family offices, private equity funds and hedge funds and institutional-quality service providers. Wildcat Investment Management provides investment management services. Richard acts as the manager of the Arnott Capital Opportunities Fund, is a director of the Arnott Opportunities (Cayman) Fund Ltd., the DelGatto Diamond Finance Cayman Ltd. Fund and WoodPoint Capital LLC. Richard is also a member of the board of advisors for Trebel Music, a member of the board of directors of Crateful, a member of the board of advisors for the Freedom Football League and a member of the board of directors for the San Diego Warriors football franchise. Richard is a registered director with Chartered Institute of Management Accountants and has served as a member of many liquidation and creditor committees.

Prior to launching Wildcat, Richard co-founded Tradex Global Advisors in 2004 and Tradex Global Advisory Services in 2014. While at Tradex, Richard served as the chief operating officer and compliance officer of the firm, director of research for the fund of hedge funds business and head of risk management for the single hedge fund business. Richard has more than 15 years of experience in alternative assets, including due diligence and allocation, management of illiquid public and private positions, risk management of hedge fund strategies, business development and management of investment teams, operational teams and service provider relationships. Prior to founding Tradex Global Advisors, Richard served as the lead analyst for the Select Access Family of Funds, a fund of hedge funds business. Richard has invested in more than 500 hedge funds and in nearly every asset class and strategy throughout his career, the majority of which have been with "emerging managers."

Richard graduated from Villanova University in 2003 with a Bachelor's degree in Economics. He has served as a Senator on the University Senate, as a member of the University's Executive Committee and as a board member and an executive committee member and treasurer of Stamford's East Side Partnership. He is currently a member of the Villanova University MBA Mentor Program and the Christopher and Dana Reeve Peer and Family Support Program.

Why do you believe cannabis-related investments are attractive?
Although investing in cannabis-related investments is risky, I do believe it can be very profitable. As in most investments we make, the quality of the management team

is of utmost importance. Management's integrity, compliance, ability to execute and make deals and their accountability are all major factors when reviewing a team. The opportunity for growth in the sector is spectacular. Similar to any sector experiencing significant political, regulatory and legal changes across many jurisdictions, the landscape is complicated and fluid. We feel that there are many places across the value chain to invest, with some being more attractive than others. Cowen projects the cannabis industry to generate $85 billion of US sales in 2030. Medical cannabis is now legal in more than 30 countries, recreational cannabis legalization efforts are making progress in many jurisdictions and CBD products are all but mainstream. It is not unrealistic to expect spectacular growth, if managed responsibly. Despite the regulatory momentum seen in 2019, public and private cannabis market valuations took a beating. Capital markets for debt and equity have all but dried up for public and private companies, creating stress industrywide. We think the confluence of stressed valuations, a need for capital, positive industry and regulatory momentum and the spectacular growth opportunity makes a well-researched, well-capitalized investment in a strong management team in the cannabis sector an incredibly attractive long-term investment over the next several years.

What are the risks associated with cannabis-related investments today and going forward?
I think there are too many risks to list. That said, I think cultivation is an incredibly risky part of the cannabis sector. Over-supply and pricing pressure in the United States and Canada are two major concerns of mine. On a related note, if more jurisdictions become legal and trade is (relatively) free, I find no reason that cannabis should be grown in regions that are not better geographically and economically suited to producing cannabis. Cannabis thrives in warm weather environments—Latin America should be a major production hub should certain barriers fall. Columbia's average temperature for the coldest month of the year is 65°F. Columbian winters have 12 hours of daylight, almost two times that of major Canadian cities. The soil in Columbia is fertile and water is abundant. The cost of labor in Columbia is a fraction of that in Canada or the United States. The cost to build in Columbia is a fraction of that in more developed markets. Hundreds of millions of dollars have been spent to build cultivation facilities covering more than 15 million square feet in the United States and Canada. If things change from a regulatory perspective, investors in those assets could be very disappointed.

Another big concern I have is illicit market risk. The illicit cannabis market size in the United States alone in 2019 was projected to be more than $27 billion. Canada's illicit market in 2019 was estimated to be between $5 billion and $7 billion. All things being equal, I do believe that most customers would rather buy products legally versus illegally. The problem is, not all things are equal. In most jurisdictions, cannabis obtained via illegal channels is meaningfully less expensive than the legal product. Multiple layers of taxes, regulatory process and procedure, compliance policies and significant operating and marketing expenses all contribute toward the higher price of legal cannabis. Additionally, in Canada, restrictions on branding and labeling have left legal buyers in legal stores uninformed, confused, and the generic packaging and significant disclaimers have made brand recognition and loyalty a very difficult achievement. If a Canadian customer walks into an illegal dispensary in Canada, because of the beautiful packaging and helpful staff, they may actually feel more comfortable than if they were in a legal dispensary. It is a very unusual dynamic that should be addressed. It is important to recognize that compliance testing on legal cannabis products worldwide is improving and as such it is not unreasonable to expect a marginally higher-priced product in exchange for certainty of quality.

What are some of the more significant due diligence or research efforts that should be considered before investing in cannabis as an asset class that can improve returns and mitigate risk?

Preservation of capital is always top of mind for me, so mitigation of risk through proper diligence is very important. There are several areas of focus where we spend a lot of time in order to gain a sense of confidence in any potential investment opportunity in the cannabis space. Some of those would include a highly experienced and diversified management team, an unwavering commitment to regulatory compliance, high-quality partnerships, high-quality products and a healthy balance sheet. My diligence, in any sector or strategy, has always started with the quality of the management team. Honesty, transparency, flexibility, creativity, experience and integrity are a few characteristics that we look for our portfolio company management teams to exemplify. Investing in a sector like cannabis can be volatile enough without adding in any extra layers of non-compliance. We are searching for management teams that operate fully legally and conservatively within their jurisdictions and who operate based on what is legal rather than what is anticipated to be legal. There is opportunity for many players in the cannabis space to partner with high-quality distribution, research, sales, cultivation and so on. Some of those partners may be mainstream, Fortune 500 types of brands that bring a wealth of experience, resources and credibility. It does depend on the circumstance, but the quality of partners and investors is an important consideration. Companies in this space generally are capital-constrained. This is still largely an unbanked area of the economy, and so finding proper and reasonable financing is one of the most significant challenges that operators face. I think it probably should go without saying that the product or service sold should be of high quality, well thought of and in demand.

Where does or should cannabis assets or opportunities fit into an investor's portfolio construction and asset allocation?

There are so many different types of investments that can be made in this space, so it is difficult to generalize. That said, I'd expect that more sophisticated investors that consider portfolio construction and asset allocation when making an investment should categorize most cannabis investing in a higher-risk, longer-term, more speculative part of their investment portfolio.

Academic Perspectives and Research

Academic articles focusing on cannabis first began to appear in the early 1900s as American researchers sought to examine the health effects of the marijuana plant brought in by Mexican migrants following the Mexican Revolution. Research on cannabis continued throughout the twentieth century, focusing on the medical, legal and ethical implications of medicinal and recreational marijuana use. According to Google Scholar, there have been 192,000 articles written about cannabis since 2010. The vast majority of these articles have studied the health effects of medicinal cannabis usage. More recently, articles have focused on the recreational usage of cannabis. Such articles studied the societal benefits or detriments that legalization would bring, the health effects of marijuana and the economics of investing in cannabis. A handful of articles have also addressed the ethics of investing in cannabis securities and the economics of cannabis investing.

One interesting article was published by the Society for the Study of Addiction, entitled "Evaluating the Public Health Impacts of Legalizing Recreational Cannabis Use in the United States." The researchers set out to describe the regulatory regimes implemented in states where recreational cannabis is legal, in order to outline their effects on cannabis use and to suggest what additional research is needed to evaluate the public health impact of these policy changes. They accomplished this by reviewing drug policy literature to identify effects of legalizing adult recreational use on cannabis price and availability, factors that may increase or limit these effects, pointers from studies on the effects of legalizing medical cannabis use, and indicators of cannabis use and cannabis-related harm that can be monitored to assess the effects of these policy changes. The report concluded that legalized recreational cannabis use will probably increase use in the long term, but the magnitude and timing of the increase is uncertain. Household, high school and college surveys should continue to be monitored, as well as the number of cannabis plants legally produced and the THC content of cannabis. Indicators of cannabis-related harms that should be monitored include car crash fatalities, emergency department visits, the frequency of addiction treatment services in use and the prevalence of regular cannabis use among young people in mental health services and the criminal justice system.[24]

Another noteworthy article from Fein Law Offices examines the ethics of investing in cannabis securities or cannabis-related investments and whether or not it breaches a fiduciary duty. The author first considers federal laws, with the most important being the Controlled Substances Act (CSA). The CSA declared cannabis a Schedule I drug in 1970, which is defined as a drug "with no currently accepted medical use and a high potential for abuse." Schedule I drugs are considered by the government to be the most dangerous drugs available. Next, the author considers rules of fiduciary duty, which means that a trustee must exercise proper care, skill and caution regarding marijuana-related securities. The author argues that the due diligence required to satisfy this standard may prove

---

24. W. Hall, "Evaluating the Public Health Impacts of Legalizing Recreational Cannabis Use in the United States," *Society for the Study of Addiction*, Oct. 2016, https://www.ncbi.nlm.nih.gov/pubmed/27082374.

difficult in the case of cannabis securities. The illegality of marijuana-related activities, the nascent state of the cannabis industry and the limited market for cannabis securities may make it difficult for a fiduciary to obtain and verify the information needed to properly assess the prudence of a particular investment. Finally, the author considers environmental, social and governance goals for fiduciaries required to invest by this standard. This would require fiduciaries to invest in furtherance of environmental, social and governance goals such as minimizing harm to the environment, preventing climate change, supporting human rights and encouraging good corporate governance. The paper concludes that it would be a breach of duty to invest in cannabis securities because the fiduciary fails to satisfy general fiduciary prudence principles and the requirements of the prudent investor rule, along with related duties.[25]

The *Journal of Real Estate Portfolio Management* published a report on investing in cannabis through real estate investment trusts (REITs). The author's purpose is to describe the rise of the cannabis industry, discuss the potential rewards and risks of investing in cannabis businesses and to identify the potential opportunities that exist for those who wish to use REITs to participate in this industry. Legal restrictions placed on banks and other financial intermediaries have prevented cannabis companies to easily access funding. Additionally, high demand for warehouse space has driven up prices and limited opportunities for cannabis companies. REITs would provide an alternative to individuals or small investor groups, who make short-term, high-interest-rate loans. REITs would offer more competitive rates, as the risk is spread across a pool of investors and across many investments. Secondly, there is high demand for land and warehouse space by cannabis companies, which means REITs can earn considerable land income in the industry. Third, a publicly traded REIT allows an opportunity for the public to invest in the cannabis industry. Some of the risks in investing in a cannabis REIT include legal risks associated with the federal government's classification of marijuana, access to capital and the infancy of the industry.[26]

Homeopathic academic articles have examined the health benefits and detriments of homeopathic medicines, with mixed results. One article by R. Sevar audited outcomes of 455 patients that were treated with homeopathic medicines. The results found that 66.8% of patients derived benefit from homeopathic treatment. 32.5% of the patients were able to stop or maintain a substantial reduction in their use of other, conventional drugs. Of the patients, the 10 most frequent clinical conditions treated were eczema, anxiety, depression, osteoarthritis, asthma, back pain, chronic cough, chronic fatigue, headaches and essential hypertension. Two patients had prolonged aggravation of their presenting complaints apparently attributable to homeopathic treatment.[27]

---

25. Melanie Fein, "Fiduciary Investments in Cannabis Securities," Fein Law Offices, Mar. 2019, https://papers.ssrn.com/sol3/papers.cfm?abstract_id=3326205.

26. Randall Guttery and Stephen Poe, "Using a Cannabis Real Estate Investment Trust to Capitalize a Marijuana Business," *Journal of Real Estate Portfolio Management*, 2018, https://www.aresjournals.org/doi/abs/10.5555/1083-5547-24.2.201.

27. R. Sevar, "Audit of Outcomes in 455 Consecutive Patients Treated with Homeopathic Medicines," *Elsevier*, July 2005, https://www.sciencedirect.com/science/article/pii/S1475491605001098#.

Another report from the *International Journal of Clinical Practice* set out to evaluate the effects of homeopathic drugs. They conducted this study by searching through five medical databases of homeopathic data. The researchers found 38 primary reports that contained data on 1,159 patients. Adverse effects in patients ranged from mild to severe, with four deaths across the 1,159 patients. The researchers concluded that homeopathy has the potential to harm patients and consumers in both direct and indirect ways and that clinicians should be aware of its risks and advise their patients accordingly.[28]

Genomic academic articles have focused on the investment into genomic research and the implications for the medical industry. One article from the medical journal *Cell* titled "Genomic Medicine—Progress, Pitfalls and Promise" set out to take stock of the progress made, as well as the hurdles to, the translation of the human genome and its effect on the nascent field of genomic medicine. The researchers summarized the key technological developments since the human genome project. They then considered the successes and challenges to genomic medicine in four areas, which were common inherited diseases, rare inherited diseases, reproductive health and cancer. Finally, the authors provided an overview of the field and suggested areas that warrant further investment to fully unlock its potential. The authors highlighted increased interest from pharmaceutical companies that are interested in investing in genomic data for rare diseases, which would increase their ability to detect rare diseases and use the genome data to introduce cures. The authors state that while large hurdles remain in genomic medicine, continued investment in basic science and technology is unquestionably necessary to overcome challenges in the industry. The investment into genomic medicine should be considered long-term, as the payoffs may not be fully realized for many decades.[29]

Summary

Opportunities to invest in marijuana and other alternative medicines are increasing. The return from investing across a wide array of platforms, direct invest and funds and related therapies also have attractive characteristics relative to traditional investments. Deregulation of cannabis in the United States will provide a major catalyst for growth.

Useful Websites, References and Additional Readings

"Cannabis Attracts Big Tobacco, Alcohol, and Pharma. Which Big Industries Will Join Next?" www.forbes.com/sites/kriskrane/2018/12/19/cannabis-attracts-big-tobacco-alcohol-and-pharma-which-big-industries-will-join-next/#206589a48daf.

---

28. P. Posadzki, A. Alotaibi and E. Ernst, "Adverse Effects of Homeopathy: A Systematic Review of Published Case Reports and Case Series," Peninsula Medical School, Dec. 2012, https://www.ncbi.nlm.nih.gov/pubmed/23163497.
29. Jay Shendure, Gregory Findlay and Matthew W. Snyder, "Genomic Medicine—Progress, Pitfalls, and Promise," CellPress, Mar. 2019, https://www.sciencedirect.com/science/article/pii/S0092867419301527.

"The Global Cell and Gene Therapy Market Is Growing at a CAGR of Over 24% During the Forecast Period 2018–2024," https://www.ptcommunity.com/wire/global-cell-and-gene-therapy-market-growing-cagr-over-24-during-forecast-period-2018-2024.

"Global Homeopathy Product Market Report 2017–2021," https://www.businesswire.com/news/home/20170920005526/en/Global-Homeopathy-Product-Market-Report-2017-2021-Growth.

"Legal Marijuana Market Size, Share & Trends Report," https://www.grandviewresearch.com/industry-analysis/legal-marijuana-market.

"Marijuana Industry Faces Challenging Tax Regime," www.forbes.com/sites/peterjreilly/2018/07/19/marijuana-industry-faces-challenging-tax-regime/#39e65b862174.

"Marijuana Sales Reports," https://www.colorado.gov/pacific/revenue/colorado-marijuana-sales-reports.

"The Next Gold Rush Is the $22 Billion CBD Business—and This Florida …," https://www.inc.com/kimberly-weisul/best-industries-2019-green-roads.html.

"North American Marijuana Index—Tracking Top Cannabis Stocks in North America," https://marijuanaindex.com/stock-quotes/north-american-marijuana-index-tracking-top-cannabis-stocks-in-north-america/.

"US boosted by Human Genome Project," https://www.ft.com/content/bf82ff12-7be9-11e0-9b16-00144feabdc0.

"Using a Cannabis Real Estate Investment Trust to Capitalize a Marijuana Business," https://www.aresjournals.org/doi/abs/10.5555/1083-5547-24.2.201.

Chapter Eleven

CRYPTOASSETS

Introduction

Investing in cryptoassets is another interesting area that has gotten a great deal of attention, both from those who are in favor and from those opposed. In this chapter, the goal is to provide a brief and simple overview of how the Bitcoin market and the broader crypto market are currently evolving and how and where investors can participate in the process today.

Definitions and Key Terms

The term cryptocurrency is a broad phrase referring to a wide range of individual coins or tokens created for different purposes. Bitcoin is the most widely known form of a cryptocurrency. A coin or token is an independent cryptocurrency. Altcoin is another example.

A coin or token is a digital measure that is created for a specific usage case. Bitcoin was created for use as a medium of exchange and payment. Other coins or tokens have other uses besides payments. The process by which real-world assets are converted into digital value via issuance of a token is called tokenization.

Mining is a process where blocks are added to a blockchain, verifying transactions. It is also the process through which new Bitcoins are created. Miners receive newly minted coins or transaction fees for spending money and resources and running algorithms that produce unique reference numbers for each coin.

A blockchain is a list of records that are linked together. Each record is referred to as a block and is securely linked to one another.

A digital or cryptocurrency exchange is a mechanism that allows its members to buy and sell cryptocurrencies for one another or to convert traditional currencies into cryptocurrencies.

Distributed ledgers are ledgers in which data is stored across a network of decentralized nodes. A distributed ledger does not necessarily involve a cryptocurrency and may be private and accessible by permission only.

An initial coin offering or token is a type of crowdfunding using cryptocurrencies as a mechanism to raise capital, similar to the use of traditional currencies in venture capital or initial public offering on an exchange. The use of an Initial Coin Offering or ICO is seen as a way to disintermediate traditional fundraising sources.

Please visit the CoinMarketCap.com website for additional definitions and a wide range of market data related to cryptoassets, coins and tokens at CoinMarketCap.com, https://coinmarketcap.com/glossary/.

Market Participants and Players

The cryptocurrency market can be broken into several segments, including coin origination, trading, distribution and usage. There are many blockchain applications that are considered cryptoassets. Bitcoin is the most well-known cryptocurrency and as such will be the primary focus of this chapter.

The type of usage case for Bitcoins is as a currency. It is intended to serve as an alternative to fiat or paper currency. Once owned, Bitcoin can be used to pay for goods and services at locations or venues that accept Bitcoin. Other cryptoassets and coins may have different usage cases.

Bitcoins, however, first need to be created before they can be utilized as currency. Unlike paper currency issued by a government and controlled by a central bank, Bitcoins are created by individuals and validated by the user community. The process of generating a single Bitcoin and validating it is called mining. Mining involves using a computer or network of computers to generate a unique identification number that is validated on the decentralized Bitcoin public ledger, also known as the blockchain. A validated entry into the blockchain is awarded a fixed number of Bitcoins by the user community. The number of Bitcoin awards for each new entry in the blockchain currently stands at 12.5 Bitcoin. A significant amount of time and computer resources are required to mine and validate each new block. There is also a maximum limit on the aggregate number of Bitcoin outstanding at any one time.

Bitcoins can be purchased on an exchange for another currency. Some ATM machines also allow for currency to be exchanged for Bitcoin. Exchanges offering Bitcoin are regulated and buyers and sellers are not anonymous. An Internet company called Cryptoradar helps individuals to quickly research and evaluate over 700 exchanges where Bitcoin and other cryptocurrencies are traded each day. Prices for Bitcoin on the various exchanges will be different, and there is no best price or single exchange where cryptocurrencies are listed or traded. Each exchange will have its own unique set of personal verification requirements and timing to open an account, they will charge different prices and fees, offer different payment methods to send or receive traditional currencies for digital ones and offer various wallet services to store coins. Exchanges will also have their own unique data protection and security environment. More information about Cryptoradar can be found on the company's website: https://cryptoradar.co/.

Holding or owning a Bitcoin requires a wallet. A wallet is where a digital key to unlock your Bitcoin on the blockchain is held. A lost key means losing access to your Bitcoin forever. Digital keys can be stored in online wallets maintained by a third party over the Internet, stored on portable hardware like an external hard drive that can be carried around by the owner or written down on paper and stored in a vault or hiding place.

Once a wallet has been created and Bitcoin purchased, then consumers can use their coins to pay for goods and services. This is an anonymous transaction. The seller of a good or service will not gather any information about the buyer. No credit card or other bank information is needed. It is the same as paying in cash. Some individuals prefer the anonymity that Bitcoin provides. Some prefer its relative ease of use or transfer and prefer Bitcoin to holding paper currency or large amounts of cash. Some also feel it is a safer form of financial transaction since it does not rely on a bank or government for storage or valuation.

Another website that is a useful source of information about the cryptocurrency market is called Cointelegraph.com. It provides details about the many players and participants in the cryptocurrency market. The site offers tutorials and plain language explanations of many of the factors investors need to consider to successfully buy and sell Bitcoins and other cryptocurrencies. For more information, visit the company website at https://cointelegraph.com/bitcoin-price-index.

Industry Associations

The Bitcoin Association is an industry association for Bitcoin users and businesses. It includes vendors, exchanges, developers, miners and other organizations that use or wish to promote Bitcoin usage. For more information visit the association's website: https://bitcoinassociation.net/.

The Wall Street Blockchain Alliance is an industry group created to promote the adoption of blockchain technology and cryptoassets globally. The organization engages regulators, policymakers, industry participants and technologists in education and communication of issues related to this industry, with the goal of helping blockchain technology achieve its full potential. For more information visit the alliance's website at https://www.wsba.co/.

Market Size and Scope

The market capitalization of cryptocurrencies was $237 billion at the end of 2019.[1] There are over 2,900 cryptocurrencies in circulation, with the largest three by market capitalization being Bitcoin (($147 billion), Ethereum ($19.4 billion) and XRP ($11.7 billion).[2] Of the major cryptocurrencies, there was an average of 648,000 transactions of Ethereum, 309,000 transactions of Bitcoin and 22,000 transactions of Litecoin.[3] According to Preqin, there are 277 hedge fund managers that operate in the cryptocurrency market.

---

1. M. Szmigiera, "Average Number of Daily Cryptocurrency Transactions in 4th Quarter of 2019," Statista, Feb. 2020, https://www.statista.com/statistics/730838/number-of-daily-cryptocurrency-transactions-by-type/.
2. M. Szmigiera, "Cryptocurrency Market Capitalization 2013–2019," Statista, Jan. 2020, https://www.statista.com/statistics/730876/cryptocurrency-maket-value/.
3. Rick Bagshaw and Coin Rivet, "Top 10 Cryptocurrencies by Market Capitalization," *Yahoo Finance*, Oct. 2019, https://finance.yahoo.com/news/top-10-cryptocurrencies-market-capitalisation-160046487.html.

Who Invests?

Today, the main investors in Bitcoin are individuals and some dedicated hedge funds. Institutional investment is still very limited at this time. A number of institutions are creating their own blockchains for the simplification of processing transactions within their own organizations. A number of governments have also considered creating a digital currency that is created and regulated by their central bank.

Opportunities and Strategies

Investors can invest and trade Bitcoin Futures on the Chicago Mercantile Exchange, buy coins directly to hold in a wallet or they can participate in the small number of mostly Canadian listed ETFs that offer Bitcoin exposure. There are also many hedge funds that now offer exposure to cryptoassets, including Bitcoin trading strategies.

A buy-and-hold Bitcoin strategy would have increased in value almost 500% from 2016 to 2019. The strategy was highly volatile with extreme gains prior to the end of the 2017 peak, followed by extreme losses in 2018 and then relatively stable price changes in 2019.

Short-selling using Bitcoin as a hedge is possible. However, it is a highly risky strategy that loses money when prices rise. Futures can be used for a short-selling strategy. Some exchanges will also allow for the borrowing and short-selling of individual coins. Contracts for differences and other derivatives can also be used to generate short-sale exposure. Some traders will own Bitcoins for long-term investment and at the same time have hedges against short-term price volatility.

Trend trading is a strategy for profiting from Bitcoin. Similar to other currencies and commodities, some traders will use trend-following algorithms to enter and exit a position. Trend following can be designed to capture short-term, medium-term or longer-term trends and profits. Trends are purely direction bets and can be based on increasing or decreasing price patterns. Trend following is based on technical analysis and pattern recognition. Other trend-following strategies include identifying breakout patterns, reversals or other patterns that can be applied when using Bitcoin futures, other futures or spot cryptocurrencies that have the necessary liquidity and daily trading volume.

Selecting a broker or exchange to execute your trades is also extremely important. There are several services that allow you to compare brokers and evaluate offerings. Brokers can be compared on several variables. Important features include liquidity, fees, leverage, short-selling, volume, customer service and privacy features. A website called Bitcointradingsites is a fast and easy way to get information and comparisons of several brokers at one time. For more information, visit the company's website at https://www.bitcointradingsites.net/brokers/.

The US Securities and Exchange Commission (SEC) has been slow to approve traditional ETFs that invest in Bitcoin for retail investors. The SEC still has issues with market manipulation and pricing related to Bitcoin and other cryptocurrencies. Several applications have been filed with the SEC and it appears only a matter of time before some get approval for trading on US exchanges.

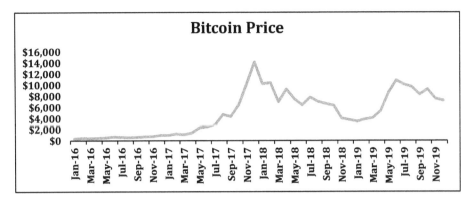

Figure 11.1. The monthly price changes for one Bitcoin from January 2016 to December 2019.
Source: Yahoo Finance

Investors that are accredited and meet minimum net worth and income tests can invest in a number of hedge funds and some ETF-like structures that offer exposure to Bitcoins and other cryptoassets.

There are a number of ETFs that invest in companies that are part of the cryptoasset ecosystem more broadly. There are funds that invest in companies engaged in the development or use of blockchain technology or use futures contracts rather than cryptocurrencies themselves to obtain exposure.

Benchmarks and Indices

Cryptocurrency prices are available from many boutiques as well as mainstream pricing services. Cointelegraph is a boutique that provides historical price information and research about Bitcoin and other cryptocurrencies. Information for this index and research data provider can be found at https://cointelegraph.com/bitcoin-price-index. Yahoo Finance (https://finance.yahoo.com) and Bloomberg (https://www.bloomberg.com) also provide a wide range of Bitcoin and cryptocurrency prices each day. Daily Futures prices for Bitcoin can be found on the CME website (https://www.cmegroup.com/).

The value of a single Bitcoin has been extremely volatile. Figure 11.1 shows the end-of-month prices of Bitcoin. This cryptocurrency rose from less than $500 in January 2016 to $7,194 at the end of December 2019. According to data reported by Yahoo Finance, the daily Bitcoin price peaked at approximately $20,000 intra-month in December 2017 before it started a two-plus-year gradual decline in price.

Firms, Funds and Platforms

Grayscale Bitcoin Trust is an investment vehicle through which investors can gain exposure to the price movements of Bitcoin without the hassle of buying, storing and selling the actual coin. Its benchmark index is the TradeBlock XBX Index 24-hour VWAP. It

Table 11.1. The performance, risk and correlation of a composite of cryptoasset investment vehicles versus the S&P 500 between January 2016 and December 2019.

	Cryptocurrency	S&P 500
Correlation	0.03	N/A
Standard Deviation	153.60%	11.56%
Average Annual Return	119.85%	14.33%
Simplified Sharpe	0.78	1.24

charges a 2% annual fee and, as of early 2020, had approximately $2 billion in assets. For more information, visit the manager's website at https://grayscale.co/.

Grayscale Ethereum Trust is an investment vehicle through which investors can gain exposure to the price movements of Ethereum without the hassle of buying, storing and selling the actual coin. Its benchmark index is the TradeBlock ETX Index 24-hour VWAP. It charges a 2.5% annual fee and, as of early 2020, had approximately $183 million in assets. For more information, visit the manager's website at https://grayscale.co/.

Amplify Transformational Data Sharing ETF is an ETF that seeks to provide investors with exposure to companies involved with the use and creation of blockchain technologies. It is managed by Amplify ETFs and has regional allocation throughout the world. For more information, visit https://amplifyetfs.com/blok.html.

Reality Shares Nasdaq NexGen Economy ETF is an ETF that seeks to provide investors with exposure to companies that are focused on the development, innovation or utilization of blockchain technology either for themselves or for others. The ETF tracks the Reality Shares Nasdaq Blockchain Economy Index. For more information, visit the company's website at https://www.realityshares.com/app/BLCN.

Leonidas Cryptocurrency Fund is a fund managed by Typhon Capital Management. According to Preqin, it trades a variety of cryptocurrencies as well as derivatives and initial coin offerings. The fund employs a quantitative approach with a combination of algorithmic strategies. For more information, visit the manager's website at https://typhoncap.com.

Composites

The returns from investing in cryptoassets are extremely volatile and will likely remain so for some time. Table 11.1 shows that between January 2016 and December 2019, the annual returns were approximately 120% with a standard deviation of approximately 150%. Despite the attractive Sharpe ratio and low correlation to the S&P 500, most investors would find this volatility way too high. However, despite the extraordinary stand-alone volatility, the case can still be made that an allocation to cryptoassets would improve a traditional portfolio's risk-adjusted returns.

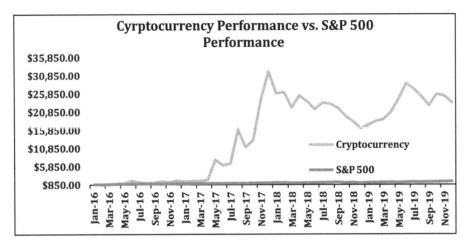

Figure 11.2. The growth of $1,000 invested in cryptoasset investment vehicles compared to the S&P 500 from January 2016 to December 2019.

A $1,000 investment in a cryptoasset composite in January 2016, shown in Figure 11.2, would have grown to an incredible $23,362 by December 2019 compared to $1,708 for the S&P 500.

Unique Risks

Limited data, a lack of history and high volatility are all challenges associated with cryptoasset investing. Investors can mitigate model risks for trend following and technical trading with the use of stop losses. Exchange operational risk and cybersecurity are important risks to consider. Investors must choose carefully when using an exchange and designing a wallet so as to avoid fraud and theft of any assets held at third parties.

Social, Legal and Ethical Considerations

There are a lot of opinions about the efficacy of cryptoassets as viable investments. Many pundits and industry observers still refer to these new forms of currencies as "Ponzi schemes" and "asset bubbles" which are destined to end in financial ruin. In some cases, there is also a negative association between cryptocurrencies and usage cases designed to avoid taxes and launder money, whether this is true or not. Many of the naysayers come from traditional trading and investment worlds and may be reacting to the fear of the unknown. On the other side of the issue are the many former traditional Wall Street traders that have set up shop to trade and profit from crypto-investing. Although the evidence is mostly anecdotal, there also appears to be a generational bias. Younger investors and millennials seem to embrace crypto much more than the older generation of Baby Boomers and most institutional investors.

Manager Perspectives and Insights

Michael Bucella, Partner, BlockTower Capital

Michael Bucella is a Partner at BlockTower Capital, an institutional cryptoasset and blockchain technology investment firm. Prior to BlockTower, Michael spent nearly a decade with Goldman Sachs in New York, most recently in the securities division as head of multi-asset sales and trading for the Canadian region, leading efforts to expand the strategy globally. Previous to this role, he led the Institutional Global Equities franchise, also for the Canadian region. He joined Goldman Sachs in 2008 as part of the Firm's Asset Management division (GSAM) where he focused on cross-asset, global investment strategies for North American institutions. Michael is a mentor for the Techstars and Creative Destruction Labs tech accelerator programs in New York and Toronto. He is also an active volunteer in multiple philanthropic organizations, as well as many personal endeavors to directly aid relief missions in disaster-stricken areas. Michael is a graduate of Fordham University's Gabelli School of Business.

What makes Bitcoin and Cryptoassets an interesting investment?
Cryptoassets and blockchain technology represent a new form of assets and technology working together in a liquid, yet inefficient market. The combination of early-stage technology, networks and business models has never met this level of liquidity, creating a ripe opportunity for uncorrelated, asymmetric, risk-adjusted returns. Contrary to most other markets, a majority of the crypto volume is retail-driven, as the adoption of the asset developed in a distinctly different format from other asset classes—beginning with the retail individual first, and only recently being picked up by the institutional community. Navigating the nuanced risks and market dynamics of cryptoassets requires a new kind of investment process with an approach operating at the intersection of traditional and non-traditional disciplines and mental models, spanning economics, game theory, regulation, cryptography, computer science, portfolio and risk management and so on. The micro opportunity in the development of underlying technologies, networks and ecosystems combines with the macro narrative of certain major cryptoassets, that is, Bitcoin, acting as an inflation hedge in the face of unprecedented central bank monetary policy, combine for what will likely be the next great cycle for cryptoassets.

What sort of investment or trading strategies work best?
The strategies in crypto markets closely resemble those in traditional assets—long-only, long/short, multi-strategy, market-neutral, systematic, venture capital, among others, each providing some measure of value. Market regimes, however, can change quickly and the ability to adapt in this market is what separates the winners from the losers. The market is developing rapidly and funds are evolving alongside the market micro-structure. New spot and derivatives exchanges, custodial solutions, trading platforms, even middle and back-office service providers are all being developed and refined by the most talented engineers from the traditional world, as they see the growing

demand from an increasingly more institutionalized set of fund managers, market makers and prop trading firms. This new infrastructure allows for hedge funds to capture the opportunity set while managing operational, execution and regulatory risk in a more meaningful way.

Venture investing is another growth area where there has been an explosion in new crypto-dedicated venture capital firms both within the major incumbent venture capital firms or spin-off of brand-name partners from the largest firms (typically with an anchor check from their former firm as a parting gift). Almost every major venture capital firm that exists today either has its own crypto-dedicated fund, has spun off a crypto fund or has made investments from its general tech funds in the blockchain and cryptoasset industries. In some cases, venture capital firms have modified their investment mandates to allow for the purchase of up to x% of their fund in Bitcoin (and other cryptoassets). These strategies, however, are taking a long view with founders which comes along with the liquidity profile of a traditional venture fund—10-year capital. Investor profile typically dictates liquidity preference—liquidity agnostic investors will find value in each of these strategies.

Seth Klarman, founder of Baupost Group and legendary investor, notes that investors are compensated by the market for taking on market risk, that is, beta, and for illiquidity. Many investors stop there, but Klarman notes that we're also compensated for complexity, operational challenges and "psychological risk." We see these additional compensated risks in spades in the cryptoasset industry. These technologies often require a degree in cryptography and engineering. They're also complex economically, in execution, security-wise and operationally—there are no established regulations, operational procedures or accounting standards to deal with cryptocurrency investing. All of these perceived risks are an investor's opportunity if they are properly underwritten and managed. The market structure, regulations and operational solutions continue to develop and will drive the industry forward, but we are still in the early innings of the market.

Who is likely to invest?

The investors base has evolved in a most unorthodox way, relative to other asset classes, as the retail market was the first to adopt cryptoassets. This evolved over the years as the market, investment products and investment strategies professionalized. The cascading interest was a function of the ability to quickly act on the evolving opportunity—ultra-high-net-worth family offices and venture capitalists were the next groups to see the opportunity and act. Today, the market is increasingly garnering the attention and capital of institutions. Sovereign wealth funds, pension plans and the majority of major endowments are now invested in the asset class. Much like David Swenson, CIO of Yale Endowment, in the early days of private equity, a few brave and brilliant investors took the first leap investing in cryptoassets when the majority shied away for fear of volatility or, worse, reputational scrutiny. Now, the majority of those same folks, led again by Swenson and a group of Endowment CIOs, have thrown their hat in the crypto ring and allocated significant pools of capital to the cryptoasset class.

Academic Research

Academic articles about cryptoassets became prevalent starting in 2008, after the founding of the blockchain and the first technology-based cryptocurrencies, starting with Bitcoin. Since then many academic articles have surfaced regarding cryptoassets, focusing on applications, investment characteristics and the risks associated with this technology. Given the infancy of the industry and lack of concrete available data, much of the current research is focused on just a few cryptoassets, such as Bitcoin, Ethereum and Ripple.

Brianne Smith of Huntingdon College described the investment characteristics, risks and regulatory environment of cryptoassets in a paper titled "The Life Cycle and Character of Cryptoassets: A Framework for Regulation and Investor Protection." In her paper, she reviews the investment indicators of cryptoassets, the conflicts and accountability in cryptoassets, as well as identifying a framework for investor protection. Smith evaluates Bitcoin as a case study in how investors think about cryptoassets. According to her research, Bitcoin investors use counterstrategy and poorly supported data to make investment decisions. Many crypto investors are speculative and rely on rumors to make investment decisions. Given this information, it is clear that Bitcoin prices are not reflective of true market conditions. Bitcoin prices, lacking any fundamentals, are primarily affected by new information, momentum, adoption, online attention, news and Google searches. Traditional currency or cash flow-based analysis doesn't necessarily apply to Bitcoin since it doesn't earn an interest rate. Because of this, Smith concludes that cryptocurrencies should not be priced with rational market thinking, which is how traditional investments are priced. Smith also goes on to say that there are both systematic and unsystematic risks associated with cryptoassets. Systematic risks include hard forks, security attacks and the dependency of crypto on other projects, as in the case of Ethereum, which is dependent on the development of smart contracts. Cryptoassets also have differing levels of security depending on the exchange they are traded on. If the exchange is not appropriately registered, it could leave the investors vulnerable to hacking. Another risk is operational risk, as the technology is difficult to operate. For example, if an investor sends cryptoassets to the wrong address or to a wallet that is not compatible, the investment is lost. Or if a hardware wallet is lost, the investment cannot be recovered. Lastly, different regulations across countries and the lack of current regulation present more challenges, particularly in Initial Coin Offerings (ICOs), which are susceptible to fraud, as crypto transactions are permanent. Given the permanence of the investment, it is likely that many projects funded through ICOs may never be completed.[4]

Smith mentions another paper by the University of Pennsylvania's Mira Nagarajan wherein she suggests four areas of governance that are needed for Bitcoin and Ethereum to function more dependably.[5] The first area relates to forks, which occur when a blockchain diverges into two potential paths forward. The problem with forks,

---

4. Brianne Smith, "The Life Cycle and Character of Cryptoassets: A Framework for Regulation and Investor Protection," *Journal of Accounting and Finance*, 2019, https://articlegateway.com/index.php/JAF/article/view/1036.
5. Szmigiera, "Cryptocurrency Market Capitalization 2013–2019."

particularly permanent forks, is that they create a break from the original chain and require the adoption of a new system. The second area is the open-sourced nature of blockchain, which allows users to track multiple transactions to the same individual, even though their identity remains anonymous. The third is regulation, as the SEC regulates cryptoasset exchanges as securities, yet does not classify cryptoassets as securities. Lastly, external governance policies remain inconsistent in the regulatory environment.[6]

An article by Guglielmo Maria Caporaleab, Luis Gil-Alanac and Alex Plastund analyzed the top four cryptocurrencies over the period 2013–17. The study included Bitcoin, Litecoin, Ripple and Dash. According to the authors, one of the largest problems with cryptocurrencies is whether their dynamic behavior is predictable, which would be inconsistent with the efficient market hypothesis (EMH). The EMH states that prices should follow a random walk, which means that cryptocurrencies, like stocks and bonds, should follow a random and unpredictable price path. This would make all methods of predicting their future prices futile in the long run. The findings of the study conclude that the cryptocurrency market exhibits persistence, which means that there is a positive correlation between its past and future values and that its degree changes over time. Such predictability represents evidence of market inefficiency, as trend trading strategies can be used to generate abnormal profits in the cryptocurrency market.[7]

Summary

Cryptocurrencies are here to stay. The real question is how big of a market and how widespread their use will become and what usage cases take hold or develop in the future. No one really knows the answer. What is more likely and easier to predict is the ability of the underlying blockchain technology to expand into applications that influence our daily life and companies of all sizes. This technology has the potential to spark innovation and may lead to improvements in productivity for many years to come.

Useful Websites and Additional Reading

"Are Bitcoin and Other Crypto-Assets Money?" https://www.riksbank.se/globalassets/media/rapporter/ekonomiska-kommentarer/engelska/2018/are-bitcoin-and-other-crypto-assets-money.pdf.

"Bitcoin and Cryptocurrency Technologies," https://www.lopp.net/pdf/princeton_bitcoin_book.pdf.

---

6. Mira Nagarajan, "An Analysis of Cryptocurrency Governance," University of Pennsylvania, 2018, https://repository.upenn.edu/cgi/viewcontent.cgi?article=1050&context=joseph_wharton_scholars.

7. Guglielmo Maria Caporaleab, Luis Gil-Alanac and Alex Plastund, "Persistence in the Cryptocurrency Market," *Research in International Business and Finance*, Dec. 2018, https://www.sciencedirect.com/science/article/pii/S0275531917309200#bib0080.

"Blockchain Challenges and Opportunities: A Survey," https://www.researchgate.net/profile/Hong-Ning_Dai/publication/328271018_Blockchain_challenges_and_opportunities_a_survey/links/5bd2706f92851c6b278f31eb/Blockchain-challenges-and-opportunities-a-survey.pdf.

"Cryptoassets: Legal, Regulatory, and Monetary Perspectives," https://www.oxfordscholarship.com/view/10.1093/oso/9780190077310.001.0001/oso-9780190077310.

"EY's Cryptocurrencies and Cryptoassets: Managing the New Asset Class," https://www.ey.com/Publication/vwLUAssets/ey-cryptocurrencies-and-cryptoassets-managing-the-new-asset-class/$File/ey-cryptocurrencies-and-cryptoassets-managing-the-new-asset-class.pdf.

"Global Cryptocurrency Benchmarking Study," https://www.crowdfundinsider.com/wp-content/uploads/2017/04/Global-Cryptocurrency-Benchmarking-Study.pdf.

"Initial Coin Offering (ICO) Risk, Value and Cost in Blockchain Trustless Crypto Markets," https://papers.ssrn.com/sol3/papers.cfm?abstract_id=3012238.

"KPMG's Institutionalization of Cryptoassets," https://home.kpmg/us/en/home/insights/2018/11/institutionalization-cryptoassets.html.

"Risks and Returns of Cryptocurrency Investing," https://www.nber.org/papers/w24877.

"SEC Spotlight on Initial Coin Offerings (ICOs)," https://www.sec.gov/ICO.

Chapter Twelve

COLLECTIBLES

Collectibles include a wide range of investments such as sports memorabilia, vintage wines and whiskey, collectable watches and vintage automobiles. Collectibles are a very niche type of exotic alternative investment. Collectibles can be purchased and held for pure enjoyment or investment or both. Historically, the market size of any individual collectibles category may be relatively small, transaction costs will be expensive and the market not very liquid, at least compared to many other types of investments. There is often a lack of reliable transaction data and experts are often needed to navigate the landscape and evaluate opportunities. Think vintage wines and whiskeys, watches, comics, limited-edition sneakers, toys, designer handbags, among other things.

Today, the landscape is evolving. Many collectibles now have exchanges and indices where you can transact and value a specific investment or benchmark performance. Many collectibles markets are still small in size and are primarily the domain of collectors and enthusiasts. In most cases, there are only direct investments available and no listed companies, ETFs or private funds that can be pursued as potential investments. Over time, however, many of these markets will grow and provide opportunities for commingled funds and a wider investor audience.

Revenue for the US collectibles industry, shown in Figure 12.1, was $1.5 billion in 2019 according to IBISWorld. The revenue has grown 5.9% per year from 2014 to 2019 and is expected to grow at an annual rate of 3% from 2019 to 2024. The industry profit margin was 5% in 2019. The revenue drivers for this industry include the amount of disposable income of consumers, the increasing presence of online retailers and competition that is driving down shipping and handling costs. The major players in the market are Heritage Auctions with a market share of 33.7%, eBay with a share of 11.1% and other firms accounting for 55.2%.[1]

The largest portion of collectibles revenue in the United States, shown in Figure 12.2, is from world currencies and coins at 32.8%, followed by sports collectibles at 28%, antiques at 17.6%, comics and animation art at 13.5%, jewelry at 6% and wine at 2.1%.[2]

---

1. Cecilia Fernandez, "Antiques & Collectibles Sales," IBISWorld, June 2019, https://www.ibisworld.com/united-states/market-research-reports/online-antiques-collectibles-sales-industry/.
2. Ibid.

Total Revenue in 2019	Annual Growth 2014–2019	Annual Growth 2019–2024	Profit Margin in 2019	Wages as a share of Revenue in 2019	Number of Businesses 2014–2019
$1.5 bn	5.9%	3.0%	5.0%	4.4%	3.9%

Figure 12.1. IBISWorld revenue and activity measures for the collectibles industry as of June 2019.

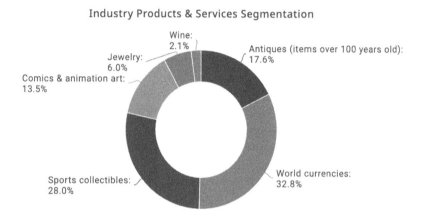

Figure 12.2. IBISWorld breakdown of the collectibles industry segments as of June 2019.

Coins

Investing in collectable currencies and coins offers an opportunity for appreciation related to the scarcity value of the item. It also gives investors an opportunity to participate in appreciation in the metal used to mint the coin itself. In 1986, the US mint began reproducing American Eagle gold coins to appeal to precious metal investors. The mint used the classic design of the Augusta Saint-Gaudens $20 gold coin. Dealers who sell coins will normally have them certified by a commercial grading company. Professional Coin Grading Service (PCGS) and Numismatic Guaranty Corp. (NGC) are the two most popular grading services. Coins with limited production and circulation are most valuable. So too are those with defects in the production process. Dealers and auction houses will take a significant mark-up when selling coins, sometimes 20% or more. Coins normally must be held as a long-term investment to make a profit. Investors need to do a great deal of due diligence and research to create a portfolio of rare coins that will appreciate. Due diligence includes making a determination of the metallic value of the coin, researching past resale value and researching the dealer's reputation.

Sports Memorabilia

The value of sports memorabilia comes from booming demand from Baby Boomers, international buyers and millennials, to name a few demographic groups. Sports memorabilia includes a wide range of items and covers many types of sports. Collectibles include uniforms and equipment used by players in games, trading cards, autographs and other merchandise. Many investors want to capture a piece of American culture that exists in something owned or used by a superstar athlete or entertainer. Private dealers include Steiner Sports, Lelands and Fanatics Authentic. Some of the most valuable sports memorabilia include items such as the 1952 Topps Mickey Mantle card, a game-worn Lou Gehrig uniform and an autographed Babe Ruth baseball. There are many platforms where investors can search for and find specific teams, apparel or other items to add to their collection. Investing in popular sports memorabilia can produce significant appreciation. For example, PWCC.com valued a Derek Jeter 1993 rookie card at $126,433 and a 1952 Mickey Mantle card at almost $500K as of January 2020.[3]

Wines

Wine is one interesting way to invest. Investors can buy premium wines from "blue chip" or they may invest in younger and newer vineyards located in premium locations. According to Statista, the overall size of the wine market is greater than $15 billion today.[4] The collectable or vintage wine market is of course only a fraction of this size. According to research done by The Wine Investment Fund, wine investing has returns similar to or greater than many global equity markets with lower volatility than equities, gold and oil. This leads to significantly higher Sharpe ratios. There is also an active wine futures market. Wine futures allow buyers to contract for a price for a vintage wine after it has been harvested but before it has been bottled. Many Bordeaux and Burgundies are "pre-sold" in the futures market to dealers and investors months or years before the wine is bottled and available for purchase. These vintage wines are sold at futures prices below the offering price that is anticipated for the wine once it is bottled and available for purchase. According to research about wine futures in the *Wine Spectator*, a 1982 Chateau Latour pre-sold in the futures market for $40 per bottle in 1983 now sells for about $1,500 per bottle. It also noted that the 2000 vintage was now worth double its release price. Despite these examples, the article goes on to say that more recently the gap or discount between the futures and secondary market prices has narrowed.[5]

3. "PWCC Market Indices," PWCC, Jan. 2020, https://www.pwccmarketplace.com/market-indices.
4. Jan Conway, "Global Wine Market Size from 2014 to 2022," Statista, Oct. 2018, https://www.statista.com/statistics/922403/global-wine-market-size/#__sid=js2.
5. "How (and Why) to Buy Wine Futures," *Wine Spectator*, Mar. 2019, https://www.winespectator.com/articles/buying-futures-3495.

Whiskey

Malt whiskey and blended whiskeys are often sought after by both connoisseurs and investors alike. A malt whiskey is made exclusively from malted barley, water and yeast. A single malt is from just one distillery or cask whereas a blended malt can come from more than one distillery or cask. Scot whiskey or blended whiskey is a mixture of malt whiskies and whiskies made from whole grains other than just barley. A type of whiskey that is American-made is called Bourbon. Bourbon uses its own set of grains and its own unique distilling process. According to Knight Frank, a provider of luxury good indices, the Knight Frank Rare Whisky 100 Index of 100 bottles of the world's most desirable rare scotch whiskeys increased by almost 40% through 2018. The index did have some losers in addition to winners. Some 21 bottles in the KFRW100 did lose value in 2018. The worst-performing 10 bottles lost 27% of their value year from 2017 to 2018.[6]

Vintage Sneakers

According to a report by Grandview research, the size of the global athletic footwear market is expected to reach $95.14 billion by 2025.[7] This is in part because limited-edition sneakers have become a much-coveted item and part of today's pop culture. Limited-edition sneakers can also provide investors with significant returns. Nike and Adidas are the two major providers of limited-edition sneakers. These brands often create versions of their sneakers that are tied to or designed by specific athletes or entertainers.

According to an article by Leigh Steinberg in *Forbes*, examples of tradable vintage sneakers include the Nike Air Yeezy "Red October," the Adidas Yeezy Boost 350 "Turtledove" and the Air Jordan 1 Off-White "Chicago."[8] These three shoes were all released in limited editions retailing at between $190 and $240, but the resale value averaged between $1,695 and $6,118 according to StockX. StockX is a company that provides trading and exchanges for collectable sneakers and other memorabilia. StockX allows investors to track portfolios, get live bids and offer prices and execute trades in vintage sneakers.[9]

Watches

Watches from manufacturers like Rolex, Audemar Piguet, Omega and Patek Phillipe are often bought for material pleasure. However, they can also be purchased and held

---

6. Flora Harley et al., "The Wealth Report," Knight Frank, 2019 https://www.knightfrank.com/wealthreport/2019/luxury-spending/luxury-investment-index.
7. "Athletic Footwear Market Size, Share, & Trends Analysis Report," Grandview Research, Apr. 2018, https://www.grandviewresearch.com/industry-analysis/athletic-footwear-market.
8. Leigh Steinberg, "The Profitable Hidden Sneaker Market," *Forbes*, Sept. 2018, https://www.forbes.com/sites/leighsteinberg/2018/09/17/the-profitable-hidden-sneaker-market/#c20e1b659256.
9. "How It Works," StockX.com, accessed Mar. 2020, https://stockx.com/how-it-works.

for investment. Each year a select number of luxury-brand high-end watches are designed in limited editions or with unique features allowing them to be "timeless" and to increase in value beyond their initial sales price. In order to retain value, watches must be in pristine condition, with their original packing and with a limited number of repairs, if any. Watches purchased and stored in a safe deposit box would be similar to other direct investments in collectibles, but a bit more convenient when it comes to storage costs and so on. In addition, watches constitute a direct investment. Watches can be a very illiquid investment and buying and selling individual watches can have very high transaction costs. Investors creating their own portfolio of watches should also have a good relationship with a watchmaker who understands vintage watches and can help appraise potential investments or provide guidance. According to data from CHRONEXT, a luxury watch dealer, if an investor in 2012 purchased the Rolex Submariner Reference 5513 and the Rolex GMT-Master Reference 1675, they would have had an investment return of 125% for the 5513 and 150% for the 1675 if sold in 2019.[10]

Vintage Automobiles

Classic automobiles are another type of collectible that offers investors an opportunity to find returns that are not very correlated to stocks and bonds. Most vintage autos are sold at public or invitation-only auctions. Three popular auctions where classic cars are bought and sold are the Barrett-Jackson auction in Scottsdale, Arizona, the Gooding and Co.'s auction at Pebble Beach and the Amelia Island Auto Auction. These auctions all feature a wide range of automobiles valued by collectors that range from blue-chip classics to American muscle. There are a limited number of funds targeting the collect-ible car market as their primary investment. Some of the more prominent funds are the Ultimate Classic Car Fund, Family Classic Cars Fund, IGA Automobile Fund and The Classic Car Fund. According to an article published in September 2018, entitled "My Kingdom for a Horse (or a Classic Car)," the average annual nominal returns from investing in classic cars from 1998 to 2017 was 5.6%. This compares to a price return of 5.43% on the S&P 500 during the same period. In this case, the returns are similar but the correlation between the investments is once again relatively low.[11]

An analysis of the Ferrari Index published by *Hagerty* from 2014 to 2018 shows a cumulative return of 222% from the 13 specific Ferraris that make up the index. This compares to a 150% commutative return from the S&P 500 during that period. Risks associated with classic automobile investments include price volatility, risk of theft or damage and illiquidity. While there are ample numbers of auctions and private sales, the

10. "How Can I Invest in Luxury Watches," CHRONEXT, accessed Mar. 2020, https://www.chronext.com/journal/buyers-guide/a-timely-question---how-can-i-invest-in-luxury-watches.
11. Dries Laurs and Luc Renneboog, "My Kingdom for a Horse (or a Classic Car)," *Journal of Financial Markets, Institutions, and Money*, Jan. 2019, https://www.sciencedirect.com/science/article/abs/pii/S1042443118303639.

Total Revenue in 2019	Annual Growth 2014–2019	Annual Growth 2019–2024	Profit Margin in 2019	Wages as a share of Revenue in 2019	Number of Businesses 2014–2019
$1.8 bn	0.7%	−0.2%	2.1%	6.0%	0.0%

Figure 12.3. IBISWorld revenue and activity measures for the classic car industry in the United States as of December 2019.

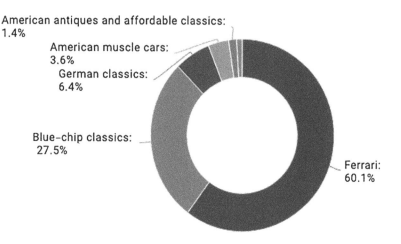

American antiques and affordable classics: 1.4%

American muscle cars: 3.6%

German classics: 6.4%

Blue–chip classics: 27.5%

Ferrari: 60.1%

Figure 12.4. IBISWorld breakdown of classic car industry segments for 2019.

demand for any specific automobile can vary greatly and impact prices. Holding a diversified portfolio of autos or investing in funds can help mitigate this risk.

According to IBISWorld data, shown in Figure 12.3, revenue for classic car dealers was $ 1.8 billion in 2019. The industry profit margin was 2.1%, with annual growth of just under 1%.[12]

The majority of classic car sales, shown in Figure 12.4, come from Ferraris at 60.1%. Blue-chip classics, German classics and American muscle cars account for almost 38% of sales and antique cars make up the rest.[13]

Benchmarks and Indices

The Knight Frank Luxury Investment Index is a good source of information about the performance of a wide range of luxury goods and collectibles. It is a broad-based index that was created in 2013. It uses third-party data to track the performance of a

---

12. Rachel Hyland, "Classic Car Dealers," IBISWorld, Dec. 2019, https://www.ibisworld.com/united-states/market-research-reports/classic-car-dealers-industry/.
13. Ibid.

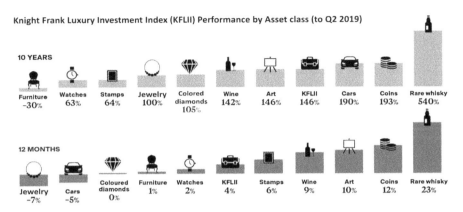

Figure 12.5. The returns from the Knight Frank Index and sub-indices for the one-year and 10-year periods that ended on June 30, 2019.
Source: Knight Frank Indices

representative basket of high-end collectibles. The index results, included in Figure 12.5, include prices related to 10 key luxury investment sectors: cars, art, wine, coins, stamps, jewelry, colored diamonds, Chinese ceramics, watches and antique furniture. It gets its data from sources such as AMR, Stanley Gibbons, HAGI and Wine Owners. The index can be found at https://www.knightfrank.com/wealthreport/article/2020-03-03-the-luxury-investment-index-2020-discover-the-worlds-mostcoveted-items.

Whiskey, coins and wine all had double-digit returns for the 12 months that ended Q2 2019. However, jewelry and vintage auto returns fell 7% and 5% for the same 12-month period.

The 10-year return from the overall index was 146%. The best performance over the past 10 years leading up to Q2 2019 was from investing in rare whiskey. Rare whiskey appreciated by 540%. Coins rose 193%. Vintage autos rose 190%. Wine rose 142%. Of course, there were also some losers during the same period. For example, vintage Chippendale furniture fell by 30% over the same 10-year period.

A sports memorabilia platform called PWCC.com maintains indices and offers a trading platform related to sports collectibles such as trading cards. The 10-year returns as of December 31, 2018, on the PWCC100 Index showed baseball cards had increased by 290% compared to 126% for the S&P 500. Some of the most valuable trading cards tracked as part of this index include the 1952 Topps Mickey Mantle, 1993 Derek Jeter, 1951 Gordie Howe, the 1957 Topps Bill Russell and the 1965 Topps Joe Namath card. The PWCC indices can be found on the company's website at https://www.pwccmarketplace.com/market-indices.

The fine wine platform Liv-ex is a global marketplace for the wine trade. The company provides trading, data, indices and technology to support a diverse group of wine businesses. The firm maintains a number of indices such as the Liv-ex Wine 50 and 100, Bordeaux 500 and the Fine Wine 1,000. More information can be found on the company's website: https://www.liv-ex.com/news-insights/indices/.

Hagerty is a comprehensive classic car information and services provider. The company's services provide vintage automobile owners access to a resale market, appraisals, insurance, financing and a wide range of products to support the classic car industry, including the provision of several classic car indices such as the Hagerty Ferrari Index. For more information, visit the company's website or its indices at https://www. hagerty.com/apps/valuationtools/market-trends/collector-indexes/Ferrari.

Firms, Funds and Platforms

The Wine Investment Fund is a vehicle to invest in fine wines. It specializes in the acquisition of Bordeaux wines. The management at the fund believes the portfolio has a low correlation to traditional investments and less volatility than other wine categories. Information about the fund can be found on the company's website at http:// wineinvestmentfund.com.

Sommelier Capital Advisors is a wine investment management company that operates a hedge fund specializing in wine investments. Sommelier Capital Holdings is an actively managed hedge fund that is managed by Sommelier Capital Advisors LLC. Information about the fund can be found on the company's website at https://www.sommeliercompany. com/investing-in-wine-investment-fund-asset-management-company.

The Classic Car Fund is a private investment fund created to provide investors with an opportunity to invest in vintage automobiles. The investment manager is assisted by an advisory board of experts in the field of classic cars. All of the automobiles owned by the fund are professionally transported, stored and insured. For more information, visit the fund's website at http://www.theclassiccarfund.com/Home_CCF.html.

PWCC Marketplace provides buyers and sellers of investment-caliber trading cards with an efficient marketplace. The goal of PWCC is to offer buyers and sellers low transaction costs, faster turnaround times, increased liquidity and greater transparency when buying and selling trading cards. Information about the PWCC Marketplace can be found on the company's website: https://www.pwccmarketplace.com.

Collectable.com is a platform and investment app that allows individuals to buy fractional ownership shares in some of the most desirable pieces of sports memorabilia. By owning fractional interests, investors can diversify more quickly and get exposure to many more items rather than investing and taking ownership of one individual item at a time. For more information, visit the company's website at https://collectable.com.

The Watch Fund is a platform that helps investors assemble a high-quality portfolio of watches on a bespoke basis. Investors get to create their own custom portfolio, wear the watches and participate in the profits when they are sold. Information about the Watch Fund can be found on the company's website at http://watchfund.com.

Liquid Rarity Exchange is an investment vehicle run by Rarity Fund advisors. The vehicle acquires collectibles and offers investors fractional ownership in items that it believes have an opportunity for significant appreciation. Each fund offering is SEC-registered and provides an opportunity to obtain exposure to individual pieces of fine art through a publicly traded investment vehicle. For more information, visit the company's website at http://liquidrarityexchange.com.

Collectors Universe is a company that provides third-party authentication and grading services to collectors, retail buyers and sellers of a wide range of collectibles. Its authentication services focus on coins, trading cards, sports memorabilia and other collectibles. Information about the company can be found at https://www.collectorsuniverse.com.

Diageo is a London-based alcoholic beverage manufacturer. Some of its largest owned brands include Smirnoff, Johnny Walker and Guinness. Diageo also holds a large minority stake in Moet Hennessy. Diageo employs over 28,000 people, has a presence in over 180 countries and produces its products from more than 150 sites throughout the world. For more information, visit the company's website at https://www.diageo.com.

Constellation Brands is a producer of alcoholic beverages including wine, beer and spirits. It owns over 100 brands and has approximately 10,000 employees across its 40 locations. The conglomerate has also recently made several investments into the medical marijuana space. For more information, visit the company's website at https://www.cbrands.com.

Ferrari is a sports car manufacturer and race team operator. In 1969, Fiat took a 50% stake in the company before spinning it off through an IPO in 2016. Ferrari sold approximately 10,000 cars in 2019, though it also generates revenue through its racing programs, merchandise and theme parks. For more information, visit the company's website at https://www.ferrari.com/en-US.

LVMH Moet Hennessy is a luxury goods manufacturer. Its various brands produce a wide variety of products including clothing, cosmetics, accessories, jewelry and more. One of its most recent acquisitions was Tiffany and Co. in 2019 for over $16 billion. The conglomerate employs over 160,000 people and operates over 75 "houses," or brands. For more information, visit the company's website at https://www.lvmh.com.

Hermes is a luxury goods manufacturer. It employs approximately 15,000 people across over 300 stores. Its various brands are active in 14 sectors including leather goods and saddlery, footwear, belts, furniture and wallpaper. For more information, visit the company's website at https://www.hermes.com/us/en/.

Amundi S&P Global Luxury ETF is an ETF managed by Amundi Asset Management that seeks to replicate the returns of the S&P Global Luxury Index, which tracks 80 major luxury-related companies. As of early 2020, the ETF had AUM of approximately $70 million. For more information, visit the manager's website at https://about.amundi.com.

Adidas is an apparel, footwear, sports equipment and accessories manufacturer. It employs over 59,000 people across the world. In 2019, Adidas produced more than 1.1 billion sports and sports lifestyle products. For more information, visit the company's website at https://www.adidas.com/us.

Nike is a sports apparel, footwear, sports equipment and accessories manufacturer. It employs over 70,000 people across more than 1,000 retail locations throughout the world. For more information, visit the company's website at https://www.nike.com.

Compagnie Financiere Richemont SA is a luxury goods holding company with a heavy presence in the watch industry among others, including jewelry, leather goods and accessories. Some of its largest and most well-known watch brands include A. Lange &

Table 12.1. The performance, risk and correlation of a composite of investments in collectibles versus the S&P 500 between January 2016 and December 2019.

	Collectibles	S&P 500
Correlation	0.71	NA
Standard Deviation	12.36%	11.56%
Average Annual Return	23.95%	14.33%
Simplified Sharpe	1.94	1.24

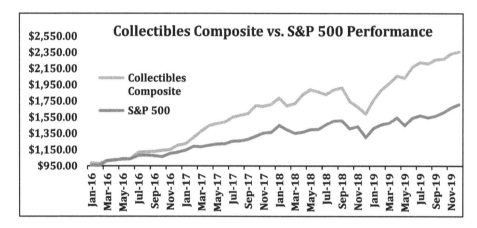

Figure 12.6. The growth of $1,000 invested in investment vehicles related to collectibles compared to the S&P 500 from January 2016 to December 2019.

Sohne, Baume & Mercier, Cartier, IWC and Roger Dubuis, among several others. For more information, visit the company's website at https://www.richemont.com.

Kering Group is a luxury goods manufacturer that has a heavy presence in the watch industry and other luxury goods, including jewelry, accessories and clothing. Some of the Kering Group major watch brands include Boucheron, Girard-Perregaux, JeanRichard and Ulysse Nardin. For more information, visit the company's website at https://www.kering.com/en/group/.

Composite

The luxury goods and collectibles composite, shown in Table 12.1, had higher returns of 23.95% versus 14.33%, similar risk of 12.36% versus 11.56% and a higher Sharpe ratio of 1.94 versus 1.24, compared to the S&P 500 for the period between January 2016 and December 2019. The composite also has a relatively low correlation of 0.71.

A $1,000 investment in a luxury goods composite in January 2016, shown in Figure 12.6, would have grown to almost $2,400 by December 2019 compared to $1,708 for the S&P 500.

Unique Risks

Collectibles are unique. However, they also share a number of common characteristics and risks. Collectibles are difficult to trade, have subjective values and are subject to fraud and theft, fire and damage. Like other exotic alternatives, they are illiquid and dealers charge significant fees. Collectibles are also not tax-efficient and generally do not qualify for capital gains treatment in the United States. Some of these risks can be mitigated via insurance and professional risk consultancy. Traditional carriers like USAA or boutique firms like Berkley Asset Protection and others offer a wide range of insurance and risk management services specifically designed for collectibles. Insurance coverage can be found for comic books, jewelry, trading cards, stamps and coins, books and manuscripts, vintage handbags, wine and sports memorabilia. Risk consulting services can help investors identify and eliminate the risk of ownership and care for a collection. Profession advice related to shaping, handling and storage, authentication and fraud protection can all ensure a portfolio is protected from catastrophic loss. In some cases, the value of a collection can also be insured against changes in market value. Insurance can also be used to fund rewards in the case of theft. For more information about how to protect collectibles, visit the Berkley Asset Protection website at https://berkleyassetpro.com/ or visit the USAA website at https://www.usaa.com/inet/pages/insurance_collectibles_main?akredirect=true.

Trends

In 2018, auctions for a wide range of collectibles experienced some of the highest prices of all time. Many individual collectibles set records for their prices at auctions or by private sales. One portrait by David Hockney was sold by Christie's for $90 million, setting the record for the most expensive work ever sold by a living artist. A bottle of Macallan 1926 was sold by Christie's for $1.5 million. Marie Antoinette's pearl pendant was sold by Sotheby's for $36 million. A 1970 Rolex Daytona "Unicorn" sold for $5.9 million. A 1962 Ferrari 250 GTO was sold by RM Sotheby's for $48.4 million. A new record for a bottle of wine was set when a 1945 Romanée-Conti was sold by Sotheby's for $558,000. One particular stamp, the 1918 Jenny Invert 24-cent, was sold by Robert A. Siegel Auction Galleries for $1.6 million. A Polish 1621 gold 100 ducat was sold by the Classic Numismatic Group for $2.2 million, making it the highest price ever for a Polish coin. The Winston Pink Legacy, a 19-carat vivid pink-colored diamond, was sold by Christie's for $50 million. Each of these set records for their particular category of collectable items in 2018.[14]

If there is a continuation of income disparity and increases in wealth generation among the richest people in the world, then the popularity and desirability of many collectibles are likely to continue. If this is the case, more money will be allocated to

---

14. Flora Harley et al., "The Wealth Report," *Knight Frank*, 2019, https://www.knightfrank.com/wealthreport/2019/luxury-spending/luxury-investment-index.

investing in a wide range of collectibles and their values will appreciate. More record prices and higher returns can be expected if global wealth increases and expands. Given its limited supply and increased demand, the asset class is likely to continue to provide investors with an opportunity for appreciation over long periods.

Academic Perspectives and Research

Academic articles related to collectibles such as vintage automobiles, wine, whiskey and a few other categories can be found starting in the 1980s. Early researchers wrote about combining passion with profit-seeking opportunities, the taxation of collectibles and strategies for collectible investing. Within the past five years, academic articles have focused on the historical returns and relationships to market benchmarks.

Benjamin J. Burton and Joyce P. Jacobsen published a paper entitled "Measuring Returns on Investments in Collectibles" in 1999. The researchers set out to determine the market for collectibles and the relationship it has with other investment vehicles. The most popular method for valuing collectibles is to create a composite index by selecting sets of items whose prices will be measured and averaged. This composite index can either be based on sets that vary over time or on a fixed market basket. The authors compared aggregate returns of three indices across collectible types that existed from Sotheby's, Salomon Brothers and the BritRail Fund. These indices indicated returns in the range of 11 to 14% over holding periods of 13–21 years, but these indices only represented post-1967 trends and were discontinued before the 1990s. Although there were some negative real return rates, they were not large in absolute value. The authors concluded that the majority of collectibles yield lower financial returns than stocks and studies that include a measure of variability over time uniformly find that collectibles embody more risk than most other financial assets. For example, the authors refer to research done by Pompe in 1996 that evaluated photographs and found them to have one of the highest annual returns of approximately 30%, after including buyer's fees. However, the research also found photograph prices to have extremely high variability, with a standard deviation of almost 300% per year. The researchers went ahead to perform a meta-analysis of several studies on collectible returns wherein they used each observation as a regression. The meta-analysis showed that none of these factors affected returns. The meta-analysis also supported the notion that while returns on collectibles may be negatively related to stock market rises, it does not provide evidence that collectibles are a good hedge against stock price falls, as their returns remain flat in bear markets. The researchers ultimately advised against making large investments in collectibles and instead encouraged investing in mutual funds as opposed to creating a collectibles portfolio.[15]

Vintage automobiles are another asset that has attracted academic research. One study by David Bonanno in 2016 focused on the vintage automotive industry as an investable asset. The authors offered three ways to value vintage autos. The first and

---

15. Benjamin Burton and Joyce Jacobsen, "Measuring Returns on Investments in Collectibles," *Journal of Economic Perspectives*, 1999, www.jstor.org/stable/2647019.

most popular way is to create a composite index in which the specific items of a set are included in a simple average. The second is to calculate a hedonic regression. This method highlights how different characteristics will influence the value of a certain asset. The third way to compute returns on collectibles is through repeat-sale regression, which occurs when an object is purchased and sold again. With enough of these observations, an index is created to show market trends. This paper used data recorded from 1994 to 2016 from the K500 Index, which covers 500 individual cars from 10 subdivisions: Pre-war and postwar European and American cars, Ferrari (pre-1958, 1958–73 and post-1973), Porsche, postwar racing cars and affordable classics. They then compared the holding period returns of each subdivision to the stock, bond and gold markets, using the DJIA, NASDAQ and the S&P 500 as a proxy for stocks, the Vanguard Long-Term Bond Index as a proxy for bonds and the Gold Fixing Price in the London Bullion Market for the price of gold. They computed standard deviations, betas and Sharpe ratios for each automotive and traditional index based on this data set. One major conclusion from the analysis is that the standard deviation for prices of vintage automobiles in the study was consistently lower than the financial market instruments. For example, the pre-1973 Ferrari and the NASDAQ have the same average returns; however, the standard deviation of the pre-1973 Ferrari is only 1.88%, while that of the NASDAQ is the highest at 10.91%. Across most subdivisions, the standard deviations tended to be below 2%, with the average standard deviation across the K500 index being 1.28%, much lower than traditional asset classes. Another finding was the very low correlation to traditional asset classes, where the S&P 500 was used as the market proxy. This suggests very low systematic risk and that this asset class can be used for diversification. Lastly, Sharpe ratios for K500 subdivisions are all higher than the S&P 500 Sharpe ratio of 0.1574. While their analysis has shown classic cars to be a sound investment, the authors warn that there is a possibility of a classic car market bubble. The entrance into the market of speculators may have caused the price to rise above market value, while recent developments seem to show that this bubble is bursting. From these findings, they conclude that classic cars may have been a wise investment if already undertaken in the past, but that prudence is needed going forward.[16]

An article in the *Journal of Alternative Investments* entitled "When Rationality Meets Passion: On the Financial Performance of Collectables" analyzes the performance of a number of different collectibles relative to traditional stock and bonds and commodities like gold. The study included visual art, fine wine, classic cars and other collectibles. The study finds impressive results for classic cars, most notably European cars. Art and fine wine did not exhibit significant relative risk-adjusted returns according to the study. The researchers also found very low betas and attractive risk coefficients on a variety of measures relative to traditional stock and bond investments. Adding collectibles to a

---

16. David Bonanno, *Classic Cars: Money Pit or Investment Star? A Study on Market for Vintage Cars under the Investor's Perspective*, Department of Economics and Finance, LUISS Guido Carli, 2016, https://pdfs.semanticscholar.org/fcfd/5c3df03fd6b693759deecadfab09cda3590f.pdf.

traditional portfolio of stocks, bonds and gold was observed to lower portfolio risk on a number of measures.[17]

Summary

Collectibles may work well in a portfolio designed for the long term and outperform during boom times, but they will not necessarily act as a hedge against economic downturns. In addition, collectibles can be expensive, are tax-inefficient, unregulated and not very liquid. They do not always beat stock and bond indices or hold their value in a market downturn. Despite these caveats, collectibles have a relatively low correlation to traditional stocks and bonds and have performed reasonably well in certain categories over specific periods. Prices tend to rise more quickly during periods of economic expansion and fall during recessions.

Useful Websites and Additional Reading

"Collecting & Investing in Wine—Costs, Risks, How to Buy," https://www.moneycrashers.com/collecting-investing-wine-costs-risks/.

"An Expert Guide to Investing in Rare Whisky," https://theupsider.com.au/rare-whisky-investing/13689.

"Measuring Returns on Investments in Collectibles," https://www.aeaweb.org/articles?id=10.1257/jep.13.4.193.

"Rules to Remember about Investing in Memorabilia," https://www.cnbc.com/id/39444167.

"The Effect of Scarcity Types on Consumer Preference in the High-End Sneaker Market," https://libres.uncg.edu/ir/asu/f/Cassidy_Nick%20Spring%202018%20Thesis.pdf.

"The New Sports Collectibles Industry: A Need For Research," https://scholarworks.bgsu.edu/cgi/viewcontent.cgi?article=1644&context=visions.

"The Wealth Report 2020," https://www.knightfrank.com/wealthreport.

"The State of the Collector-Car Market," https://www.automobilemag.com/news/collector-car-market-buy-hold-sell-classic-vintage/.

"Watches Are Yet Another Easy Way Rich People Make Their Money into More Money," https://www.nytimes.com/2019/03/20/style/collectible-watches.html.

"Why Sneakers Are a Great Investment," https://www.ted.com/talks/josh_luber_why_sneakers_are_a_great_investment?language=en.

---

17. Phillippe Masset and Jean-Phillippe Weisskopf, "When Rationality Meets Passion: On the Financial Performance of Collectables," *Journal of Alternative Investments*, Oct. 2018, https://jai.pm-research.com/content/21/2/66/tab-article-info.

Chapter Thirteen

INVESTOR PERSPECTIVES AND INSIGHTS

During the research for this book, I was able to speak to a number of industry participants, investors and portfolio managers about investing in exotic alternative investments. Broadly speaking, investors appear to be attracted to the specific exotic alternative assets because they believe they will have little or no correlation to stocks and bonds or other alternatives like hedge funds. Some investors are attracted only to those exotic alternatives with cash flows, despite their uncertainty, while others are investing for appreciation alone. Some individual investors stressed the fact that they look to invest at the early stage of a business that has significant growth potential and a low correlation to the markets.

Institutional investors seem to think more in terms of credit products and are looking for cheap risk-adjusted cash flows. They treat exotic alternative asset classes with known or estimated cash flows as part of their overall credit investment portfolio. Insurance-linked securities, royalties and litigation claims fall into this category. In these cases, exotic or illiquid private credit allocations could range from 0% to 50% of an institution's credit portfolio.

Some investors seem to avoid exotic asset classes such as life settlements, litigation funding, catastrophic loss bonds and cannabis due to perceived complexity, moral or ethical concerns or simply based upon a lack of consensus or a strong diversity of opinions about the suitability within their organizations. Anecdotally at least, it appears that asset allocation to exotic alternatives ranges anywhere from a low of 0% to as high as 15% of the overall assets.

In the section that follows, we review feedback from several investors who have had some experience with exotic alternative investments. The responses are both positive and negative. The interviews that follow were conducted with a range of industry professionals covering both institutional and individual investors as well as allocators and consultants active or interested in this space.

Peter Brady, Independent Consultant

Peter Brady is a business developer and marketing professional in the alternative asset management industry. He has more than 15 years of business development, investor relations and marketing experience in hedge funds, dating back to 2004. From 2013 to 2018, he was head of business development at a start-up event-driven equity hedge fund. Before that, he held senior business development positions at Larch Lane Advisors, Prisma Capital Partners and FRM. Mr. Brady has published articles in the *Journal of Alternative Investments* and the *Journal of Taxation of Investments*. Mr. Brady received his BA in Economics from Columbia University in 1993 and his JD/MBA from Columbia University in 1998.

What is your view on the appetite for institutions to invest in exotic alternative investments today?
All of the investors I spoke to were familiar with most of these strategies and in most cases had at a minimum reviewed presentation material from one or more investment managers pursuing such strategies. Moreover, all of the investors had invested in or recommended that their clients invest in one or more exotic alternative investment strategies prior to 2020.
One common theme shared by the investors was that the two primary appeals of all of these strategies were the potentially uncorrelated returns and the potential for consistent returns/yield well in excess of their targeted return for the portfolio. The most common reasons cited for not allocating to many of the strategies were concerned about a limited track record to evaluate, potential "headline risk" or social policy concerns within the organization, a lack of liquidity and issues related to operational risk and fraud potential.

What feedback did you get on specific types of exotic alternative investment products?
Reinsurance was a strategy that was the most widely adopted among the investors with whom I spoke. Most had invested with one or more managers focused on this strategy. This strategy appears to offer the appealing characteristics cited above while addressing most of the potential concerns. Specifically, investors cited the fact that collecting premiums for insuring against catastrophic weather events is clearly uncorrelated to capital markets and the potential for attractive yields is appealing (albeit with the potential for "left tail" risk in the event of one or more large catastrophes occurring in a short time frame). In terms of the concerns, there have been institutional-focused investment managers pursuing this strategy since the first decade of the 2000s, so allocators generally feel they have sufficient return data from which they can evaluate the strategy. In addition, investors can typically access this strategy through a relatively liquid vehicle and it does not appear to present significant concerns about the headline or operational risk. If anything, some investors indicated that this strategy may have attracted too much institutional capital, which has compressed expected future returns, thereby reducing one of the primary appeals of the strategy.
Investor sentiment about life settlements was generally less favorable compared to reinsurance. While it offers a similar appeal in terms of potential for consistent, uncorrelated returns, investors expressed more concern about possible headline risk related to this strategy. In particular, multiple investors indicated that their organization would not be comfortable pursuing a strategy that essentially profits when groups of individuals die earlier than predicted by insurance company mortality estimates. Indeed, this strategy falls squarely in the category of "headline risk" as there have been articles in the *Wall Street Journal* and elsewhere questioning whether it is unsavory to pursue this strategy. Also, investors that have any type of socially responsible investing (SRI) mandate are highly unlikely to pursue this strategy. Interestingly, more than one person that I interviewed indicated concerns that the morality of this strategy may be

misplaced, but at an organizational level, it is easier to simply avoid this strategy rather than try to convince people that potential concerns may be overstated.

Cannabis was an investment where none of the investors interviewed had pursued this strategy or even seriously considered an investment. Investors consistently cited concerns about the murky legal status of cannabis and CBD where state and federal statutes conflict. Investors generally do not feel comfortable accepting the high legal/regulatory risk associated with investing in this area. In some cases, cannabis also may be an unacceptable strategy for investors with an SRI policy. On top of these issues, investors did not believe that this strategy offered uncorrelated returns, which is an appealing characteristic of other exotic alternatives.

Crypto was also a strategy where none of the investors interviewed had pursued the strategy or even seriously considered an investment. However, the reasons given for avoiding the strategy were not the same. In the case of digital currency, the primary concerns cited were extreme volatility combined with very limited track records. For most institutional investors, the combination of high volatility and limited data to evaluate makes digital currency a non-starter. When you add in the fact that there have been high-profile cases of fraud in the space and that funds are populated with smaller, less-established managers, it is easy to understand why institutional adoption is very low in this area.

Collectibles is one area where a few investors had looked at managers that invest in artwork and other collectibles, but none had made or recommended an investment. While investors believe that investments in various collectibles potentially offer uncorrelated returns, most expressed significant concerns about liquidity and the lack of reliable performance data. Most investors viewed these investment categories as very limited niches, so they also expressed concerns about potential capacity constraints and whether they could invest sufficient capital into such a strategy to justify the time and effort required to conduct proper diligence and monitoring of such an investment.

How did investors think about asset allocation to exotic and direct investing versus the use of managers and funds?

In most interviews, investors tended to group strategies such as litigation financing and royalties from intellectual property together as niche credit strategies. Litigation financing appears to have attracted a relatively high level of interest from institutional investors. Most of the investors interviewed had either invested in or recommended litigation financing. This is likely due to the fact that this strategy offers the same potential advantages of other exotic alternatives (attractive, uncorrelated returns) while effectively addressing most of the concerns that prevent institutions from investing in some of the other strategies. A number of well-established firms have been pursuing this strategy for a sufficient time to allay most concerns about the lack of track record and liquidity. While the investors with whom I spoke generally indicated that they were willing to consider investing in a vehicle that captures the income stream from royalty payments, several also believed this strategy lacked sufficient capacity to have broad institutional appeal.

Most of the institutional investors and consultants interviewed indicated that they would only invest in these strategies through an investment manager rather than making direct investments into a specific security or deal. Investors recognized that each of these areas requires knowledge and expertise that their organization did not possess. As such, the preferred approach was to invest with a specialized manager. Investors are willing to pay fees to a manager for sourcing and managing investments. In most cases, managers accessed exotic alternative investments via a commingled fund, although some investors were also willing to co-invest in specific deals alongside a manager rather than in a commingled fund. Investors were generally agnostic about the exact structure of a fund; they indicated that their primary concern was that the fund terms be reasonable and that the liquidity offered should be consistent with the strategy. As such, for less liquid strategies, investors were comfortable investing in a vehicle with a multi-year lock-up and potentially a commitment of capital that would be drawn over time.

Tom Ehrlein, City National Rochdale

Tom Ehrlein joined City National Rochdale in 2005. He is the head of investment solutions and his work is an essential part of asset allocation and investment decisions at the firm. Mr. Ehrlein's responsibilities include product development, investment research and due diligence and asset allocation modeling. As of October 2019, the firm as a whole managed $45 billion and Mr. Ehrlein is responsible for a significant amount of those assets under management. Previously, Mr. Ehrlein held positions at FactSet Research Systems (Investment Management Consultant) and ABN-Amro (Middle Market Lending/Securitization). He earned his BS in Finance from the University of Scranton and his MBA in Finance from Hofstra University. City National Rochdale is a wholly owned subsidiary of the Royal Bank of Canada.

Please tell me about your firm, its products and services and its mission or unique value proposition.
City National Rochdale is an investment firm that typically focuses on high-net-worth and ultra-high-net-worth individuals. We have a diverse set of clients and we act as a registered investment advisor and follow the highest standards of fiduciary care for our investors. The firm has approximately $40 billion assets under management and we are backed by one of the largest financial institutions in the world, the Royal Bank of Canada.

What is your professional experience in raising capital, evaluating or recommending exotic alternative investments such as life settlements, litigation finance, airline leases, storage units, tax liens, art finance, cryptoassets, intellectual property rights/royalties or other "off-the-run" assets with low correlation to traditional stocks and bonds?
Our firm has allocated to what we call non-traditional asset classes for the better part of the past two decades. We typically don't view investment or product allocations as exotic, rather, as a business decision that most investors understand but would not otherwise be able to access the opportunity.

Historically, we have allocated to investments that have an identifiable cash flow metric and additional potential investor benefits. More growth-based or speculative areas are typically not in our wheelhouse. This is not to say an area of potential long-term high growth is not a good investment, but as an investment firm, we try to understand our limitations and our client needs.

Our investment criteria framework is fairly simple. Our due diligence process then takes a lengthier amount of time and includes checking for unique, differentiated and uncorrelated opportunities, durability and structural persistence, fundamental economic underpinning, income generation, tax efficiencies and capital preservation. We also look to avoid beta plays, untested managers or strategies, unsustainable opportunities or trades, unjustified or unrewarded illiquidity as well as limited downside protection.

How do you think about these asset classes when it comes to traditional asset allocation and portfolio construction?

From an asset allocation standpoint, we don't view these investments very differently than traditional asset classes. From a discussion and communication standpoint, they are very different. The illiquidity aspect of these asset classes makes the conversation with investors extremely important.

As an investment firm, we look at asset classes from a high-level picture in four main categories: equities, core fixed income, opportunistic income and real assets. Depending on the client's situation, we might add a fifth category of alternative investments. Although we might segregate alternative investments, we usually feel they are a part of the main four categories. Cryptoassets, although interesting, would not be an area we would pursue for our client base in the current state.

For example, we view our leasing strategies as real assets and insurance-based solutions as opportunistic income. However, since these might be very different from a global real estate mutual fund or a high-yield bond, we might call them out to explain the strategy and the liquidity profile more directly with our investors.

In terms of fit within our investor's portfolio, that is really dependent on the individual's goals, needs and risk profile. If we were running unconstrained portfolios, allocations to these strategies would likely be higher than they currently are. Our typical client has between 10% and 20% exposure related to their overall portfolio.

Ken Shoji, View Capital Advisors

Ken Shoji is the chief investment officer of View Capital Advisors, a wealth management firm in Dallas. Ken has over 30 years of experience in trading and asset management. Before joining View Capital, he founded an advisory firm serving family offices, ran a quantitative hedge fund and managed the alternative investment business for an international bank. He has also held positions in derivatives sales and trading at Deutsche Bank, Bankers Trust and J. P. Morgan, in New York, London and Tokyo, respectively. Ken is a CFA charter holder and graduated with an MA with Honors from the University of Edinburgh and an MBA from the Harvard Business School.

Please tell me about your firm, its products and services and its mission or unique value proposition?
View Capital Advisors is an independent wealth management firm founded 15 years ago
to grow wealth for a select group of families, executives and entrepreneurs. We provide our clients with comprehensive wealth management strategies that include wealth
planning, estate structuring and investment management. Our clients tend to have an
entrepreneurial spirit, are highly driven and embrace non-traditional views and are
individuals who see us as peers, subject matter experts and investment partners. They
demand insight, candor and alternative approaches to the status quo. Since a significant number of our clients are international investors, we have developed extensive
expertise in multi-jurisdictional tax planning and investment structuring. We foster a
performance-driven culture that promotes intellectual excellence and curiosity, analyt-
ical rigor and operational efficiency.

For most of our larger clients, we manage "endowment style" portfolios with a significant
allocation to alternative strategies. We allocate capital through external investment
managers in both traditional and alternative asset classes. We look for exceptional
investment managers that have top-tier performance, institutional quality infrastructure and demonstrate a fiduciary mind-set and integrity.

Our investment team has extensive experience in sourcing, researching and conducting
manager due diligence. We bring partner-level professionals who have been trained at
major institutional investment firms. We participate in hundreds of investment manager meetings per year and devote a considerable amount of time speaking to our
collective network of major endowments, foundations, pension and sovereign wealth
funds in order to stay abreast of new investment strategies, managers and academic
research.

Our value proposition is that we can offer the highly customized and personalized advisory service of a boutique firm with the investment sophistication, thought leadership
and product breadth of the most advanced institutional investors. Our strength in
alternative investments gives us a competitive edge in our target client markets.

*What is your professional experience in raising capital, evaluating or recommending exotic alternative
investments such as life settlements, litigation finance, airline leases, storage units, tax liens, art finance,
cryptoassets, intellectual property rights/royalties or other "off-the-run" assets with low correlation to
traditional stocks and bonds?*
I have been researching and investing in non-traditional investments on behalf of institutional investors and family offices for over a decade, including those related to operating assets, insurance, intellectual property, real assets and collectibles. Operating
assets include aircraft leasing, railcar leasing, operating real estate (cold storage, data
centers), cell towers and cannabis farms. Insurance includes life settlements and catastrophe insurance. Intellectual property includes music royalties, film finance and
litigation finance. Real assets include cattle, water infrastructure and water rights.
Collectibles would primarily include artwork.

At View Capital, we have invested in these areas through funds sponsored by external
asset managers. In a few cases, we have invested directly, primarily in co-investments
with fund managers. We have established an internal vehicle (View Wireless Fund) to

invest directly in cell towers, DAS systems, 5G technology and related communication assets.

We have been very selective in the type of managers we have chosen to work with in these fields. Our experience is that the most successful managers are those who have deep subject-matter expertise derived from tenure in the relevant industry, and who have acquired an understanding of the best practices necessary to run an institutional-quality fund. For example, we have met art advisors who clearly have tremendous expertise in contemporary art but have little financial discipline when it comes to buying art for investment purposes and are unable to meet the operating transparency, reporting and investor communication requirements that an institutional investor would expect from a fiduciary manager. Conversely, we have met former Wall Street traders who are financially sophisticated but lack the art history and art market background to be able to make nuanced acquisition decisions. We have found that the best managers in these non-traditional asset classes need to have both skill sets.

Another important tenet we hold is that fund sponsors need to be very active asset managers; in other words, they need to generate alpha above the "buy-and-hold" beta of the asset class. While this may seem obvious, managers in many of these strategies are working with assets whose value can be enhanced significantly with proactive management. For example, a music royalty manager can buy a publishing right and passively collect royalty income. However, an active manager can aggressively market the music to media companies to have the music played in films, television programs, commercials, video games and even toys ("synchronization", in industry parlance). Each additional use of the music not only generates additional income but also enhances the equity value of the asset. In the area of life settlements, for example, a fund may simply buy and hold policies until the insured's death. An active manager, however, may conduct extensive monitoring and research on the insured's health and lifestyle on an ongoing basis, which might result in insights into the insured's longevity that could lead to profitable trading of the policy.

Finally, we believe that it is critical for investors to have a thorough understanding of the operational practices involved in these strategies. In catastrophe insurance, an understanding of how investor capital can be "trapped" (as in, a situation in which cash collateral is held in escrow until the liability arising from a natural disaster claim is assessed and settled) is critical to determining the amount of exposure an investor has at risk at any given time. An understanding of valuation methodologies is obviously critical in all of these strategies.

How do you think about these asset classes when it comes to traditional asset allocation and portfolio construction?

While we invest in traditional alternative investments such as hedge funds, private equity, private credit and real estate funds, we do not take the approach of carving out a small percentage of a client's "alternatives" bucket for "exotic" investments. In fact, in many client portfolios, such investments represent the bulk of risk exposures.

We build customized portfolios based on the client's specific investment objectives, risk tolerance, time horizon, tax situation and other constraints. In practice, however, we have found that many portfolios fall into common types, such as multi-generational growth or retirement income. We create model portfolios to provide a starting point for many asset allocation proposals and to provide an internal benchmark for performance tracking.

We design portfolios based on three principal dimensions: risk premia, liquidity and cash flow. While we can bucket assets along traditional lines such as equities, mutual funds or alternatives, we find that such asset labels don't always help us or our clients understand the purpose of each investment in their portfolio. A risk-based analysis provides better information about what return and risk drivers are present in each investment. Equity risk, necessary for long-term growth, can come from both marketable equities and private equity funds. Credit exposure exists in not only marketable bonds but also private credit strategies and real estate. For example, our investments in net-lease real estate funds have exposure to corporate lessee credit risk, as well as to equity risk and duration, since the value of long-term leases are sensitive to interest rates. Aircraft leasing also involves exposure to corporate credit, but it is also sensitive to global travel growth, which in turn is sensitive to global GDP growth. Music royalty cash flows have historically been unaffected by economic slowdowns or recessions, so they may provide capital protection in those environments. By focusing on the contribution of investments to fundamental risk factors such as equity, credit and duration, we believe we can get a better sense of how portfolios will behave under different economic and market conditions.

In determining the relative allocations to risks in portfolios, we are guided by our assessment of the macroeconomic environment, asset valuations and market structure dynamics. If we see that we are at the end of a business or market cycle, we may overweight allocations to risks that may outperform in a deflationary or recessionary environment.

Finally, we also have to balance the optimal risk allocations with the client's liquidity tolerances and cash flow requirements. While a portfolio of middle-market lending funds may meet the desired exposure credit risk, it may exceed the client's target tolerance for liquidity if they are all 10-year lock-up vehicles or it may be unable to meet their cash flow needs if they do not make distributions until the end of the fund's stated investment period. Conversely, a strategy such as aircraft leasing can generate high quarterly distributions compared to traditional fixed-income funds.

So, our portfolio construction process is to first determine the appropriate mix of risk factors that meets the client's investment objectives and then allocate to the right combination of liquid and private funds that results in the target exposures.

We devote a great deal of time educating our clients about these investments. We write white papers describing strategies, invite clients to listen to manager presentations and host an annual investment conference dedicated to these themes. Intellectual property investments were the theme of our 2019 conference and operating assets the theme of our 2017 conference.

We do not believe that exotic alternatives are only appropriate for the largest investors. We typically negotiate smaller minimum investment sizes than the manager's stated minimum, allowing us to allocate amounts as small as $100,000 to a private fund whose stated minimum might be $5 million.

One feature of these strategies where we are very cautious is their correlation to other investment strategies. These strategies are often marketed as having little or no correlation to the public equity or bond markets. However, as with many assets whose returns are subject to serial correlation effects, their statistical correlation relative to public markets need to be taken with a large grain of salt. For example, the occurrence of natural disasters such as hurricanes and earthquakes may be random events unrelated to the financial markets. However, we have seen that the occurrence of major natural disasters can impact the performance of public markets. The tsunami that hit the Pacific coast of Japan in March 2011 led to over $35 billion in insured losses that resulted in significant losses for reinsurance funds, but it also triggered an 18% collapse in the Nikkei stock index, a loss that the market did not recover from for 21 months. There was a causal relationship between the natural catastrophe and the stock market that had an impact on the investor portfolio.

The limited capacity of many of these strategies makes them vulnerable to capital flows. We have seen significant yield compression in strategies that involve discounting of future cash flows, such as life settlements, music royalties and film finance.

Ron Suber, Venture Capitalist

Ron is an entrepreneur, business executive, sales and marketing professional, branding expert, mentor, student and coach. He has a long history of creating and executing successful strategies, raising debt and equity for fintech ventures, collaborating and having fun on winning teams. He enjoys engaging with entrepreneurs to help with their marketing, product development, strategy, sales process, hiring, focus and execution of key metrics. Ron is on the board of directors of Qwil and YieldStreet and the advisory board member to Juvo, Unison, Money360, House Canary, MoneyLion, Earnup, Even Financial and eOriginal. He has been married for 28 years, has two grown children and lives in San Francisco, California.

Please tell me a little about your background with respect to alternative investments, both traditional ones such as hedge funds, private equity, venture and real estate and the more exotic like litigation finance, art finance, farmland, vintage auto, life settlements or others.

I spent 20 years on Wall Street in the custody, finance, operations, technology and trading of hedge funds. Having watched it all, observing the wins, losses and lessons, I decided to allocate a portion of my personal assets into the lending to alternatives across commercial and residential real estate, art, shipping, consumer, small business, trade finance, invoices and litigation. The net yield on these assets is 8%–12% with a term of one to four years. These investments are best held in tax-deferred accounts. I have decided not to invest in the life settlements space as advances in medicine are making this category less profitable and "hoping someone dies" just doesn't feel right. I was an investor in the early days of peer-to-peer lending. The business generated 9%–10% net returns but limited volume. As the demand from retail and institutional investors grew, starting in 2014, the volume increased and the returns decreased as rates lowered and defaults increased.

How do you think about any or all of these more exotic alternative investments when it comes to asset allocation and portfolio construction?
Personally, for my portfolio, asset allocation falls into three main buckets: passive, low-cost, tax-efficient equities via ETFs, investments in private companies hoping to make 10 times, alpha and full exits and liquidity within 10 years and fixed income, including cash, municipal bonds and lending into private credit. For me, the allocation is 30% equities, 25% privates and 45% fixed income (cash, municipal bonds and specialty credit). Investments in exotic alternatives would fit into the private investment or lending bucket depending on the specific case.

Seth Weinstein, Individual Investor

Seth Weinstein is a private investor in early-stage technology start-ups, currently with more than 30 active investments with a focus on emerging fintech businesses. He is the founder, managing director and CEO of Morgan Stanley Fund Services Inc. (2005–17), established as a wholly owned subsidiary of Morgan Stanley, providing a comprehensive suite of technology-enabled services to leading hedge funds and investors across the United States, Europe and Asia and supported by over 700 professionals based in New York, London, Dublin, Glasgow, Hong Kong, Mumbai and Bengaluru, administering assets in excess of $250 billion. He began his career within Morgan Stanley's prime brokerage business in 1988 and joined BPB Associates in 1994 as the managing director, leading engagements with hedge funds, investment banks, broker-dealers and service providers. He joined NatWest Securities in 1996 as executive vice president and global head of technology for the institutional equity division. He later joined Deutsche Bank as a managing director as part of that firm's acquisition of NatWest's global equity derivatives businesses. Finally, he rejoined Morgan Stanley in 2000, as managing director and co-head of US prime brokerage.

What is your background and current position in the market?
I recently retired after a 30-year career in financial services. My current focus is on early-stage venture investing, with a bias toward fintech. I have made approximately 40 active private investments thus far.

What is your experience in investing in exotic alternatives such as litigation finance, life settlement, art finance, farmland, rare minerals, cannabis, collectibles, Bitcoin or blockchain, intellectual property rights, eSports or other non-correlated asset classes (either directly, via funds or listed companies in the space)?
I have invested in several direct, seed-stage angel investments in various alternative asset management businesses, including a quantitative investment firm for art assets called Arthena, an artificial intelligence–powered litigation finance company called Legalist and a quant fund using predictive analytics to trade electricity called

Gaiascope. Other investments in start-ups that may represent exotic alternatives platforms and infrastructure providers, including a novel prediction market, essentially a para-mutual betting platform for the outcome of events called Kalshi, and two "pick and shovel" companies in the digital (crypto) currency space, one enabling a protocol for tokenized debt agreements called Dharma and another focused on anti-money-laundering compliance and transaction monitoring for digital assets called TRM Labs.

Where do you see these sorts of opportunities fitting into a portfolio and what type of investors do you think they are best suited for?

I maintain a 25% allocation to alternatives within my overall investment portfolio, including hedge funds, private equity, venture capital, real estate and commodities. Within this alternatives bucket, I've allocated approximately 20% to direct venture or angel investments, or about 5% of my total investment portfolio, which I expect to expand over time as I allocate more capital to new deals and participate in follow-on funding rounds via pro-rata rights.

I see exotic alternatives fitting into an overall asset allocation strategy for both institutional and high-net-worth investors, as they have the potential to offer non-correlated returns in less-crowded niche markets. Although my current exposure to exotic alternatives comes through direct investment activities in start-ups, I can see investing in ETFs or funds as compelling product offerings emerge.

I can also see the appeal of such products more generally to retail investors as more products become available in the form of liquid individual securities, mutual funds and ETFs.

Greg Kiernan, Sonostar Ventures

Greg Kiernan is the managing partner and CEO of Sonostar Ventures LLC, an investment, private equity and venture capital firm established in 1997, which currently invests in early to mid-stage venture capital opportunities and provides fee-based investment and consulting services. Prior to founding Sonostar, Greg worked at Lehman Brothers, Salomon Brothers and then for 10 years as a managing director at PaineWebber where he was a member of the firm's executive operating, risk management and commitment committees. He served as a director on the executive committee of the Public Securities Association. Before starting his Wall Street career, Greg worked for Cravath, Swaine and Moore as an attorney admitted to practice law in New York State. Greg holds a JD degree from Harvard Law School and a BA from Amherst College (Magna Cum Laude, Phi Beta Kappa). Greg is a board member of several companies that Sonostar has financed and is involved in a number of charitable and civic ventures. Until recently, he served on the executive committee of the San Miguel Academy of Newburgh where he was a board member and a founding council member. He is a recipient of the Amherst College Alumni Distinguished Service Award. He resides in Chappaqua, New York, with his wife, Vera, with regular visits from their five children and grandchildren.

Please tell me about your firm.

Sonostar Ventures was started in 1997 with initial capital provided by its two founding partners: Greg Kiernan and David Moore. The firm's primary emphasis is on early-stage venture capital; however, because the invested assets use the personal capital of its founders, the firm can also invest in any public or private opportunity that presents itself in the marketplace.

What sort of unique investments do you like to pursue and what are your objectives?

Over the years, Sonostar and its principals have invested in more than two dozen venture capital deals representing a variety of different entrepreneurial opportunities. The list of investments is long, but for at least a portion of our portfolio, our goal has been to find opportunities and investments that are not correlated to the stock market and the overall economy. We attempt to achieve superior returns by finding uncorrelated investments. The firm has provided the initial capital for a range of companies. Investments have included Marquis Jets—the first of its kind, 25-hour private jet card that enabled travelers to experience the luxury of private air travel with a fixed cost, 25-hour annual membership card—and Paradigm Direct, a direct-to-consumer performance marketing firm that sells cell service, long-distance service, home alarm services and other monthly subscription services for large brands.

The challenge is that in one sense, nearly every investment has some correlation to the market and the economy. So, for example, when we invest in some intriguing new science in the biotech sector (as we did successfully at a very early stage with both Kite Biopharmaceuticals and Allogene Therapeutics in immune-oncology), we expect the assets to be generally tied to the performance of the biotech sector in the market, including how that sector may impact capital-raising opportunities for our companies, valuation for successful compounds, merger opportunities and exit strategies. But we understand that the primary determinant of whether our investment will be successful or not is not driven by the market per se, it is driven by the success or failure of the underlying science. Do the drugs work? If they do, our early investment will have significant positive returns, irrespective of whether the market is up or down. Similarly, if our companies' specific drugs do not work, it will not matter if the biotech sector is hitting all-time highs; our returns will suffer.

While we cannot deny that "the market" has at least some impact on everything we invest in, we have nevertheless been able to find investments in certain businesses where the performance has been non-correlated or, in any event, less correlated with the markets and the overall economy.

Our most successful business has been our investment in the residential window replacement business for one of the leading high-quality window manufacturers in the United States. While there is no question that the business flourishes during times of economic strength, we have been surprised to learn that even when housing starts have slowed or declined, our business has maintained a positive trajectory. It turns out that consumers are most likely to replace their windows as a fix-up in preparation for a move, as an upgrade and home improvement shortly after a move or as a lifestyle enhancement when the real estate market has slowed and folks are staying put. Our window business has weathered multiple economic cycles and has grown to the point where it will do more than $400 million in combined revenues in 2019. Our projection is for continued growth with a modest correlation to the housing market.

One failure we invested in was Golden Goal Soccer and Lacrosse tournament park, a 300-acre sports park featuring state-of-the-art synthetic and natural turf fields and housing for youth teams. Before we invested, we did careful due diligence on Cooperstown Dreams Park, the Little League predecessor equivalent of what we were trying to build. Our research showed that at Cooperstown, total revenues and the numbers of teams participating had consistently grown year after year, irrespective of the strength of the economy. Armed with that data and analysis showing that youth soccer and lacrosse participation and the development of corresponding league play were expanding exponentially, we invested in our new facility. The first two or three years showed strong early success, we broke even by the third year, but the recession of 2008–9 led to a complete collapse in our business. Dozens of teams that had signed up for one of our 14 one-week programs dropped out, forfeiting their deposits. Meanwhile, as it turns out, Cooperstown continued to thrive. We learned that the parents of soccer and lacrosse players are much more closely attuned to the performance of the markets and the economy than the parents of Little League baseball players, and as the recession progressed, under the burden of significant indebtedness, our investment ceased operations, costing us most of our investment.

Recently, Sonostar's principals purchased a portfolio of taxi medallions from a distressed seller in New York City. At one time medallions traded for as much as $1.3 million, and for more than 10 years they had traded well above $500 thousand per medallion, until Uber. The introduction of Uber, Lyft, Juno and a host of other rideshare services have decimated the New York City taxi industry. Medallion prices have collapsed and many medallion holders who had borrowed to purchase medallions have been unable to cover their debt payment obligations resulting in foreclosures. We believe that there are a host of factors that make this an opportune investment. The city has approved legislation capping the number of new Uber and Lyft drivers that will be licensed to offer service in New York City. The result is that for the first time in the past three years, the average monthly lease rates for medallions have actually started to modestly increase, at the same time that medallion prices have reached new lows. As a depreciable asset, taxi medallions offer attractive tax-advantaged current cash flow along with potential capital appreciation if the current market dislocations work themselves out. We believe that our purchase will prove timely and will show meaningful returns uncorrelated to the behavior of the overall markets.

How do these less or uncorrelated investments fit into your overall portfolio?

Concerning public stocks and fixed income investments, we have found that we are able to significantly enhance our returns by dedicating a meaningful portion of up to 25% of our portfolio to these "uncorrelated" investment opportunities. The majority of our portfolio is dedicated to more typical plain vanilla venture capital investments.

Other Investor Perspectives

A recent article in *Bloomberg Wealth* by Suzanne Woolley, Edward Robinson, Katya Kazakina and Devon Pendleton entitled "Where to Invest $1 Million Right Now," updated on April 28, 2020, discussed changes in asset allocation and investment strategies with five prominent investors and fund managers. Investors and allocators seemed keen to allocate to new ideas within traditional stock and bond, private equity or hedge fund portfolios. Their suggestions included ideas related to companies that make batteries, investments in copper, private equity secondary market investments, cybersecurity and healthcare. Each expert was also asked to discuss other less traditional ways to invest for the future. Some of these ideas included topics covered in this book, such as art, wine, collectibles and sports memorabilia. Other topics discussed included waste management and rental homes in the Hamptons. The complete article and interviews with the five experts can be found by going to the Bloomberg website: https://www.bloomberg.com/features/how-to-invest-a-million-dollars/?srnd=premium.

Chapter Fourteen

PORTFOLIO RETURN AND RISK USING EXOTIC ALTERNATIVE INVESTMENTS

In this chapter, we will explore the properties of individual exotic alternative investments as well as a master composite portfolio created from the investments in public companies, ETFs, mutual funds and private LPs discussed in this book.

The master composite only includes the exotic alternatives categories that have been previously identified and that have publicly traded shares, mutual funds and ETFs or those private funds with semi-liquid structures such as hedge funds. The goal of creating a master composite is to understand how the return and risk characteristics of each exotic alternative category interact with one another and how they compare to traditional stock portfolios as well as traditional alternative investments such as hedge funds, private equity and real estate. The master composite used in our analysis includes a total of 97 investment vehicles. There are 83 public companies and ETFs and 14 hedge funds in the master composite. The investment vehicles were grouped by exotic investment category and then an evenly weighted composite was computed using the returns from each category.

Analysis of Master Composite Returns, Standard Deviation and Correlation Versus Stocks and Traditional Alternatives

The return and risk from investing in a master composite of exotic alternative investments is shown in Table 14.1. It had an annual return of almost 40% for the period between January 2016 and December 2019. The annual return significantly exceeded the S&P 500 return of 14.33% and the return of 7.95% from a composite of traditional alternative investments such as hedge funds, real estate and private equity. Not surprisingly, the stand-alone volatility of the exotics composite was also the highest at 18.96%, compared to the S&P 500 at 11.56% and traditional alternatives at 8.94%.

A complete list of the individual constituents of the exotic master composite and of the indices used to evaluate traditional alternatives is also included in Appendix 1.

A correlation matrix of the exotics composite, the S&P 500 and traditional alternatives from the period from January 2016 to December 2019 is shown in Table 14.2. The correlation of the exotics composite to the S&P 500 was 0.44. The correlation to traditional alternatives was 0.42. The correlation of the S&P 500 to traditional alternatives was quite high at 0.88.

Table 14.1. The annualized return of a master exotics composite versus the S&P 500 and an index of traditional alternative investments between January 2016 and December 2019.

	Exotics	S&P 500	Alternatives
Annual Return	37.70%	14.33%	7.95%
Standard Deviation	18.96%	11.56%	8.94%

Table 14.2. A correlation matrix of exotics, stocks and traditional alternatives for the period between January 2016 and December 2019.

	Exotics	S&P 500	Alternatives
Exotics	1	1	
S&P 500	0.44		
Alternatives	0.42	0.88	1

The higher return and relatively low correlation of the exotics composite to the S&P 500 and traditional alternatives mean that adding exotics to a traditional portfolio asset allocation should have positive portfolio effects and improve portfolio diversification.

Analysis of Master Composite Return and Risk Versus Stocks and Traditional Alternatives

Portfolio returns need to be analyzed on both an absolute and a risk-adjusted basis. Exotic alternatives had a higher absolute return and more volatility than stocks or traditional alternatives for the period from January 2016 to December 2019. However, despite their higher volatility, exotic alternatives are not necessarily a riskier investment than traditional investments.

Why is this? One reason is that the standard deviation is a measure of volatility alone. It does not consider the returns relative to volatility or risk. A Sharpe ratio is a better measure because it considers the returns associated with risk. It is a better gauge than simply comparing returns or risks alone. The use of a standard deviation as a risk measure also assumes that all returns are normally distributed. This is not the case with many investments, including exotic alternative investments. When returns are not normally distributed, it is best to supplement traditional volatility analysis based on standard deviation alone with any number of alternate risk measures. Some useful alternate return and risk measures commonly used for portfolio analysis when returns are not normally distributed include the worst-case drawdown and recovery, the worst- and best-case months, the number of positive and negative months and the distribution skew or kurtosis. Evaluating returns using Sharpe ratios and these alternate risk measures tells a different story. The exotics portfolio returns and risk appear much less extreme and are, in fact, better than the S&P 500 or traditional alternatives on both an absolute and a risk-adjusted basis.

Table 14.3. The comparative return and risk statistics for the master exotic composite, the S&P 500 and a traditional alternatives composite between January 2016 and December 2019.

	Exotics	**S&P 500**	**Alternatives**
Sharpe Ratio	1.98	1.24	0.89
Worst-case month	−8%	−9%	−6%
Best-case month	26%	9%	8%
Skew	1.89	−0.85	−0.19
# Positive months	37	36	35
# Negative months	11	12	13

The master exotic alternatives portfolio in Table 14.3 had a Sharpe ratio of 1.98. This significantly exceeded both the S&P 500 at 1.24 and traditional alternatives at 0.89. It also had a lower worst-case month of −8%, a higher best-case month of 26% and more positive months at 37 when compared to the S&P 500. Exotics also had a higher best-case month, more positive months and less negative months than traditional alternatives.

The exotic alternatives composite had a positive skew of 1.89 compared to a negative skew for both the S&P 500 and traditional alternatives. Positive skew is highly desirable as it implies that an investment will have more unexpectedly large positive monthly results relative to a normal distribution. It is also a measure of non-normality. A skew of less than −1 and more than +1 indicates the returns are not normally distributed. Since this is in fact the case for exotic alternatives, it is best to use alternate risk measures and not just a standard deviation or Sharpe ratio.

It is now quite clear from a purely statistical analysis, that a portfolio of exotic alternatives had better risk-adjusted returns and less risk than traditional investments between January 2016 and December 2019. This implies that exotic alternatives are more attractive than either the S&P 500 or traditional alternatives. This is true on both an absolute and a risk-adjusted basis. It is true regardless of whether observations are based on a risk-adjusted measure like a Sharpe ratio or on alternate risk measures that are more suitable for non-normally distributed data sets. However, there is more to be considered. A portfolio of exotic alternatives will have a number of additional risks that are not always or equally present when investing in stock or even traditional alternatives. These additional risks are not captured in any quantitative analysis of monthly returns. It is important that investors consider these risks before making any investment or asset allocation decision. Exotics have many more significant issues and risks related to liquidity, operational risk and valuation than traditional investments or other alternative investments. Exotic alternatives portfolios will have substantially more illiquidity, increased valuation risk and higher operational risk than either stocks and most traditional alternative investments. These additional risks are factors that significantly limit the amount of money investors can put into exotic alternative investments on a stand-alone basis or as part of a complete portfolio.

Investors who want to add exotics to traditional portfolios will need to perform both quantitative analysis and significant due diligence on each investment before finalizing any asset allocation decision. This additional due diligence will include both quantitative

Table 14.4. The comparative return, standard deviation and Sharpe ratio for the master exotic composite, the S&P 500, a traditional alternatives composite and a blended portfolio of all three investment composites between January 2016 and December 2019.

	Exotics	S&P 500	Alternatives	Evenly Weighted Portfolio
Annual Return	37.70%	14.33%	7.95%	19.75%
Standard Deviation	18.96%	11.56%	8.94%	11.00%
Sharpe Ratio	1.98	1.24	.89	1.80

analysis and qualitative analysis of the individual investments, pricing sources, platforms and fund managers being considered.

Impact of Exotic Alternative in Portfolio Construction

Our return and risk statistics show exotics outperform both stocks and traditional alternatives on both an absolute and a risk-adjusted basis. It also should not be a surprise that the relative low correlation to traditional investments means that adding exotics to a portfolio of stocks and traditional alternatives will lower portfolio risk and improve portfolio returns. A review of the data in Table 14.4 shows that between January 2016 and December 2019, an evenly weighted composite of stocks, exotics and traditional alternatives had returns of 19.75%, a standard deviation of only 11% and a Sharpe ratio of 1.80. When including exotic alternatives in a traditional portfolio, returns improve more than risk, thereby increasing the Sharpe ratio. This is due to the relatively low correlation of the exotics composite to traditional and alternative investments.

The growth of a $1,000 invested in stocks, exotic and traditional alternatives is shown in Figure 14.1 along with an evenly weighted portfolio of each investment. This blended portfolio of stocks, exotics and traditional alternatives would have grown from $1,000 in January 2016 to $2,056 in December 2019, exceeding the value of $1,708 for the S&P 500 alone and $1,357 for a composite of traditional alternative investments.

The scatter chart shown in Figure 14.2 visually illustrates the relationship between risk and reward for the individual categories of exotic alternative investments (excluding cryptoassets), the exotic master composite, the S&P 500, traditional alternatives and an evenly weighted portfolio. Among the individual categories, life settlements had the lowest risk at 3.67%, litigation finance had the highest return at 62% and alternative medicines had the highest risk at 37%. The evenly weighted portfolio had higher returns and lower risk than the S&P 500 and higher returns with only slightly higher risk than traditional alternatives. Litigation finance had the best Sharpe ratio of 2.06 followed by collectibles at 1.8 and life settlements at 1.7, respectively. Cryptoassets (not shown in Figure 14.2) had a return of 142% and a volatility of 154% and a Sharpe ratio less than one.

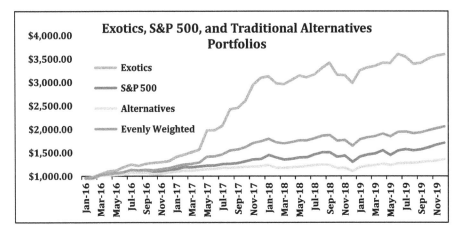

Figure 14.1. The growth of $1,000 invested in the master exotic composite, the S&P 500, a composite of traditional alternatives and an evenly weighted composite from January 2016 to December 2019.

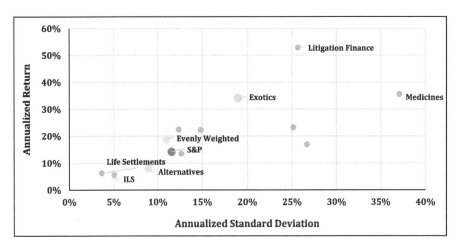

Figure 14.2. A plot of the risk and returns of individual exotics, the master exotic composite, the S&P 500, traditional alternatives and a blended portfolio.

Investing in Liquid Exotic Alternative Investments

The exotic alternative investment composite analyzed thus far, as shown in Tables 14.1 and 14.2 and illustrated graphically in Figures 14.1 and 14.2, includes both liquid securities that trade on exchanges (public companies and ETFs) and hedge funds that do not trade on exchanges and only offer investors monthly or quarterly redemption options. Investing in the master composite would only be an option for accredited investors who are able to invest in private vehicles like hedge funds and would exclude retail investors who are not accredited.

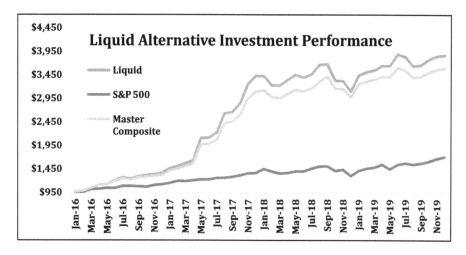

Figure 14.3. The growth of $1,000 invested in liquid exotics, the master exotic composite and the S&P 500 from January 2016 to December 2019.

How would an exotic alternative investment composite suitable for retail investor, comprised of only public companies and ETFs, performed from January 2016 to December 2019? Figure 14.3 shows the growth of $1,000 invested in a purely liquid exotic composite of public companies, ETFs and mutual funds, the master exotics composite and the S&P 500. The liquid composite had grown to $3,871 versus $3,595 for the master composite and $1,708 for the S&P 500. The composite of only the liquid exotic alternative investments, weighted by category, outperformed both the exotics master composite and the S&P 500.

The differential in performance between the liquid and exotic master composite is due to the fact that no public companies or ETFs were available for investment in the life settlements category. The liquid composite has no exposure to life settlements. Since this was one of the lowest returning and least risky categories in the master composite, the performance of the liquid composite should be higher and so should the volatility. This means that the liquid portfolio is slightly riskier and less diversified, since it excludes any investments in life settlements. This is exactly what was observed. The liquid composite had a return of 41.73% and volatility of 21.4% compared to the return of the master composite of 37.7% and volatility of 18.96%. This higher volatility and increased concentration does not nullify the benefits of this composite for retail investors who otherwise would not be able to invest at all.

Retail investors would still benefit from some, if not all, of the positive portfolio effects associated with investing in exotic alternative investments such as an improved Sharpe ratio and a higher portfolio return. The liquid portfolio for retail investors had a Sharpe ratio of 1.95 compared to 1.98 for the master composite and 1.24 for the S&P 500. The correlation of both the liquid and master exotics composites to the S&P 500 were 0.44, respectively.

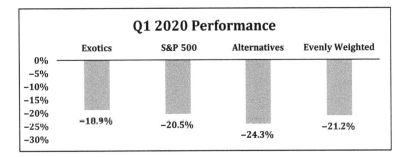

Figure 14.4. The quarterly performance an exotic alternatives composite, the S&P 500 and traditional alternatives for the first quarter of 2020.

Impact of Q1 2020 Recession and the COVID-19 Market Meltdown on Exotic Alternative Investments Relative to the S&P 500 and Traditional Alternatives

We have established that during our initial sample period between January 2016 and December 2019, exotic alternatives offered attractive absolute and risk adjusted returns during periods of economic growth and reasonable levels of market volatility. The next question is how well do these investments do during a recession or when the market is extremely volatile? To answer this question data from the first quarter 2020 recession and market meltdown due to the COVID-19 pandemic was analyzed for the S&P 500, traditional alternatives and exotic alternative investments. The first quarter of 2020 provides us with a data set to evaluate if the previously observed outperformance is persistent during an economic contraction or if exotics offer any downside protection relative to the S&P 500 or traditional alternatives.

The peak value and all-time high for the S&P 500 occurred on February 19, 2020. By March 23, the S&P 500 index had dropped approximately 34%, which is the steepest and fastest decline in history. The biggest single daily drop during this period was approximately 11% or over 2,000 index points on March 16. The biggest gain during this period was a daily increase of approximately 9% on March 13. Over the entire first quarter, the S&P 500 index fell 21%.

The bar chart in Figure 14.4 shows the full quarter losses for the exotic composite, the S&P 500, traditional alternatives and the evenly weighted composite for the quarter ended March 31, 2020. The data shows that the exotic alternatives portfolio, which had significantly outperformed the S&P 500 from January 2016 to December 2019, also outperformed the S&P 500 during the first-quarter market meltdown, albeit marginally. This is significant. While it did not preserve capital or avoid losses, the exotic alternatives portfolio did perform better than both a traditional investment in stocks and an investment in traditional alternatives.

From January 2016 to March 2020, over market cycles that included both economic expansion and a recession, investments in exotic alternatives using public and private funds and vehicles outperformed stocks, with better absolute and risk-adjusted returns.

This extended period of data analysis makes it clear that adding exotic funds and vehicles to traditional portfolios *should* improve portfolio Sharpe ratios and should be considered as a part of an asset allocation model.

More data and testing and longer time horizons will no doubt provide additional useful information for asset allocation decisions. Past performance is never a predictor of future returns and correlations, but it is a useful guide and an important input for decision making.

Summary

Our analysis thus far supports the case for allocating some of an investor's assets to exotics, both during a growth phase in the economy and during an economic contraction. Our analysis indicates that these exotic investments capture significant upside when markets expand and also outperform marginally when markets contract. Exotics have better absolute and risk-adjusted returns in good times and in bad, at least based on our data analyzed from January 2016 to March 2020. In fact, it appears to be a *compelling* argument that exotic alternative investments *should* be included in the asset allocation process for many investors.

The only questions that remain now are how to best execute on individual decisions to use direct investments when appropriate, which commingled vehicles should be considered for investment and how much should be allocated to exotic alternative investments. The last question is the simplest to answer. How much is the ideal or optimal amount of exotic investments to add to any portfolio? The immediate answer is easy—it should be greater than zero. But *how much greater* is a more difficult question to answer. The answer will not come from data analysis alone. It will also be a function of the amount of money an investor is willing to spend upfront to research each asset class, investment vehicle and manager under consideration. Answering this question needs to include an in-depth analysis of available liquidity and a determination of how much operational risk one is willing to take on. In most cases, it will be illiquidity and operational risk that will be the binding constraints on portfolio construction and asset allocation to exotic alternative investments. No amount of research and due diligence may be able to expand capacity, improve liquidity or enhance a valuation model in the short run. Frustratingly, some investors may find themselves limited as to the amount they can comfortably invest in exotic alternatives and in the number of investment choices available today.

For now, constructing a portfolio of exotic alternatives as part of any asset allocation process will involve making many tradeoffs between direct investments, liquid vehicles like ETFs and investing in vehicles that have longer lock-up terms like hedge funds, private equity and venture capital opportunities.

The good news is that as time passes and more investors participate in the exotics market, it is likely that liquidity, infrastructure and capacity will improve. Over time, more managers will launch funds dedicated to exotic alternative investments and more publicly traded investment options will emerge. Those investors who start early and begin to build a portfolio and framework of analysis will capture the most attractive opportunities and have the best outcomes.

Chapter Fifteen

FINAL THOUGHTS ON EXOTIC ALTERNATIVE INVESTING

Here are some final thoughts about the various types of exotic alternatives and how to invest in them. Hopefully, it will be useful to reflect on some of the principles that many of these asset classes share when evaluating opportunities now and in the future.

1. Investors need to be dispassionate about the underlying investment being considered. In other words, they should think only about the financial opportunities and risks when considering investing. In this sense, it is not the beauty of a piece of art nor the morality of a lawsuit that is of primary concern, but rather the return on investment and the downside risk alone.

2. Diversification matters. Exotic alternatives have complex value drives. Tastes and preferences can change over time. Individual claims, collectibles or death benefits can vary dramatically, very quickly rendering any single investment worthless. A well-diversified portfolio of assets within a specific exotic category that has more winners than losers can benefit from the high returns or resale value of the winners, often with triple-digit returns relative to the losses, which are always limited to 100% of any investment.

3. Ethical and legal issues may be present in many exotic alternatives. One primary example is that of marijuana. Another is investing in mortality or life settlements or providing funding for lawsuits. Each may lead to a variety of ethical and legal considerations or debates within an organization or between investors with different perspectives.

4. Leveraging a winning investment can create outsized gains. Leveraging an underperforming investment can produce outsized losses. Leveraging an already volatile investment is dangerous. So, leverage should not be a primary driver of exotic alternative investment returns or portfolios.

5. For most exotic investments, returns are not highly correlated with traditional stocks and bonds, have a low correlation to each other and to traditional alternatives, like hedge funds and private equity. Stand-alone risk and return are less important than portfolio effect when it comes to exotic alternatives.

6. Payoffs are often asymmetrical. Losses can be mitigated or small and limited to the initial investment, whereas gains can be large, often several times the value of the initial investment. Limiting the downside risk is a very important factor to consider when dealing with exotic alternative investments.

7. Both execution and operational risk can be significant in many types of exotic alternative investments. In many cases, the operational risk will be larger than the market or credit risk. Exotic alternatives with cash flows are subject to interest rate, liquidity and credit risk like any other fixed-income instrument.

8. Valuations often present a challenge when involving exotic alternative investments. The market data and transaction history available to investors are almost always limited. Models with unobservable inputs are often required, making estimated IRRs a challenge.

9. There is a high return on resources spent on research and risk that allows investors to demystify investments and capture excessive complexity or uncertainty-related risk premia.

10. It is important to avoid the mania and bubbles that can emerge in exotic alternatives.

11. Funds and commingled vehicles as well as those who manage them may have limited track records, thereby requiring more due diligence than traditional investments.

12. Remember, returns and valuations are all relative and should always be adjusted for risk. Alternative risk measures like worst-case drawdown, skew and positive months versus negative months may be more useful for non-normal datasets.

13. Be mindful that in some cases there is significant operational risk due to limited infrastructure and a lack of institutional best practices.

14. Many types of exotic investments, particularly collectibles, are pricey, illiquid and not regulated beyond industry associations.

15. Portfolios tend to be concentrated or derive their returns from a small portion of their investments. Finding benchmarks and comparable indices may not be easy given the limited data set and idiosyncratic nature of many categories of exotic alternatives.

16. Always remember that many of the factors impacting exotic alternative investments are fluid. Markets are evolving and changing all the time, as are the returns, risks and opportunities related to exotic investments.

17. Due diligence must be done on the asset class, the portfolio of specific investments and on any third-party platform, manager or advisors who help create or manage the portfolio.

18. Exotic alternative investments are not normally distributed. They should be evaluated using both risk-adjusted and alternate risk measures.

19. The optimal portfolio weight for exotics is greater than zero!

20. Operational risk, liquidity and due diligence resources are binding constraints on portfolio construction using exotics.

21. Exotics may also offer investors some downside protection in addition to breakout return opportunities.

22. Only accredited investors can invest in hedge funds and private vehicles offering exotic exposures.

23. Retail investors can invest in public companies, exchange-traded funds, closed-end funds and trusts to get exposure without sacrificing performance or beneficial portfolio effects.

24. Investors who start early will benefit from future improvements in exotic alternative liquidity, infrastructure and the emergence of more investable funds over time.

25. The question is not whether you should invest in exotic alternative investments, but rather how much!

APPENDIX ONE

MASTER EXOTIC ALTERNATIVES COMPOSITE CONSTITUENTS DATA

Indices

Alternative Investment Composite Indices	Category	Source
Red Rocks GLPE Index	Private Equity	glpeindex.com
HFRI Fund Weighted Composite Index	Hedge Funds	hedgefundresearch.com
FTSE NAREIT US Real Estate Index	Real Estate	reit.com

Hedge Funds

Category	Manager	Fund Name	Category	Assets under Management
Life Settlements	AIR Asset Management	AIR US Life Fund I	Hedge Fund	$67.9M
Life Settlements	Leadenhall Capital Partners	Leadenhall Life Insurance-Linked Investment Fund	Hedge Fund	$564.3M
Life Settlements	Managing Partners Group	Augury Hedge Fund—USD Arbitrage Class	Hedge Fund	N/A
Life Settlements	SL Investment Management	BlackOak Investors	Hedge Fund	$38.6M
Life Settlements	GI Asset Management	GIS General Fund	Hedge Fund	$53.01M
Life Settlements	Laureola Advisors	Laureola Investment Fund—USD Class	Hedge Fund	$60M
Life Settlements	Ress Capital	Ress Life Investments—USD Class	Hedge Fund	$182.7M
Life Settlements	Vida Capital	Vida Longevity Fund	Hedge Fund	$2.31B

(continued)

Hedge Funds

Litigation Finance	Pravati Capital	Pravati Credit Fund III	Hedge Fund	$50.27M
Insurance-Linked Securities	Nephila Capital	Nimbus Weather Fund Ltd	Hedge Fund	N/A
Insurance-Linked Securities	Securis Investment Partners	Securis Non-Life Fund Class A	Hedge Fund	$1.13B
Insurance-Linked Securities	Fermat Capital Management	GAM FCM Cat Bond—USD Initial Series	Hedge Fund	$1.72B
Alternative Medicines	Navy Capital	Navy Capital Green Fund	Hedge Fund	$75M
Cryptoassets	Typhon Capital Management	Leonidas Cryptocurrency Fund	Hedge Fund	$520K

Source: https://www.preqin.com/ as of March 31, 2020.

Listed Equity, ETFs, Trusts and Mutual Funds

Category	Name	Ticker	Category	Market Capitalization
Litigation Finance	IMF Bentham (Omni Bridgeway)	IMF (OBL.AX)	Listed Equity	$972.70M
Litigation Finance	Burford Capital Ltd.	BUR.L	Listed Equity	$1.04B
Intellectual Property	Ligand Pharmaceuticals Inc.	LGND	Listed Equity	$1.51B
Intellectual Property	XOMA Corp.	XOMA	Listed Equity	$267.66M
Intellectual Property	PDL BioPharma Inc.	PDLI	Listed Equity	$394.88M
Intellectual Property	San Juan Basin Royalty Trust	SJT	Listed Equity	$107.67M
Intellectual Property	Franco-Nevada Corp.	FNV	Listed Equity	$25.76B
Intellectual Property	Sandstorm Gold Ltd.	SAND	Listed Equity	$1.50B
Intellectual Property	Royal Gold Inc.	RGLD	Listed Equity	$8.27B
Insurance-Linked Securities	Swiss Re AG	SREN.SW	Listed Equity	$20.2B
Insurance-Linked Securities	Everest Re Group, Ltd.	RE	Listed Equity	$8.03B
Insurance-Linked Securities	PartnerRe Ltd.	PRE-PH	Listed Equity	$2.63B

Listed Equity, ETFs, Trusts and Mutual Funds

Taxes and Leasing	AerCap Holdings N.V.	AER	Listed Equity	$3.13B
Taxes and Leasing	Air Lease Corp.	AL	Listed Equity	$2.49B
Taxes and Leasing	Triton International Ltd.	TRTN	Listed Equity	$2.15B
Taxes and Leasing	Textainer Group Holdings Ltd.	TGH	Listed Equity	$429.54M
Taxes and Leasing	Public Storage	PSA	Listed Equity	$33.69B
Taxes and Leasing	Extra Space Storage Inc.	EXR	Listed Equity	$11.83B
eSports and Gaming	Manchester United, plc	MANU	Listed Equity	$2.66B
eSports and Gaming	The Liberty Braves Group	BATRA	Listed Equity	$1.01B
eSports and Gaming	Madison Square Garden Sports Corp.	MSG	Listed Equity	$5.69B
eSports and Gaming	Rogers Communications Inc.	RCI	Listed Equity	$21.19B
eSports and Gaming	BCE Inc.	BCE	Listed Equity	$36.66B
eSports and Gaming	Churchill Downs Inc.	CHDN	Listed Equity	$3.93B
eSports and Gaming	World Wrestling Entertainment Inc.	WWE	Listed Equity	$3.47B
eSports and Gaming	Vail Resorts Inc.	MTN	Listed Equity	$6.80B
eSports and Gaming	Activision Blizzard Inc.	ATVI	Listed Equity	$49.33B
eSports and Gaming	Electronic Arts Inc.	EA	Listed Equity	$32.81B
eSports and Gaming	Nintendo Co. Ltd.	NTDOY	Listed Equity	$51.27B
eSports and Gaming	NetEase Inc.	NTES	Listed Equity	$45.13B
eSports and Gaming	TakeTwo Interactive Software Inc.	TTWO	Listed Equity	$13.92B
eSports and Gaming	Sony Corp.	SNE	Listed Equity	$76.51B
eSports and Gaming	Huya Inc.	HUYA	Listed Equity	$3.45B
eSports and Gaming	Glu Mobile Inc.	GLUU	Listed Equity	$1.19B
eSports and Gaming	GameStop Corp.	GME	Listed Equity	$348.71M

(continued)

Listed Equity, ETFs, Trusts and Mutual Funds

eSports and Gaming	NVIDIA Corp.	NVDA	Listed Equity	$179.14B
eSports and Gaming	VanEck Vectors Video Gaming and eSports ET	FESPO	ETF	$123.51M
eSports and Gaming	VanEck Vectors Gaming ETF	BJK	ETF	$21.98M
eSports and Gaming	Roundhill BITKRAFT eSports and Digital Entertainment ETF	NERD	ETF	$10.27M
eSports and Gaming	Wedbush ETF MG Video Game Tech ETF	GAMR	ETF	$72.84M
Farm, Air, Water, Timber	Weyerhaeuser Co.	WY	Listed Equity	$16.10B
Farm, Air, Water, Timber	Rayonier Inc.	RYN	Listed Equity	$3.36B
Farm, Air, Water, Timber	Potlatch Deltic Corp.	PCH	Listed Equity	$2.36B
Farm, Air, Water, Timber	American Water Works Co. Inc.	AWK	Listed Equity	$22.86B
Farm, Air, Water, Timber	Aqua America (Essential Utilities Inc.)	WTRG	Listed Equity	$10.81B
Farm, Air, Water, Timber	FlexShares Morningstar Global Upstream Natural Resources Index Fund	GUNR	ETF	$2.97B
Farm, Air, Water, Timber	iShares Global Timber and Forestry ETF	WOOD	ETF	$176.06M
Farm, Air, Water, Timber	Invesco MSCI Global Timber ETF	CUT	ETF	$70.38M
Farm, Air, Water, Timber	The Organics ETF	ORG	ETF	$6.05M
Farm, Air, Water, Timber	Invesco Water ETF	PIO	ETF	$164.55M
Farm, Air, Water, Timber	Invesco S&P Global Water Index ETF	CGW	ETF	$567.64M
Farm, Air, Water, Timber	Invesco Water Resources ETF	PHOETF		$904.06M
Farm, Air, Water, Timber	First Trust Water ETF	FIW	ETF	$442.41M

Listed Equity, ETFs, Trusts and Mutual Funds

Farm, Air, Water, Timber	Tortoise Global Water ESG Fund	TBLU	ETF	$13.8M
Farm, Air, Water, Timber	AllianzGI Water Fund Class A	AWTAX	MF	$549.74M
Cannabis and Medicine	Aurora Cannabis Inc.	ACB	Listed Equity	$992.45M
Cannabis and Medicine	Canopy Growth Corp.	CGC	Listed Equity	$5.93B
Cannabis and Medicine	Cronos Group Inc.	CRON	Listed Equity	$2.23B
Cannabis and Medicine	Tilray Inc.	TLRY	Listed Equity	$876.16M
Cannabis and Medicine	Illumina Inc.	ILMN	Listed Equity	$45.06B
Cannabis and Medicine	Exact Sciences Corp.	EXAS	Listed Equity	$11.41B
Cannabis and Medicine	Myriad Genetics Inc.	MYGN	Listed Equity	$1.12B
Cannabis and Medicine	Boiron SA	BOI.PA	Listed Equity	$577.80M
Cannabis and Medicine	ETF MG Alternative Harvest ETF	MJ	ETF	$473.2M
Cannabis and Medicine	Evolve Marijuana Fund	SEED.TO	ETF	$50M
Cannabis and Medicine	Horizons Marijuana Life Sciences Index ETF	HMMJ.TO	ETF	$337.71M
Cannabis and Medicine	ARK Genomic Revolution ETF	ARKG	ETF5	13.03M
Cannabis and Medicine	American Growth Fund Series Two Class E	AMREX	MF	$703.81K
Cryptoassets	Amplify Transformational Data Sharing ETF	BLOK	ETF	$71.54M
Cryptoassets	Reality Shares Nasdaq NexGen Economy ETF	BLCN	ETF	$51.1M
Cryptoassets	Grayscale Bitcoin Trust	GBTC	Trust	$1.542B
Cryptoassets	Grayscale Ethereum Trust	ETHE	Trust	$244M
Collectibles	Ferrari N.V.	RACE	Listed Equity	$39.25B
Collectibles	Collectors Universe Inc.	CLCT	Listed Equity	$185.68M

(continued)

Collectibles	LVMH Moet Hennessy	MC.PA	Listed Equity	$179.64B
Collectibles	Hermes International	IRMS.PA	Listed Equity	$70.53B
Collectibles	Adidas AG	ADDYY	Listed Equity	$43.17B
Collectibles	Nike Inc.	NKE	Listed Equity	$138.82B
Collectibles	Compagnie Financiere Richemont SA	CFRHF	Listed Equity	$32.14B
Collectibles	Kering SA	KER.PA	Listed Equity	$58.38B
Collectibles	Diageo plc	DEO	Listed Equity	$79.46B
Collectibles	Constellation Brands Inc.	STZ	Listed Equity	$31.86B
Collectibles	Amundi S&P Global Luxury ETF	GLUX.MI	ETF	$120.91M

Source: Yahoo Finance and manager websites as of April 27, 2020.

APPENDIX TWO

IBISWORLD REPORTS INDEX

Anna Miller, "Art Dealers in the U.S.," IBIS World, December 2019.
   Cecilia Fernandez, "Antiques & Collectibles Sales," IBIS World, June 2019.
   ———, "Medical & Recreational Marijuana Growing," IBIS World, November 2019.
   Devin McGinley, "Commercial Aircraft Leasing," IBISWorld, December 2019.
   Nick Masters, "Video Games in the U.S.," IBISWorld, December 2019,
   Qing Zheng, "Storage and Warehouse Leasing in the U.S.," December 2019.
   Rachel Hyland, "Classic Car Dealers," IBIS World, December 2019.
   Ryan Roth, "Intellectual Property Rights Licensing in the US," IBIS World, August 2019.
   ———, "Sports Franchises in the US," IBIS World, November 2019.
   Thomas Henry, "Timber Services in the US," IBISWorld, March 2020.
   Victor Adeleke, "Settlement Funding Companies," IBIS World, December 2018.

For more information about IBISWorld research and data, go to the company's website at https://www.ibisworld.com.

GLOSSARY

Abstract Art is art that does not attempt to represent external reality but seeks to achieve its effect using shapes, forms, colors and textures.

Air Rights are a developmental right to develop a specific amount of unused air space above real property.

Air Rights Lease Agreements give one party the rights to use a specific air space parcel for development in exchange for rents or fees.

Air Space Parcels are certain volumes of air space that are owned and can be sold, leased or rented.

Alpha is a measure of the active return on an investment, the performance of that investment compared with a suitable market index.

Appraisal is an auction house's evaluation of an artwork's market or insurance value.

Art Collectors are people who buy artwork to adorn offices, buildings or in their homes.

Art Gallery is a private business that works with one or more artists to promote their work

Art Investors are people who are interested in portfolio diversification by using art as an investment.

Art Speculators are investors who purchase art as an attempt to realize short-term gains as a result of their appreciation in value.

Auction House is a place where artwork is bought and sold in a competitive setting.

Blockchain is a system in which a record of transactions made in Bitcoin or another cryptocurrency is maintained across several computers that are linked in a peer-to-peer network.

Bond Indenture is a contract associated with a bond, which typically includes a description of the bond features, restrictions placed on the issuer and the actions that will be triggered if the issuer fails to make timely payments.

Cannabidiol (CBD) is the chemical ingredient from the hemp plant that is used mostly in cosmetic or pharmaceutical applications.

Capital Lease is a lease where the lessor transfers the ownership rights of the asset to the lessee at the end of the lease term.

Cash Rent is computed per acre based on a farm's tillable acres and is normally paid in full before any crops are planted.

Cash Surrender Value is the amount available in cash upon voluntary termination of a policy before it becomes payable.

Catastrophic Loss Bond is a derivative debt investment vehicle issued by insurers and reinsurers designed to raise investor capital to cover catastrophic loss events

Celebrity Bond (Bowie Bond) is a commercial debt security issued by a holder of fame-based intellectual property rights to receive money upfront from investors in exchange for assigning investors the right to collect future royalties.

Claim is a creditor's assertion of a right to payment from a debtor or the debtor's property.

Class Action Lawsuit is when one or more members of a large group or class of individuals or other entities sue on behalf of the entire class.

Collective Bargaining Agreement (CBA) is a written legal contract between an employer and a union representing the employees.

Compound Annual Growth Rate (CAGR) is the rate of return that would be required for an investment to grow from its beginning balance to its ending balance.

Copyright is a protection given to an original song, sound, artistic work, dance or design.

Crop Share Arrangement is an arrangement where the landowner is paid a rent based on a percentage of the crop's revenue. In this case, the landlord and the farmer both assume the risk.

Cryptocurrency is a digital currency in which encryption techniques are used to regulate the generation of units of currency and verify the transfer of funds, operating independently of a central bank.

Cryptocurrency Wallet is a device, physical medium, program or a service which stores the public and/or private keys and can be used to track ownership, receive or spend cryptocurrencies.

Default Risk Premium is the difference between a debt instrument's interest rate and the risk-free rate.

Defendant is an individual or business against whom a lawsuit is filed.

Dispensary is a store that can legally sell cannabis products, either for medical or recreational use.

Distributed Ledger is a database that is consensually shared and synchronized across multiple sites, institutions or geographies.

Due Diligence is a comprehensive appraisal of a business undertaken by a prospective buyer, especially to establish its assets and liabilities and evaluate its commercial potential.

Duration is the weighted average of the time until cash flows are received. It can be used as an approximate measure of a bond's price sensitivity to changes in interest rates

Edible Cannabis Products refer to those cannabis products that are orally consumed and can include brownies, gummy bears and other foods or beverages.

eSports is a multiplayer video game played competitively for spectators, typically by professional gamers.

Event-linked Bonds are debt instruments that are linked to specific insurance activities underwritten by an insurance company.

Expansion Space means all air space located directly above an air space parcel extending upwards without limitation.

Face Amount is the amount that will be paid to a beneficiary in the case of the death of the insured under the policy.

Fantasy Sports is a type of game, often played using the Internet, in which participants assemble imaginary or virtual teams of real players of a professional sport. These teams compete based on the statistical performance of those players in actual games.

Fine Art is a type of art that includes paintings, sculptures, printmaking and other works.

Flex-Lease is a hybrid arrangement that combines a cash base lease with a revenue-sharing arrangement if commodity prices reach certain levels.

Foreclosure is a legal process in which a lender attempts to recover the balance of a loan from a borrower who has stopped making payments to the lender by forcing the sale of the asset used as the collateral for the loan.

Grower is someone who plants and cultivates either traditional cannabis or hemp plants.

Initial Coin Offering (ICO) is the cryptocurrency industry's equivalent to an Initial Public Offering (IPO).

Hard Fork is a radical change to a network's protocol that makes previously invalid blocks and transactions valid or vice-versa.

Hemp is the name given to the strain of the cannabis plant with a low THC component and a high CBD component.

Hurdle Rate is the minimum rate of return on an investment required by a manager or investor.

Hydroponic Farming is a high-tech growing method in which vegetables are grown without soil.

Infringement is the action of breaking the terms of a copyright law or license agreement.

Judgment is the official decision of a court finally resolving the dispute between the parties to a lawsuit.

Kurtosis is a measure of "tails" of the probability distribution of a real-valued random variable.

Landmark Transfers allow the owners of landmarks to transfer unused development rights to adjacent parcels to any lot on another corner that touches the same intersection.

Lessee is a person who holds the lease of a property, such as a tenant.

Lessor is a person who leases or lets a property to another, such as a landlord.

Licensee is the party that pays a royalty to the licensor or owner of the protected asset.

License Agreement outlines the rights, responsibilities and terms between an owner and a licensee of intellectual property.

Life Annuity is an annuity, or series of payments at fixed intervals, paid while the purchaser is alive.

Life Expectancy is the probability of an individual living to a certain age.

Life Settlement is a transaction in which a life insurance policyowner sells his or her policy to an investor in exchange for a lump-sum payment and assumption of future premium obligations.

Lien is a right to keep possession of property belonging to another person until a debt owed by that person is discharged.

Longevity Bonds pay high interest rates in return for taking on the risk of a reference portfolio of people living longer than a specific period. Investors lose some or all remaining coupons and principal if the set threshold is achieved.

Macaulay Duration is the weighted average term to maturity of the cash flows from a bond.

Mean is the average of a set of the numbers used to measure the central tendency of a dataset.

Medical Marijuana is a form of a CBD produced for medical use and only obtainable by prescription.

Meta-analysis is an examination of data from a number of independent studies of the same subject, in order to determine overall trends.

Mining is the processing of transactions in the digital currency system, in which the records of current Bitcoin transactions, known as a block, are added to the record of past transactions, known as the blockchain.

Monte Carlo Simulation is a broad class of computational algorithms that rely on repeated random sampling to obtain numerical results. The underlying concept is to use randomness to solve problems that might be deterministic in principle.

Mortality is the incidence of death at each age.

Mortality Bonds pay high interest rates in return for taking on the risk of a reference portfolio living less than a specific period. Investors lose some or all remaining coupons and principal if a set threshold is realized.

Non-Recourse Loan is a secured loan that is secured by a pledge of collateral, typically real property, but for which the borrower is not personally liable

Operating Lease is the rental of an asset from a lessor, but not under terms that transfer ownership of the asset to the lessee.

Pandemic Bonds are bonds that pay high interest rates in return for taking on the risk of losing some or all remaining coupons and principal if a pandemic occurs.

Price Elasticity is a measure of the relationship between a change in the quantity demanded of a particular good and a change in its price.

Patent is a protection given by a regulatory authority, government or the courts with a specific jurisdiction that limits the use of a specific technology, invention or process for a specific timeframe.

Patent or Copyright Infringement occurs when one party is accused of using a protected asset without permission or without paying for it.

Permanent Crops are trees and plants that produce fruit annually and only get planted once.

Plaintiff is a person or business that files a formal complaint with the court.

Policyowner is the person who owns a life insurance policy.

Premium is the payment that a policyowner makes in exchange for an insurance policy.

Prior Appropriation Rights allow a landowner to establish access rights and withdraw water on a first come first serve basis.

Provenance (of a piece of art) is a reference to the chain of custody or trail of ownership associated with a potential investment.

Real Assets is an investment asset class that covers investments in physical assets such as real estate, energy and infrastructure.

Real Estate Investment Trust (REIT) is a company that owns, operates or finances income-producing properties.

Recourse Loan allows the lender to collect from the debtor and the debtor's assets in the case of default.

Regression Analysis is a measure of the relation between the mean value of one variable and the corresponding values of other variables.

Reinsurance is when insurers transfer portions of their risk portfolios to other parties by some form of agreement to reduce the likelihood of paying a large obligation resulting from an insurance claim.

Riparian Rights is a system for allocating water among those who possess land along its path.

Row Crops are single-season commodities such as soybeans that get planted and harvested annually.

Royalty is a payment from one person or party to another associated with the use of an intellectual property.

Scalping is selling (a ticket) for a popular event at a price higher than the official one.

Scarcity Value is the economic factor that increases an item's relative price based upon artificially low supply.

Sharpe Ratio measures the performance of an investment compared to a risk-free asset, after adjusting for its risk.

Smart Contracts is a computer protocol intended to digitally facilitate, verify or enforce the negotiation or performance of a contract.

Special Purpose District Transfers are used to tailor zoning to specific neighborhoods.

Standard Deviation is a measure of the amount of variation or dispersion of a set of values.

Stranger-Originated Life Insurance (STOLI) is an arrangement in which an investor holds a life insurance policy without an insurable interest.

Streaming Media is multimedia that is constantly received by and presented to an end-user while being delivered by a provider.

Tax Credits are incentives given to a business or investor by the Internal Revenue Service or other government agencies that are designed to incentivize certain types of investment behavior.

Tax Lien is a lien imposed by law upon a property to secure the payment of taxes.

Term Life Insurance guarantees payment of a stated death benefit during a specified term.

Tetrahydrocannabinol (THC) is a chemical that comes from the marijuana plant that is responsible for most of cannabis's psychological effects.

Title Insurance is a form of indemnity insurance that protects the holder from financial loss as a result of defects in a title to a property.

Tort is a wrongful act or an infringement of a right (other than under contract) leading to civil legal liability.

Trademark is a protection given to a picture, logo or word associated with a product or service.

Trade Claims are assertions of rights to payment by one counterparty to another.

Trigger Events are events that result in risk sharing between the buyer and the seller of insurance-linked security.

Universal Life Insurance is permanent life insurance with an investment savings element and offers low premiums like term life insurance.

Value at Risk (VaR) is how much a set of investments might lose (with a given probability) given normal market conditions, in a set period such as a day.

Viatical is a policy of a person with a terminal illness and less than two years of life expectancy.

Waterfall Payment is a repayment system by which senior lenders receive principal and interest payments from a borrower first and subordinate lenders receive principal and interest payments after.

Weather Hedge is a security or product that allows a buyer to reduce or eliminate weather or climate risk.

Whole Life Insurance is permanent life insurance.

Zoning Lot Merger is when owners combine adjacent lots into a shared lot and pool together their development rights.

INDEX

Lightning Source UK Ltd.
Milton Keynes UK
UKHW012331070121
376629UK00001B/34